MW00612081

Hiking California's Mount Shasta Region

HELP US KEEP THIS GUIDE UP TO DATE

Every effort has been made by the author and editors to make this guide as accurate and useful as possible. However, many things can change after a guide is published—trails are rerouted, regulations change, facilities come under new management, and so forth.

We welcome your comments concerning your experiences with this guide, and how you feel it could be improved and kept up to date. While we may not be able to respond to all comments and suggestions, we'll take them to heart, and we'll also make certain to share them with the author. Please send your comments and suggestions to the following address:

Globe Pequot
Reader Response/Editorial Department
246 Goose Lane
Guilford, CT 06437

Or you may e-mail us at: editorial@falcon.com

Thanks for your input, and happy trails!

Hiking California's Mount Shasta Region

A Guide to the Region's Greatest Hikes

Bubba Suess

FALCONGUIDES

GUILFORD, CONNECTICUT
HELENA, MONTANA

FALCONGUIDES®

An imprint of Rowman & Littlefield
Falcon, FalconGuides, and Outfit Your Mind are registered trademarks of Rowman & Littlefield.

Distributed by NATIONAL BOOK NETWORK

Copyright © 2015 by Bubba Suess
Maps: Daniel Lloyd © Rowman & Littlefield
All photos by the author.

All rights reserved. No part of this book may be reproduced in any form or by any electronic or mechanical means, including information storage and retrieval systems, without written permission from the publisher, except by a reviewer who may quote passages in a review.

British Library Cataloguing-in-Publication Information available

Library of Congress Cataloging-in-Publication Data available

ISBN 978-1-4930-0984-8 (paperback)
ISBN 978-1-4930-1509-2 (e-book)

∞™ The paper used in this publication meets the minimum requirements of American National Standard for Information Sciences—Permanence of Paper for Printed Library Materials, ANSI/NISO Z39.48-1992.

The author and Rowman & Littlefield assume no liability for accidents happening to, or injuries sustained by, readers who engage in the activities described in this book.

To my wonderful wife, Harmony, who gave me the mountain, made this book possible, and continues to make me a better man.

Contents

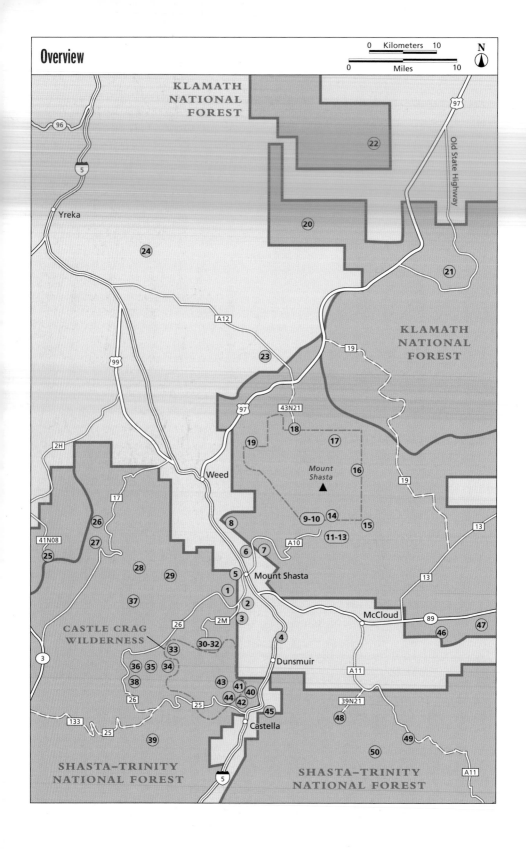

0   Kilometers   10

0   Miles   10

N

Acknowledgments

First and foremost, I would like to thank my wife, Harmony, who has hiked many of these trails with me and encouraged me every step of the way. Her patience is beyond measure, and her wisdom and judgment continue to amaze me. Great, heartfelt thanks go to my parents, Ron and Jane Suess. Their moral and logistical support was invaluable. How they have maintained such a vast reservoir of energy while contending with their grandchildren is a mystery. I would also express my deep gratitude to my brother, Matt Suess. He has been my hero from my earliest memories and his sense of adventure, perseverance and integrity have guided me my entire life.

I would like to offer a special thanks to my friend Caleb Marchi. He first introduced me to Mount Shasta many years ago. When time permits, he continues to accompany me on memorable adventures throughout Northern California. I am also grateful to his parents, Robert and Sylvia, whose generosity was essential when I first moved up to Mount Shasta.

Jim and Velma Nile have been instrumental in adding to my knowledge of the geography, flora and fauna, and lore of Mount Shasta. They have lived at the foot of the mountain since the early 1950s and their love for this area is as infectious as it is deep. They continue to influence new generations of wilderness lovers. They need a peak named in their honor.

A few people hiked the trails with me and their company was a great help on this journey. In addition to my wife, my children Carson and Laramie joined me on many hikes. My brother, his wife Dana, and their children Connor, Nathan, and Rachel were also welcome companions on some of the trails. Velma Nile spent a great day with my family and me at South Gate Meadow. Caleb Marchi, Mark Volle, Ben Gerber, and Jake Cole hiked with me. We had some special times on the trails.

The members of the Mount Shasta Trails Association deserve a great deal of praise for the incredible work they have done building and maintaining trails around Mount Shasta. Many memories will be built on the paths they have given to the community.

Introduction

As lonely as God and white as a winter moon, Mount Shasta starts up suddenly from the heart of the great black forests of California.

You would hardly call Mount Shasta a part of the Sierras; you would say rather that it is the great white tower of some ancient and eternal wall, with here and there the white walls overthrown.

It has no rival! There is not even a snow-crowned subject in sight of its dominion. A shining pyramid in everlasting mail of frosts and ice, the sailor sometimes, in a day of singular clearness, catches glimpses of it from the sea a hundred miles away to the west; and it may be seen from the dome of the capitol 340 miles distant. The immigrant coming from the east beholds the snowy, solitary pillar from afar out on the arid sage-brush plains, and lifts his hands in silence as if in answer to a sign.

—Joaquin Miller, *Life Amongst the Modocs*, 1874

These famous words were written by famed nineteenth-century poet Joaquin Miller to express his obvious admiration for Mount Shasta, California's most awe-inspiring and majestic mountain.

Miller lived for a time around the mountain, and it made an indelible impression upon him. By the time he laid eyes on Mount Shasta, people had been drawn to it from before recorded history. The mountain still exerts this inexorable pull on people today. Travelers to or through the area find their eyes always gazing upward at its icy spire.

Mount Shasta has no peer in sight. The mighty volcano towers over 5,000 feet above Mount Eddy, its tallest neighbor. Most of the other mountains are far shorter. As if to embellish the great cone's already astounding proportion, Mount Shasta is surrounded on three sides by flat valleys. This puts its full 10,000 feet of relief on display, causing every other landmark to shrink in stature.

Height is not the only way the Mount Shasta impresses. At its base it is nearly 20 miles in diameter, which is roughly the same length as the nearby Trinity Divide or Scott Mountains, and about half the distance from the summit to the Oregon border, more than 40 miles to the north.

For all of its intimidating proportions, Mount Shasta is an inviting mountain to explore. Its lower flanks are covered in vast forests and dotted with springs; meadows are scattered about its slopes. Wildflowers erupt from the small patches of grass nourished by water of such purity that people travel great distances to drink it.

Travel is easy along the tree line, and the views are unrelentingly spectacular. In some ways, the mountain's mammoth scale makes it a mountain range on its own. For the hiker, this means that the geography does not demand that trails climb steeply up difficult slopes. Instead, hikes travel through valleys, across plains, along creeks and on the rim of staggering chasms.

The sunrise illuminates Mount Shasta's icy towers.

Yet, because Mount Shasta is what it is, even the easiest trail has an overabundance of awe-inspiring scenery.

Joaquin Miller may have claimed justly that Mount Shasta has no rival around it, but the mountains around the solitary volcano are not insignificant. The seemingly boundless Klamath Mountains lie to the west, and those who have had the good fortune to explore the stunning alpine splendor of the Trinity Alps or the beautifully unusual Marble Mountains know that these are mountains with a capital "M."

The tallest subrange of the Klamath, the Trinity Divide, lies just to the west of Mount Shasta. Resulting from a completely different geological history, the Trinity Divide has many features absent on Mount Shasta, most notably large alpine lakes. The trails along the ridges, canyons and glacial cirques are beautiful in their own right and are blessed with views of the volcano towering in regal solitude over its domain.

Alpine mountains are not the only landscapes that make hiking in the Mount Shasta area a memorable experience. The wild granite spires of the Castle Crags, the McCloud and Sacramento Rivers, and the high desert terrain in Mount Shasta's enormous rain shadow all add an amazing degree of variety not often found so close together. Motivated hikers could watch the sun rise from a lush tree-line meadow on Mount Shasta, witness enormous, thundering waterfalls on the McCloud River, spend an afternoon exploring a seemingly unfathomable lava cave in the desert north of the mountain, and then watch the sunset on Mount Shasta's icy tower while sitting on the edge of an alpine lake set in towering, glaciated cliffs. Mount Shasta is a grand place indeed.

Geography

Mount Shasta lies at the nexus of two wildly different geologic regions. The mountain itself is a part of the great Cascade Range, a series of mountains created from extensive volcanic activity. Immediately to the west of Mount Shasta lie the Klamath Mountains, an orphaned relative of California's mighty Sierra Nevada. The Klamaths are the result of massive seafloors being uplifted and punctuated by igneous rock intrusions.

Despite their radically different origins, the two mountain ranges have been forced into contact with one another. The summits of Mount Shasta, the highest point in the California Cascades, and Mount Eddy, the highest point in the Klamath Mountains, lie only 16 miles apart. The lower periphery of the ranges is separated by only a couple of miles.

The Cascade Range begins to the south, around Lassen Peak, and continues north past Mount Shasta, through Oregon and Washington, and into southern British Columbia. South of Lassen is a broad depression in the mountains occupied by Lake Almanor and the Mountain Meadows Reservoir. This low area roughly forms the division between the Cascades and the Sierra Nevada. South of the depression, the Sierra Nevada extend southward, with geology related to the Klamath Mountains.

The California section of the Cascades is basically divided in two. The Lassen Cascade is the southernmost section and includes Lassen Peak and the great, active highlands of Lassen Volcanic National Park. The namesake peak is a large plug dome volcano, the new cone built up over the remnants of an older, decimated mountain. The former peak is referred to as Mount Tehama, and is believed to have once been nearly as tall as Mount Shasta. Lassen Peak was the most recent volcano to erupt in the continental United States until the Mount St. Helens eruption in 1980. It was active for several years in the early twentieth century, including a major eruption in 1915.

Active geothermal features persist around the base of Lassen Peak, evidence that powerful forces are still at work beneath the surface of Mount Tehama's ruins. Beyond the immediate Lassen area, the southernmost part of the Cascades includes lava flows, cinder cones and a chain of tall, volcanic peaks extending to the north along the crest of the range.

Crater Peak and Burney Mountain are the tallest and most significant mountains north of Lassen Peak. North of Burney Mountain flows the Pit River, roughly forming the boundary between the Lassen Cascade and the Shasta Cascade.

The Shasta Cascade covers the area between the Pit River and the Oregon border, where the range subsides briefly and is bisected by the Klamath River. Although Mount Shasta utterly dominates the region surrounding it, there are other notable volcanic features in the Shasta Cascade.

An epic view of Mount Shasta, Mud Creek Canyon, and Mud Creek Falls from the Clear Creek Trail.

East of the big mountain are the Medicine Lake Highlands, a large shield volcano. This type of volcano is built up through slow, successive flows of runny, fluid lava. Medicine Lake is located in the large caldera, surrounded by several large, dramatic lava flows. The Medicine Lake Volcano is the largest single volcanic peak by volume in the Cascade Range. North of Medicine Lake is Lava Beds National Monument, a collection of lava flows, lava caves and cinder cones.

Mount Shasta lies well to the west of Medicine Lake and the Lava Beds—so much so that it is really an outlier of the Cascade Crest. The central part of the range lies just east of the mountain and extends north toward Oregon. Prominent peaks like Ash Creek Butte, the Whaleback, and the Goosenest are all large, ancient volcanoes, evidence that this area has seen a significant amount of eruptive activity.

Mount Shasta, the second highest peak in the Cascades after Mount Rainier, is an enormous stratovolcano. Unlike shield volcanoes, stratovolcanoes are built up from much more violent eruptions that produce lots of ash and thicker, more viscous lava. The denser material moves swiftly away from the point of eruption, which causes the material to pile up. Mount Shasta built up to its present size over several eruptive periods. The mountain's great girth is enhanced by the presence of a massive, secondary cone named Shastina. Taken by itself, this peak would be the third highest summit in the Cascades.

Several other features on the mountain warrant some mention as well. Chief among them are the seven glaciers that blanket its upper slopes. On the north and east side are four large sheets of ice: Whitney, Bolam, Hotlum, and Wintun. These are the four largest glaciers in California. On the mountain's south side, there are three smaller glaciers: Konwakiton, Mud Creek, and Watkins. All of the hikes on the east and north sides of Mount Shasta enjoy excellent views of these awesome chunks of ice.

Another notable feature on the mountain is Mud Creek Canyon. This epic gorge is the deepest and longest of the many canyons that radiate out from the summit. The chasm is nearly 1,000 feet deep and 1 mile wide in places, and is almost 7 miles long.

To the west of Mount Shasta lie the great Klamath Mountains, the impressive counterpart to the Cascade Range. Where the Cascades are volcanic in origin, the Klamaths are the result of massive uplifting. It is believed that at one time the Klamaths were beneath a great deal of water, and great forces thrust them upward.

A significant amount of the range is composed of yellow-red, ultramafic peridotite. While this rock makes up the vast majority of the earth's mantle beneath the sea, it is relatively uncommon in high concentrations above the water. Interspersed throughout the ultramafic rock are large swaths of gabbro, a rock similar to granite but with a different chemical composition. Granite itself is present in sizable plutons, or masses of igneous rock. These were once great bubbles of lava that cooled beneath the earth and were later thrust upward, while the rest of the surroundings were eroded away. Other types of rock, including marble, were all accreted together to form an amazingly complex mountain range.

The Klamath Mountains extend from the North Yolla Bolly Mountains west of Red Bluff all the way to regions north of the Rogue River in Oregon, a distance of more than 180 miles. Large rivers are one of the defining characteristics of the Klamath Mountains, chief among them the great Trinity River, but the range also includes the Scott, Salmon, and Shasta Rivers. These swift-moving rivers travel through deep canyons and all feed into the long Klamath River.

Several major subranges exist within the Klamath Mountains. The Trinity Alps, Marble Mountains, and Siskiyou Mountains are all large, alpine blocks comprising hundreds of thousands of acres. Lesser-known ranges within the Klamaths include the North Yolla Bollys, the Kalmiopsis area in Oregon, the Scott Mountains, and the Trinity Divide. These last two are of particular importance to us, since they are in closest proximity to Mount Shasta.

The Trinity Divide is roughly 20 miles long, stretching from Red Mountain in the south to China Mountain in the north. The range is so named because it forms the divide between the headwaters of the Trinity River and the Sacramento River, the longest in California. Like most of the Klamath Mountains, the range is a mixture of different rock types. Large sections of these mountains are composed of gabbro or serpentine or peridotite.

Mount Eddy, a large massif at the north end of the divide, is both the range's and Klamath Mountains' high point, at just over 9,000 feet. The northern third of the range, which includes Mount Eddy, is significantly higher than the rest of the divide, and is referred to as the Eddy Range or simply "the Eddys." The central third of the Trinity Divide is a long ridge that runs east from the main crest. This ridge is flanked by the South Fork of the Sacramento River. Most of the Trinity Divide's trails in this guide are found along this section of the mountains. The southernmost part of the Trinity Divide has some spectacular scenery, but it has also seen extensive logging activity. Significant pockets of pristine country are still found here, but this area is still healing from past hurts.

The Scott Mountains are geologically similar to the Trinity Divide, but most of the range is composed of serpentine and peridotite, with fewer intrusions of other kinds of rock. They meet the Trinity Divide at China Mountain, the fourth tallest peak in the Mount Shasta area. From there they extend westward and connect to the vast Trinity Alps. The eastern half of the Scotts forms the divide between the headwaters of the Trinity River and the Scott River. Only the easternmost end of these mountains is near Mount Shasta, so they tend to be overlooked. Nonetheless, these are tall, beautiful mountains.

Between Mount Shasta and the Trinity Divide lies the Strawberry Valley, the gap between the two vast mountain ranges. Other broad, flat areas lie to the north and south of Mount Shasta. The Shasta Valley lies to the north, and is drained by the Shasta River. The McCloud Flats spread out to the south of Mount Shasta and are drained by the McCloud River. The high mountains are not the only places in the Mount Shasta area that have great trails. All three of the flat lowlands around Mount Shasta have excellent hikes and wonderful scenery.

History

The Mount Shasta area was inhabited by Native Americans for thousands of years before the arrival of European explorers. The lands were occupied by several different tribes, including the Klamath, Shasta, Wintu, and Modoc. The mountain was a natural draw to them and it was considered with awe and reverence.

Early explorers' accounts refer to sightings of a peak that may have been Mount Shasta, but the first reference to the peak by name was made in 1826 by Peter Skene Ogden, a trapper for the Hudson Bay Company. Though some believe he had actually sighted Oregon's Mount McLoughlin, history has accorded him the honor of discovery and naming. Mount Shasta was the last of the great Cascade volcanoes to be discovered, and is the only one to retain its Native American name. Despite taking its name from the original people who lived around it, the mountain's naming was not as simple as it sounds. Ogden originally named the peak Sastise, but several other names would be applied before the modern variation of its original name would be generally accepted. Other names for the peak included Pitt Mountain and Mount Jackson.

By the 1840s, fur trappers and explorers were traveling through the area regularly. John C. Fremont's third expedition, which included famed mountain man Kit Carson, passed the east side of the mountain and camped north of Mount Shasta on

Klamath Lake. In his notes, Fremont noted that Mount Shasta looked so high as to be unclimbable.

Over the course of the next decade a gold rush in the Klamath Mountains brought many prospectors, while settlements began to form around the base of the volcano. The town of Yreka, to the north of Mount Shasta, was a thriving boomtown that sprang up in support of the prospectors. Mining proliferated throughout the Klamath Mountains, though it was particularly heavy in the Trinity Alps. The Castle Crags was the site of several mines as well.

In 1855 the Battle of the Castle Crags took place. Starving Native Americans came down to miners' camps near Castella to raid food. The usual salmon runs that had supported the natives had been damaged by mining activity, leaving them with little to eat. Miners, including the famous poet Joaquin Miller, chased the tribe up into the mountains above the crags, and a pitched battle occurred on the ridge sepa-rating Castle Lake from the main block of the Castle Crags. Toward the end of the decade the mining boom was fading out but the first lumber mills were built, begin-ning another chapter in the economics of the Mount Shasta area.

Another boom was about to take place as well. Elias Pearce, a merchant from Yreka and a member of the state legislature, was the first to summit the mountain in 1854. Following his ascent, tourism became an increasingly prominent part of Mount Shasta life. Parties attempted the summit regularly. An early resident, Justin Sisson, established a tavern at the foot of Mount Shasta in the Strawberry Valley, near the present-day fish hatchery and Mount Shasta Sisson Museum. His tavern became a prominent hotel and way station for the stagecoach and its weary travelers. It was also a popular place to begin climbs up the mountain. This was the beginning of the modern community of Mount Shasta City.

However, not all who climbed the mountain were tourists. In the latter half of the nineteenth century, many luminaries of the exploration of the American West were drawn to Mount Shasta. Josiah Whitney and William Brewer were enthralled by the mountain and spent a great deal of time on it. Clarence King was admittedly haunted by Mount Shasta, made ascents to the top, and did a great deal of scientific research on it. His 1870 discovery of the giant Whitney Glacier was the first scientific confirma-tion that glaciers were active in the United States.

The following decade, famed explorer and ethnologist John Wesley Powell dwelt around the mountain, documenting the languages of the local Native American tribes. Great western painter Albert Bierstadt visited the area, and painted Mount Shasta. In the 1880s, the great USGS geologist Joseph Diller studied Mount Shasta while on an expedition in the Cascades that also included Lassen Peak and Crater Lake.

It was in the wake of these other travelers and explorers that one of Mount Shasta's most famous visitors arrived. John Muir first came to Mount Shasta in 1874. Though he is well known for his devotion to the great Sierra Nevada, Muir had fallen in love with Mount Shasta before he even reached the base of the mountain:

*When I first caught sight of it over the braided folds of the Sacramento Valley, I
was fifty miles away and afoot, alone and weary. Yet all my blood turned to wine,
and I have not been weary since.*

—John Muir, *Letters*, 1874–1888

The world-renowned naturalist returned to Mount Shasta more than a dozen
times over the next couple of decades. In a way, it was his home away from the Sierra.
On one famous occasion he and a guide climbed to the top of the mountain, only
to be overtaken by a sudden storm. He and his companion survived the night on top
of Mount Shasta by huddling over the active sulfur vents near the summit. He wrote
frequently about the mountain and his love for it. One of his strongest recommenda-
tions was to circumambulate the mountain, rather than attempt the summit. Another
recommendation made by Muir was the creation of Mount Shasta National Park.

*The Shasta region is still a fresh unspoiled wilderness, accessible and available for
travelers of every kind and degree. Would it not be a fine thing to set it apart like
the Yellowstone and Yosemite as a National Park for the welfare and benefit of
all mankind, preserving its fountains and forests and all its glad life in primeval
beauty?*

—John Muir, "Picturesque California," 1888

John Muir's desire to see the mountain enshrined as a national park never came
to pass. Many of the great forests that surrounded the mountain fell to the logger's ax,
and progress had its sway over the area. Yet the mountain withstood, and its beauty
and majesty remain unabated. The teachings of John Muir and other conservation-
ists were finally taken to heart by the American public and government when the
Wilderness Act was passed in 1964. On the twentieth anniversary of the act's passage,
in 1984, Congress passed the California Wilderness Act. This established the Mount
Shasta Wilderness, and at least a part of Muir's vision was brought to fruition. The
mountain was henceforth protected in its primeval state.

Perspective and Change

One of the most fascinating features of Mount Shasta is the amazing way its appearance seems to change depending on where you stand to observe it. The presence of
Shastina makes an enormous difference in the mountain's profile. From the west, it
seems like a giant, broad shoulder, balanced out by Sargents Ridge. From that perspective, Mount Shasta seems to lack a conical shape and does not look like a traditional
stratovolcano. If you view the mountain from the south Shastina is barely visible, but
the mountain takes on a very craggy, layered appearance. Conversely, Shastina is in
full view from the north, and the mountain appears much more conical. Only when

The Castle Crags highlight the view from the confluence of Castle Creek and the Sacramento River.

viewed from the east is Shastina completely obscured, and Mount Shasta takes on the traditional shape of a stratovolcano. So different are the perspectives, it almost seems as though you are looking at a different mountain from one side to another.

The appearance of the mountain is not the only aspect that changes. Mount Shasta is famous for its incredible displays of oddly shaped lenticular clouds. The clouds often appear as large discs aloft in the sky. They can be solitary, or in stacks, or scattered around and about the mountain. At times they will sit right on, or over, the summit. Other times the lenticular clouds will be somewhere adjacent to the mountain but not actually making contact. These clouds occur with some frequency, particularly when weather patterns are changing. Even if you have gazed on the mountain every day for a year, the amazing cloud displays ensure that you can never tire of the mountain or assume that it will be the same when you look upon it next.

Weather

The weather in the Mount Shasta area is typical of Northern California's mountain regions: The winters are cold with ample precipitation, and the summers are warm and dry. This is great for hikers. Even though snow can persist well into spring, many trails at lower elevations can be hiked when the higher trails are still inaccessible. Late spring, summer, and fall often have gorgeous weather, perfect for hitting the trail.

Even when it is hot in town, you can always drive up onto Mount Shasta or the Trinity Divide to find trails in cooler temperatures.

Not surprisingly, Mount Shasta has a lot of influence on the weather, creating the potential for unpredictable conditions. Snow has fallen on the mountain every month of the year, and storms can develop very suddenly. Some of the high points on Mount Shasta, especially Green Butte, draw lightning; it is best to get off of these if you see a storm developing. The same is true for mountains in the Trinity Divide, especially Mount Eddy.

Not all of Mount Shasta's sway over the weather, and its resultant unpredictability, is bad. One of the highlights of viewing the mountain is the opportunity to witness its famous lenticular clouds, which often presage changes in the weather. The endlessly different formations add a layer of visual majesty that embellishes a mountain that needs no embellishment.

Biological Diversity

The region surrounding Mount Shasta is world renowned for its unusual biological diversity. In particular, the Klamath Mountains are an incredibly rich botanical reservoir, due to their placement in proximity to many of the major mountain regions of the Pacific Southwest and Northwest: the Cascades, the Coast Ranges, the Sierra Nevada, and even the extensive basin-and-range province of the Great Basin. Species of all these areas are present in the Klamaths. The classic example is in the Russian Wilderness, a collection of granite peaks only 20 miles west of Mount Eddy, adjacent to the Scott Mountains. In one square mile of the Russian Wilderness, 17 different conifer species have been documented. This is the highest concentration of different conifers in the world. Although some of the species found in the Russian Wilderness are not present in the Scott Mountains and the Trinity Divide, most of them are, and many of the hikes in this book explore areas where these rare and unusual trees grow.

The amazing botanical features of the Klamath Mountains do not end with mere diversity. In addition to the range's proximity to other biological regions, the unique geology of the Klamaths has produced a number of endemic species—types of trees and plants that grow nowhere else in the world except within these mountains. The abundance of peridotite and serpentine, both of which produce poor, inhospitable soil, has forced adaptation onto many species. Look out for the Port Orford cedar, the Brewer spruce (also called a weeping spruce because of its droopy branchlets) and the *Darlingtonia*, a carnivorous pitcher plant sometimes referred to as a cobra lily. The last was considered such a significant find that Asa Gray, the greatest American botanist of the nineteenth century, accompanied John Muir to Mount Shasta to observe the plant and collect samples.

Not all of the notable trees are found in the Klamath Mountains. Although Mount Shasta does not have the unique species that proliferate in the mountains to the west, it does boast cathedral-like groves of Shasta red fir, as well as great stands of large mountain hemlock, a less common tree for the region.

Mount Shasta also presents hikers with the opportunity to observe *krummholz* at tree line. The several species of pine that can survive there are stunted and grow close to the ground, almost like a ground-cover plant in some cases. This phenomenon is typical at tree line elsewhere, but the opportunity to enjoy easy hikes through *krummholz* is not as common.

Hazards

Hiking the trails around Mount Shasta is not without its dangers. The four most common dangers are bears, mountain lions, rattlesnakes, and poison oak. The last is only found on a couple of trails in this book, at the lowest elevations. In most cases the trails pass through stands of the bush and careful walking will allow you to avoid touching it.

Bears: There are plenty of bears in the Mount Shasta area, though it is uncommon to encounter one on the trails. The best thing to do is to be alert and, if possible, travel in groups. Make noise to make your presence known to any bears in the area. Clapping and speaking loudly are effective ways to do this. If you do encounter a bear, do not run. Stay still until the bear has left. If they continue approaching you, fall to your stomach and lie still until the bear departs. If you are actually attacked by a bear, fight back. Bears generally do not expect prey to hit and kick them, which can deter them from continuing to attack.

Mountain lions: Mountain lions live throughout the mountains in this area, but are rarely seen. It is unlikely that you will encounter one on the trail. As always, hiking in groups is safer than hiking alone. If you do encounter a mountain lion, pick up any small children. The cats consider smaller animals easier to catch. Do not run. Mountain lions expect their prey to flee and running will cause them to pursue. Try to look as large as you can and do not crouch, kneel, or sit. People do not resemble a lion's normal prey when they are standing. Lastly, as with bears, if you are attacked, fight back. Mountain lions can be made to flee.

Rattlesnakes: Rattlesnakes are found around the Mount Shasta area. Be alert to what is on the trail. If you see a rattlesnake, do not try to handle it. Stay at least 6 feet away—the farther away, the better. Be especially careful when climbing up rock piles and similar places where snakes may be hiding.

Camping

The Mount Shasta area has a variety of lodgings suitable for any budget. It also has a great selection of places to camp. The USDA Forest Service maintains several campgrounds scattered throughout the mountains and canyons around Mount Shasta.

Some campgrounds, like the ones at Castle and Gumboot Lakes, are located in beautiful alpine lake basins. The Fowlers campground is right on the McCloud River, only minutes away from the waterfalls. A pair of great campgrounds are on Mount Shasta: The McBride Springs Campground is just outside of Mount Shasta City on the Everitt Memorial Highway, while Panther Meadows is found near tree line, high on the mountain.

The forest service also permits dispersed camping in the national forest, so long as you do not camp in an area where it is expressly prohibited. Dispersed camping means that there are no amenities, including no water and no restrooms. Popular dispersed spots include the South Fork of the Sacramento River and Bunny Flat. Other areas, farther from Mount Shasta, have forest service campgrounds as well. One great example is the beautiful spot at Orr Lake, in the secluded country northeast of Mount Shasta.

The Lake Siskiyou Resort operates a large campground with great access to the lake and the Lake Siskiyou Trail. It is also conveniently located near many of the hikes in this guide. Castle Crags State Park maintains three campgrounds: a large one close to park headquarters, and two primitive environmental camps near the Flume Trail and the Sacramento River. Lastly, there is a public campground at Lake Shastina on the north side of Mount Shasta. If the lake is full, this can be a pleasant spot.

Water

The Mount Shasta region is well known for its high-quality water. In addition to the Sacramento and McCloud Rivers, there are dozens of creeks and a vast array of springs. Indeed, the water was one of the first attractions that brought tourists to Mount Shasta. Resorts like Shasta Springs and Ney Springs were popular with travelers who came to the mountains to enjoy the fantastic scenery, imbibe the pure waters, and relax. While most of these resorts have long since closed, the water remains a powerful draw. It is available for purchase far and wide from name-brand bottled water companies. The springs themselves attract those looking for pure, cold water gushing forth from the earth. The most popular of these is in the Mount Shasta City Park. The springs there, colloquially referred to as the headwaters of the Sacramento River (they aren't, the river begins in large lakes and meadows high in the Trinity Divide), are prolific. People enjoying the waters and bottling it up to take home are a constant presence here.

Hikers in the Mount Shasta area are fortunate to enjoy many sources of water while on the trail. A particularly edifying benefit is the number of springs along the trails. Like their counterparts closer to populated areas, these produce exceptionally pure, cold water and it is not necessary to filter it. While you are on the trail, you can simply enjoy the earth's bounty and drink the water without treating it. The same is true for the well-known springs in the Trinity Divide, such as the Indian Spring in the Castle Crags. This water flows from the rocks, some of which is diverted just downstream and used by the State Park's campground.

Though the springs have exceptional purity, the water from the lakes and streams should still be treated. Many consider the water to be safe, but caution is still in order and treating the water from these sources is recommended.

The Deadfall Lakes Basin.

Dogs

Hikers accompanied by their canine friends will find the Mount Shasta area particularly dog friendly. Other than hikes in the Mount Shasta Wilderness and Castle Crags State Park, most of the trails in this guidebook are open to hikers with dogs. The only trail on Mount Shasta that is open to dogs is the Old Ski Bowl Trail, which lies outside the wilderness boundary. Dogs are permitted on the trail, but it is important not to cross over the ridge into the wilderness area. Even though Castle Crags State Park prohibits dogs, there still some hikes in the Crags where canines are welcome. The hike on the Pacific Crest Trail to Burstarse Falls is completely outside of the state park and dogs are permitted. The short access trail to the PCT is named the Dog Trail because it allows hikers with dogs to bypass the state park. It is also possible to follow the PCT east for a ways with dogs, but a shuttle hike is not feasible, since it enters the state park. The only other trails in this guide where dogs are not allowed are Hike 24 in the Shasta Valley Wildlife Refuge and Hike 50 in the McCloud River Preserve.

Maps

Numerous maps of the Mount Shasta region are available for hikers. For good overviews of the area, the official maps of the Shasta–Trinity and Klamath National Forests are great resources. These large maps, produced by the forest service, are waterproof and printed in full color. One especially nice feature is the color-coded properties, indicating the land status of salient points. The one drawback to these maps is their scale, which is so large that it is not great for trail detail. The forest service has also produced a nice map that has good detail for the Mount Shasta and Castle Crags Wilderness areas.

If you are looking for a little more detail for hiking in the Mount Shasta Wilderness, Thomas Harrison has produced a nice map for the mountain. Though it has a few minor errors (none of which will really steer you wrong), it is easy to read and fairly comprehensive. It also has the convenience of indicating the mileage between points.

For trails in any area around Mount Shasta, the USGS topo maps are good and are generally reliable. A few of the hikes in this guide do not appear on these maps because the trails were recently constructed or the maps are in need of updating, but overall they are still reliable resources.

Trail Finder

	Great Views	Wild-flowers	Peak Baggers	Lakes	Rivers and Creeks	Waterfalls	Canyons	Remark-able Trees	Interesting Geology	History Buffs	Back-packers	Kids	Hikeable Offseason
Mount Shasta City Trails													
1. Lake Siskiyou	•	•		•	•							•	•
2. Box Canyon Trail					•		•			•		•	•
3. Ney Springs Creek					•	•	•					•	•
4. Hedge Creek Falls					•	•	•		•	•		•	•
5. Elsa Rupp Preserve					•							•	•
6. Spring Hill	•		•									•	•
7. Gateway Trail	•												
8. Black Butte	•		•						•				
Mount Shasta Trails													
9. Horse Camp	•	•								•	•		
10. Green Butte Ridge	•		•										
11. Panther Meadow	•	•			•							•	
12. Gray Butte	•	•	•					•					
13. South Gate Meadow	•	•			•						•		

	Great Views	Wild-flowers	Peak Baggers	Lakes	Rivers and Creeks	Waterfalls	Canyons	Remark-able Trees	Interesting Geology	History Buffs	Back-packers	Kids	Hikeable Offseason
14. Old Ski Bowl	•									•			
15. Clear Creek	•	•				•					•		
16. Brewer Creek	•				•	•	•				•		
17. North Gate	•												
18. Whitney Falls	•				•	•	•		•				
Shasta Valley & Cascade Crest													
19. Black Lava Trail	•							•	•			•	•
20. Goosenest	•		•					•	•				
21. Orr Lake	•			•	•							•	•
22. Juanita Lake				•								•	
23. Pluto's Cave	•								•			•	•
24. Trout Lake	•			•								•	•
Scott Mountains													
25. Kangaroo Fen & Bull Lake	•	•		•							•		
26. Caldwell Lakes	•			•							•		
27. Bluff Lake & Cement Bluff	•			•					•		•		

	Great Views	Wild-flowers	Peak Baggers	Lakes	Rivers and Creeks	Waterfalls	Canyons	Remark-able Trees	Interesting Geology	History Buffs	Back-packers	Kids	Hikeable Offseason
Trinity Divide													
28. Deadfall Lakes & Mount Eddy	•	•	•	•	•			•			•		
29. Sisson–Callahan Trail	•	•		•	•		•	•		•	•		
30. Castle Lake Shore				•								•	•
31. Little Castle Lake & Mount Bradley	•		•	•									
32. Heart Lake	•		•	•									
33. Gray Rock Lakes	•			•							•	•	
34. Soapstone Trail	•												
35. Cliff Lakes	•			•				•				•	
36. Gumboot Lake	•			•								•	
37. Porcupine & Toad Lakes	•	•		•							•		
38. Seven Lakes Basin	•	•		•							•	•	
39. Tamarack Lake & Twin Lakes				•									
Castle Crags													
40. Root Creek					•	•						•	•
41. Castle Dome	•								•				

	Great Views	Wild-flowers	Peak Baggers	Lakes	Rivers and Creeks	Waterfalls	Canyons	Remarkable Trees	Interesting Geology	History Buffs	Back-packers	Kids	Hikeable Offseason
42. Flume Trail					•					•		•	•
43. Burstarse Falls					•	•	•		•			•	
44. Lower Castle Crags Traverse	•				•				•				•
45. Sacramento River					•			•	•			•	•
McCloud River													
46. McCloud Falls					•	•	•	•	•			•	•
47. McCloud River Trail		•			•			•	•	•		•	•
48. Squaw Valley Creek		•			•	•		•				•	
49. Ash Camp to Ah-Di-Na					•		•			•	•		
50. McCloud River Preserve					•		•						

Map Legend

Municipal

≡⬡5⬡≡ Interstate Highway

≡⬭97⬭≡ US Highway

≡⬭89⬭≡ State Road

═══════ Local/County Road

≡⊡A10⊡≡ Forest Road

═ ═ ═ ═ Unpaved Road

├──┼──┤ Railroad

Trails

------ Featured Trail

------ Trail

·········· Off-Trail Hike

Water Features

⬭ Body of Water

Marsh

River/Creek

Intermittent Stream

Waterfall

Spring

Symbols

⧖ Bridge

▲ Backcountry Campground

Boat Launch

■ Building/Point of Interest

⋀ Campground

∩ Cave

× Elevation

Lava

🅿 Parking

⧓ Pass

▲ Peak/Elevation

⊞ Picnic Area

Scenic View

○ Town

⑳ Trailhead

❓ Visitor/Information Center

Land Management

National Park/Forest

Wilderness Area/
Natural Landmark

State/County Park

Miscellaneous Area

Part I: Mount Shasta City Trails

Mount Shasta City is nestled in the Strawberry Valley, a wide depression lying between Mount Shasta on the east and the Trinity Divide on the west. The north end of the valley is secured in dramatic fashion by the giant pyramid of Black Butte, while the south end is open, quickly falling away into the canyon of the Sacramento River, which flows south from its headwaters in the Trinity Divide all the way to San Francisco Bay.

Like many of the communities in Siskiyou County, Mount Shasta City's roots lie in the timber industry. Now it is the recreational epicenter of southern Siskiyou County. Most trips to the area begin in town, where logistical needs can be met and there is a good assortment of restaurants and lodgings.

The trails around the town can be divided into two areas, each accentuating different features of the Strawberry Valley.

South of town, the trails orient around the Sacramento River and its tributaries. Whether it is the impounded waters of Lake Siskiyou, rushing tributary creeks racing to join the Sacramento, or the large river itself as it surges through the Box Canyon, these trails revolve around water. Hiking here is easy, refreshing, and pleasant, yet sacrifice nothing in terms of great scenery.

In contrast, the trails north of town are dedicated to exploring volcanic terrain. Climbing peaks like Black Butte, Spring Hill, and the lower flanks of Mount Shasta, these are hikes that celebrate great views of Mount Shasta. Whichever trail you follow, the hikes around Mount Shasta City are a great way to familiarize yourself with the area.

1 Lake Siskiyou

Circumnavigating beautiful Lake Siskiyou, this easy hike has great views of Mount Shasta, Mount Eddy, and the surrounding mountains. There are also beaches at the Sacramento River's inlet and at the Lake Siskiyou Resort. Although it encircles the lake, the trail is often broken up into hikes along the north and south shores, especially in the winter and spring when the bridges across the Sacramento River are removed. This is one of the most popular trails in the Mount Shasta area.

Total distance: 6.2 miles
Trail type: Loop or out and back
Elevation gain: Minimal
Difficulty: Easy to moderate, depending on destination
Trail surface: Pavement; packed dirt
Hiking time: About 4.5 hours
Season: Year-round, but the loop is incomplete from November to April due to seasonal bridge removal

Fees and permits: There is a per-person fee to enter the Lake Siskiyou Resort.
Canine compatibility: Dogs are permitted.
Land status: Siskiyou County
Trail contact: Siskiyou County Public Works, 1312 Fairlane Rd., Yreka, CA 96097; (530) 842-8250; www.co.siskiyou.ca.us;
Other: Water and other supplies are available at the Lake Siskiyou Resort.

Finding the trailhead: From the city of Mount Shasta, head west on West Lake Street, crossing over I-5. At the stop sign, turn left onto Old Stage Road. After 0.3 mile veer right onto W A Barr Road. Continue south, turning right into the parking lot just before crossing over the dam that impounds the Sacramento River and forms Lake Siskiyou. GPS: N41° 16' 51.10" / W122° 19' 45.41"

The Hike

Nestled at the foot of the Trinity Divide and enjoying outstanding views of Mount Shasta, Lake Siskiyou is one of the prettiest reservoirs in California. It is also one of the premier features of Mount Shasta City, a community that boasts a cornucopia of outdoor attractions.

The encircling Lake Siskiyou Trail may be the least wild trail in the Mount Shasta area, but it still supplies plenty of beautiful scenery highlighted by fantastic views of Mount Shasta, Mount Eddy, and Battle Rock, the high point of the Castle Crags.

Many amenities are scattered around Lake Siskiyou, particularly along the south shore, where the Lake Siskiyou Resort offers an extensive campground, a boat ramp, beach, and associated stores and restaurants. Despite this, there are still many opportunities to enjoy a natural setting while hiking around the lake. This is particularly important in the off-season, when the high country is covered in snow. At that time, the Lake Siskiyou Trail still offers hikers the chance to enjoy the outdoors and appreciate spectacular vistas.

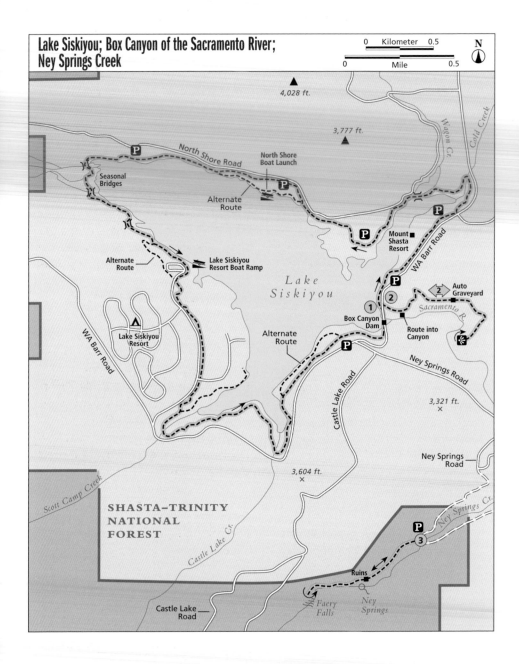

0   Kilometer   0.5

0   Mile   0.5

N

▲ 4,028 ft.

▲ 3,777 ft.

North Shore Road

North Shore Boat Launch

Seasonal Bridges

Alternate Route

Alternate Route

Lake Siskiyou Resort Boat Ramp

Mount Shasta Resort

WA Barr Road

Auto Graveyard

Lake *Siskiyou*

Lake Siskiyou Resort

WA Barr Road

Alternate Route

Box Canyon Dam

Route into Canyon

Sacramento R.

Ney Springs Road

3,321 ft. ×

3,604 ft. ×

Castle Lake Road

Ney Springs Road

SHASTA–TRINITY NATIONAL FOREST

Scott Camp Creek

Castle Lake Cr.

Wagon Cr.

Cold Creek

Ney Springs Cr.

Ruins

Castle Lake Road

Faery Falls

Ney Springs

Because the Lake Siskiyou Trail rings the lake, there is not a clear beginning or end. There are, however, distinct sections of the trail that have varied personalities. The north and southeast shores are the most natural and undeveloped portions of the trail. The bulk of the south shore route passes through the campground and buildings of the Lake Siskiyou Resort, while the northeast section of the trail passes by the edge of the Mount Shasta Resort and along the road that accesses the lake from Mount

Shasta City. For those not attempting the entire loop, one popular section is the north shore, usually from a parking area on W A Barr Road to the Sacramento River's inlet, a distance of about 2.25 miles. Another runs from the dam to the edge of the Lake Siskiyou Resort, which is also about 2.25 miles. However, whenever possible, the loop around the lake is a great way to enjoy the trail.

One can start at any of the six trailheads or at the Lake Siskiyou Resort. This description of the trail will begin at the Box Canyon Dam Trailhead, which is located immediately north of the dam. This is the best place to start a loop around the lake because (assuming a counterclockwise circumnavigation) it gets the section through the Mount Shasta Resort and along the busy road over with first, places the Sacramento River inlet as a sort of mid-point highlight, and saves the incredible views of Mount Shasta from the southeast corner of the lake as the climax of the entire hike. From there it is a short jaunt back to the trailhead. While the trail can be done in a number of permutations, this pattern puts the emphasis on the trail's scenic qualities and the fantastic views of Mount Shasta.

Beginning at the parking area on the north side of the Box Canyon Dam, the trail heads north along W A Barr Road. Walk through the parking lot looking for the wide path heading north, running parallel to the road. This section, stretching to the north for about 0.8 miles, suffers the most vehicular traffic and is by far the least natural part of the hike. About 0.5 mile from the trailhead, the Lake Siskiyou Trail passes another parking area, across the street from the main entrance to the Mount Shasta Resort. The path continues north along the road and then descends a switchback that crosses a creek and descends into a narrow gully, finally taking on a natural setting.

Cold Creek begins only a short distance to the north, emerging from springs near the fish hatchery. The trail follows the creek until the rushing waters are stilled as they meet the impounded water of Lake Siskiyou. The path proceeds west, staying 50 feet or so above the lake, then traveling along the spine of a very narrow spit of land that extends out into the lake. At the west end of the spit, the great arch of the recently constructed Wagon Creek Bridge rises above the water. For many years the Lake Siskiyou Trail was incomplete and a full circuit around the lake was not possible. With the completion of the bridge, all sections of the trail are now linked together.

On the far side of the bridge, the trail hugs the lakeshore, staying 30 feet above the water. About 0.3 mile past the bridge the route arrives at the third parking area. Though not part of the official trail, it is worthwhile to continue to the south, where a narrow peninsula extends out into the water and has great views of the lake.

To continue on the Lake Siskiyou Trail, return to the parking lot and look for the trail continuing on the west side. The route passes along the edge of a grassy meadow before making a lazy arc to the north, where the trail intersects an old road that now functions as the trail and soon leads to the edge of Lake Siskiyou again.

The trail splits here. The main route stays high and nears the road as it skirts the edge of the large bowl that holds the lake. Though the trail is generally in the trees along this stretch, there are plenty of views of the lake and Battle Rock. The alternative route drops down to the lake's level and stays near the shore as it heads west. This area is open and grassy, adding variation to the trail.

Whichever route you choose, they both arrive at a large parking and picnic area after 0.3 mile. The trails continue for another 0.4 mile until they meet again. At the junction the grassy, level area crossed by the alternate route ends and the two trails, now joined, continue through the trees high above the lake. Another 0.3 mile leads to the final parking area before the crossing of the Sacramento River's inlet.

To get to the inlet, stay on the trail as it heads west. It drops down a slope before a sign points the proper direction. The path turns to the south and crosses a series of small overflow creeks choked with riparian vegetation before depositing hikers on the banks of the river. Metal bridges set on top of thick wire baskets filled with river rock provide an easy way across the rushing waters. Note that these bridges are removed from November through April. During the winter it may be possible to cross the river anyway. Once the spring runoff comes, the Sacramento is a raging torrent and should not be crossed.

On the far side of the river, the trail continues through the river's wash, which is covered with river rock. The lake's inlet is popular with picnickers because of a beach between the Sacramento River's two channels. The highlight, however, is the view to the west, where Mount Eddy looms 6,000 feet overhead.

The sandy path cuts through the area for 0.2 mile to the far side of the wash, where a second channel of the Sacramento is revealed, spanned by another set of seasonal bridges. The trail then makes one short switchback up the embankment and begins the long eastward journey along the lake's south shore.

Once on the south shore, the wide trail passes through mixed forest just above the lake. It soon crosses a seasonal creek on a well-built, heavy wooden bridge, and continues to parallel the edge of the lake, eventually arriving at a trail junction marked by a gate with hiker pass-throughs. Note that the official route of the Lake Siskiyou Trail turns right at the junction and heads uphill on a dirt road.

The trail then veers off the road and passes through chaparral until it emerges in the southwest corner of a large parking lot at the Lake Siskiyou Boat Ramp. This section of the trail has no views, is hot, and has minimal shade. Instead of going this way, stay straight at the gate and continue hiking by the lake. The path passes occasional picnic tables with views across the lake of Mount Shasta emerging from behind Rainbow Ridge.

The trail soon reaches the boat ramp. There are good, clean bathrooms on the far side of the ramp.

Whichever option you take to get to the boat ramp area, there is minimal signage indicating where to go from here. The best course is to head toward the little store at the parking lot. From there, follow the road for a few yards and look for a sign indicating the Lake Siskiyou Trail, which heads off the road to the east. Hike through the trees along the rock-lined trail. At the telephone pole turn right, and walk the rest of the way to the road. Be sure not to stay straight at the telephone pole. Though the trail is well established, it only leads into the campground.

Lenticular clouds and Mount Shasta highlight the view from the south shore of Lake Siskiyou.

Once at the road, the trail cuts through the heart of the Lake Siskiyou Resort. During the summer months there is an incredible amount of activity in this bustling vacation community. Staying along the road, the path proceeds east. Along the way it passes campgrounds, a laundromat, a playground, the general store, and the Lake Sis restaurant. Beyond the general store area, the trail crosses a road and the activity begins to fade significantly.

As the woods thicken, a sign indicates a side trail branching off to the east, toward the lake. Though this trail is not part of the loop around the lake, for those with the time, it is a pleasant option that leads along the Scott Camp Creek arm of the lake. The path eventually arrives at the edge of the main body of the lake and turns back to the west, leading to the resort's beach. Here there is an iconic view of Mount Shasta. The beach has a snack shack and all sorts of aquatic recreation available.

Resuming the loop around the lake, the trail departs the resort on a wide dirt road. It hugs the contours of the water as it first heads west, along Scott Camp Creek. It crosses the creek and then returns to the east, following the south side of the creek. It is possible to climb down to the water, and there are some nice pools in the creek that make great spots for relaxing.

The route then turns to the right around a little ridge and begins to parallel the impounded waters of Castle Lake Creek, which emerges from Castle Lake. The trail follows this arm of the lake to the creek's inlet and makes another crossing. Once on the east side of the creek, the trail heads north a short distance to another trail junction. Here the main path cuts straight through the woods to the trail's final parking area. A much more scenic option is to take the singletrack alternate route, which stays close to the water and has views. The perspective is particularly good for Mount Eddy, whose immense bulk is impressive from here.

This path eventually ends at an area with picnic tables on the south shore. From this point hikers can appreciate one of the most spectacular views of Mount Shasta to be found anywhere. The great mountain towers high overhead and reflects in the lake's clear waters. It is a tremendous climax to the trip around the lake. This spot is also easily accessed from the aforementioned parking area, and is a great easy-to-get-to place to take pictures of Mount Shasta.

When you are finally able to pull away from the incredible view, head up the wide path toward the parking area. A signed junction marks the return to the main branch of the Lake Siskiyou Trail. Turn left and continue through the woods to the Box Canyon Dam. Be sure to cross the dam on the east side to catch glimpses of the awesome canyon of the Sacramento River. On the far side of the dam is the parking lot from which you set out.

Miles and Directions

0.0 Start by hiking north on the Lake Siskiyou Trail from the north end of the Box Canyon Dam parking lot.

0.6 Arrive at Cold Creek and follow it to the inlet at Lake Siskiyou.

0.9 Cross over the Lake Siskiyou Bridge.

1.2 Reach a large parking area. Continue east through a gate and skirt the edge of a meadow.

1.6 The trail splits. The main route stays high while the alternate route follows the edge of the water.

1.8 Both trails meet at the north-shore boat launch.

2.7 The trail descends a short hill and comes to the first of two channels of the Sacramento River.

3.3 After crossing the second channel of the Sacramento, climb to the edge of the lake and follow the shore west to a junction. Stay left and continue to the Lake Siskiyou Resort boat ramp.

3.5 Turn right at the boat ramp and follow the road past the store.

3.6 Turn left on a marked dirt path cutting through the trees. It quickly comes to an end on the side of the main campground road.

4.1 Follow the camp road through the Lake Siskiyou Resort, passing the store, campground, and other structures. When the road turns right, veer left onto an old dirt road. A spur trail to the left connects to the resort's beach.

5.4 Hike along the dirt road as it rounds Scott Camp Creek and Castle Lake Creek's inlets into Lake Siskiyou. On the east side of Castle Lake Creek, the road reaches a junction.

5.9 Arrive at the south shore picnic area and enjoy the incredible view of Mount Shasta.

6.2 Continue across the dam, reaching the Box Canyon parking lot and completing the loop.

2 Box Canyon of the Sacramento River

Just below Lake Siskiyou is the Sacramento River's Box Canyon, a narrow gorge with tall cliffs. The trail meanders along the rim of the canyon with frequent views down into the interior. An unusual car cemetery in the woods makes an interesting feature for history and car buffs. The trail ends at a large rock outcropping with a great perspective on the river that races along the bottom of the canyon. A spur route near the beginning of the hike leads to a short, via ferrata-esque descent down the cliffs to the river using iron ladders and ropes.

See map on page 22
Total distance: 1.5 miles
Trail type: Out and back
Elevation gain: Minimal
Difficulty: Easy
Trail surface: Packed dirt
Hiking time: About 1 hour
Season: Year-round

Fees and permits: None
Canine compatibility: Dogs are permitted.
Land status: Siskiyou County
Trail contact: Siskiyou County Public Works, 1312 Fairlane Road, Yreka, CA 96097; (530) 842-8250; www.co.siskiyou.ca.us
Other: There is no water on the trail.

Finding the trailhead: From the city of Mount Shasta, drive west on West Lake Street, crossing over I-5. At the stop sign, turn left onto Old Stage Road. After 0.3 mile, veer right onto W A Barr Road. Continue south, turning right into the parking lot just before crossing over the dam that impounds the Sacramento River and forms Lake Siskiyou. Walk across the street and look for the sign hanging from a tree, marking the beginning of the Box Canyon Trail. GPS: N41° 16' 51.10" / W122° 19' 45.41"

The Hike

The Box Canyon of the Sacramento River is most often observed from the Box Canyon Dam, which impounds the Sacramento River to form Lake Siskiyou. The canyon, a narrow trough lined with 200-foot-high cliffs, channels the river along a fast-paced course just after being released from the dam. Unfortunately, the view that most people get from the dam is marred by the protective fencing that lines the dam's sidewalk. They usually gaze down into the canyon with interest and move on.

Fortunately, there is another, better option to experience canyon. The hike has many things to recommend it. First, it is a scenic trail that has interesting routing and offers several vistas down into the canyon. Second, it is an easy trail: At about 1.5 miles round-trip, it is short and level. Third, the trail has fascinating historical artifacts, namely an old car and appliance graveyard where the old metal skeletons, some dating back as far as the 1930s, are piled up along the path. Lastly, the Box Canyon Trail includes a spur that offers an exciting descent to the bottom of the canyon, next to the river.

Old cars line the Box Canyon Trail.

The trail begins on the north side of the Box Canyon Dam with a very mild descent, passing through a mixed forest of ponderosa pine, cedar, and oak, as well as brush, mostly manzanita. After only 0.1 mile, a trail splits off to the right. This is the route that descends into the bottom of the Box Canyon.

Stay left, crossing a broad, arcing slope of the canyon wall that is covered with thousands of river rocks, which appear to be in place to prevent erosion. Above the stone embankment you can see the edge of the Mount Shasta Resort's golf course. As you hike the wide path above the stones, look downstream into the canyon to observe a pretty waterfall dropping down the cliffs into the Sacramento River.

Beyond the stone embankment and the golf course, the trail narrows and soon passes a small, spring-fed creek with an attractive, narrow gorge of its own. Beyond the creek, the trail maintains an easterly course along the Box Canyon rim.

Keep an eye out for a few rusty barrels, which are followed by a couple of old, rusty cars that are in states of deep decay. This is just a harbinger of the extensive auto-appliance graveyard ahead, where earlier residents of Mount Shasta City would push their unwanted cars and appliances down the hill to dispose of them. At the time, the slope must have been clear of trees. Now it is heavily wooded, and some cars even have trees growing through them. Some narrow tracks leave the trail to wind their way through the extensive collection of antiques. This makes an interesting excursion all its own. The graveyard adds an interesting angle to the Box Canyon Trail and seems more like a piece of history than an old dump.

The trail next crosses another small stream, this time utilizing a small bridge made of piled logs. The angle of the canyon's slope has steepened considerably by this point, and the path is now well below the canyon rim, though it is still just above the most vertical part of the cliffs that make up the Box Canyon proper. When the canyon makes a broad bend to the south, good views open up down to the bottom.

The path has a little more exposure than before and the canyon falls away steeply to the right. Watch for a well-established spur trail branching off to the right. Follow this to a series of rock outcrops. You can carefully climb out onto the rocks and get great views down into the canyon. This is the best view of the canyon, other than those along the route to the bottom. Back on the main trail, the path proceeds a little farther, to another rock outcropping, but the views here are not as good.

Canyon Access

One of the best features of the Box Canyon Trail is the opportunity to climb down into the seemingly inaccessible canyon. At the junction near the beginning of the trail, stay to the right. The trail drops steeply down the side of the canyon, toward the large stone embankment. Just before reaching the rocks, the trail turns to the right. It steepens and begins to climb down into the rocky, inner gorge. Though not necessary, thick ropes have been securely fastened to aid the descent. At the bottom of the rope section, the trail utilizes iron ladders mounted to the cliffs to finish the trip to the bottom.

Once inside the canyon, a broad, rocky bench is flanked by the Sacramento River. You can scramble over the rocks upstream and get a rare glimpse of the Box Canyon Dam from the bottom. It is much more imposing from below. If you scramble downstream, there is perhaps the best view of the whole trip, where the canyon narrows and the river crashes against cliffs on both sides of the canyon. To complete the picture, a small but attractive waterfall cascades into the river.

Miles and Directions

0.0 Start by crossing the road and hiking on the Box Canyon Trail.

0.1 Reach the spur that climbs down into the canyon. Descend into the canyon now, or on the return.

0.5 Arrive at the auto graveyard.

0.75 Reach the large rock outcrop with views down into the canyon. Retrace your steps.

1.5 Arrive back at the trailhead.

3 Ney Springs Creek

This short hike enters a lush canyon; home to nineteenth-century ruins, a well-developed rock climbing area, a crashing creek, and a beautiful waterfall. Using an old dirt road as a trail, the path climbs through the canyon, just above beautiful Ney Springs Creek. A side trail visits exquisite Faery Falls. This is a good trail in the off-season.

See map on page 22
Total distance: 1.5 miles
Trail type: Out and back
Elevation gain: 300 feet
Difficulty: Easy
Trail surface: Old dirt road
Hiking time: About 1 hour
Season: Year-round (best in spring)

Fees and permits: None
Canine compatibility: Dogs are permitted.
Land status: Shasta-Trinity National Forest
Trail contact: Mount Shasta Ranger District, 204 W. Alma St., Mount Shasta CA 96067; (530) 926-4511; www.fs.usda.gov/stnf
Other: Water is available in Ney Springs Creek. Do not disturb the old resort ruins.

Finding the trailhead: From the city of Mount Shasta, head west on West Lake Street, crossing over I-5. At the stop sign, turn left onto Old Stage Road. After 0.3 mile, veer right onto W A Barr Road. Continue south, crossing over the dam that impounds the Sacramento River and forms Lake Siskiyou. Just past the dam, make a left turn onto Castle Lake Road. Immediately, make another left turn onto the well-maintained gravel of Ney Springs Road. Continue straight, passing the turn to the Ney Springs/Cantara Wildlife Area at 1 mile. The road turns to the west. After another 0.5 mile, a large clearing appears on the left. Park here and hike up the road on the right. It is possible to continue driving up the road, but the surface degrades significantly beyond the clearing. GPS: N41° 15' 57.85" / W122° 19' 26.73"

The Hike

This hike, following an old road, enters a densely forested canyon through which raucous Ney Springs Creek crashes over boulders and small cataracts. At the upper end of the road are ruins of nineteenth-century Ney Springs Resort. Little remains other than some walls, cisterns, fountains, and some steps leading down into the creek. Nonetheless, these ruins are a fascinating glimpse into the type of tourism that used to be found throughout the Mount Shasta area. Ney Springs Resort was one of many camp resorts that dotted the region, from Dunsmuir to north of Weed. Beyond the ruins, the trail culminates at Faery Falls, where Ney Springs Creek tumbles into the canyon.

The old road that makes up the Ney Springs canyon's trail begins at a junction in a clearing. The main road crosses Ney Springs Creek and continues east on the south bank of the creek. The hike heads west, staying on the north side of the creek. It is a short trail, directly above the creek, passing through dense forest canopy. The creek

Faery Falls.

moves swiftly through the canyon, pouring over small waterfalls and rapids. Enormous boulders line the edge of the creek, adding a sense of drama.

After 0.4 mile of slight climbing, the road reaches the ruins of the Ney Springs Resort. The first section of the ruins is difficult to make out because it is overgrown. If you are interested in exploring the ruins, find the obvious retaining walls, cisterns, and fountains and such, then backtrack to find the large foundations of cut stone.

In its heyday, the resort boasted an extensive complex and drew guests for many years. John Ney discovered the springs in 1887, and within a few years the resort had been established. At its height, the resort boasted a hotel that could accommodate fifty people, a bathhouse, and various outbuildings including a barn and a carriage house. Boardwalks were reportedly constructed through the forest as well. Today, little remains of the resort. The most obvious sections are a large retaining wall that once housed a fountain, and another retaining wall leading down to a stone platform and cisterns next to the creek. Some of the pipes used to transport the spring water can still be found, and in places they have broken and the water continues to flow out of the breach.

A hundred yards or so below the primary ruin, a level, raised area created by piling rocks may once have been the barn or carriage house. The way the forest has reclaimed the area gives it an attractive, albeit eerie, quality.

Past the ruins, the trail continues to climb up the canyon just above the creek. A rough road branches off to the right, leading to the rock climbing area. To reach

Faery Falls, stay left on the main road. It continues past the resort ruins for 0.25 mile. Look for a cairn-marked use trail that drops down to the creek. Here are several good vantages for the falls and it is possible to climb all the way to the base.

Faery Falls is an attractive, 40-foot cataract. Today, the falls draw most people into Ney Springs Canyon, and its proximity to the resort suggests it was equally popular with the canyon's guests in the nineteenth century. The fall has two tiers, first shooting through a narrow slot in the cliff and crashing into a small bowl. The creek then pours out of the bowl, splits in two, and fans out over the rock. Late in the season, half of the second tier fan disappears.

Miles and Directions

0.0 Start by leaving the parking area in the clearing, and begin hiking up the canyon alongside Ney Springs Creek.

0.4 Arrive at Ney Springs Resort ruins.

0.75 Descend the short spur trail to Faery Falls. Retrace your steps.

1.5 Arrive back at the trailhead.

4 Hedge Creek Falls

Hedge Creek Falls, a pretty little waterfall in a small city park north of Dunsmuir, is just off of I-5. The falls are the main attraction, but the trail is full of unusual geology, interesting routing, and a great view of Mount Shasta. This short hike has a lot to offer.

Total distance: 0.8 mile
Trail type: Out and back
Elevation gain: 200 feet
Difficulty: Easy
Trail surface: Packed dirt; rocky
Hiking time: About 1 hour
Season: Year-round, but best in spring when the falls are full

Fees and permits: None
Canine compatibility: Dogs are permitted.
Land status: Dunsmuir city park
Trail contact: City of Dunsmuir Parks and Recreation, 4841 Dunsmuir Ave., Dunsmuir, CA 96025; (530) 235-4740; www.dunsmuir parks.org
Other: Water is available at the trailhead.

Finding the trailhead: From I-5 heading north, pass through Dunsmuir and take the Siskiyou Avenue exit. Turn left, pass under the freeway and immediately turn right onto Mott Road. The parking lot is on the right.

From I-5 heading south from Mount Shasta, take the Siskiyou Avenue exit. Turn right, and then right again. The parking area is immediately on the right. GPS: N41° 14' 11.02" / W122° 16' 11.00"

The Hike

As I-5 leaves Dunsmuir and begins its climb up toward Mount Shasta, signs proclaim the presence of nearby Hedge Creek Falls. Travelers may be curious about the waterfall, but usually don't stop. They keep driving toward the giant volcano farther up the highway. This leaves Hedge Creek Falls to locals, for the most part. Despite the lack of attention, this is a great little hike with surprising diversity. Of course, the primary attraction is the waterfall, a 30- to 35-foot plunge that pours out of a large notch cut through a hanging wall of columnar basalt. Its proportions are not grand but it is perfectly packaged and very pretty, with the added attraction of a trail routed behind the waterfall. The trail then descends down along Hedge Creek, passing numerous smaller cataracts. It ends at an observation deck high over the creek's confluence with the Sacramento River, commanding a fantastic view of Mount Shasta. Despite a little exposure at the end, its short length and numerous attractions make this a great trail to hike with small children.

The path to Hedge Creek Falls begins at a small picnic area just across the road from the parking area. There is a table, gazebo, water fountain (only operational from late spring to fall) and some displays on the area, the whole of which is perched right

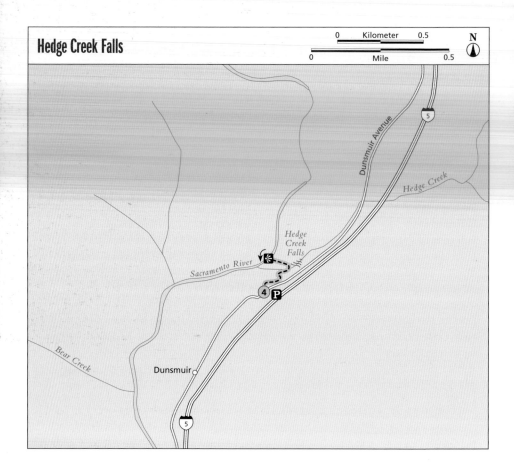

on the edge of the canyon above Hedge Creek and the Sacramento River. The trail leaves the picnic area and descends at a very moderate grade. It immediately crosses a small, seasonal stream, then proceeds down a couple of switchbacks as the falls become audible. The grade levels off as you arrive at the waterfall.

Hedge Creek Falls is a scenic little waterfall that's more intimate than awesome. The most notable element of the waterfall is the cliff through which it flows. The wall, a popular destination for rock climbers, is composed of columnar basalt, a formation caused when lava cools and cracks to form vertical, roughly hexagonal-shaped columns of rock. The wall is actually about 10 feet above the ground because the lowest section has collapsed, creating a cave of sorts. As the trail approaches the falls, it comes alongside the creek and then enters the cave behind the falls. The path becomes a little rockier as the spray pelts stepping stones, positioned to help hikers avoid the muddy ground.

Once on the far side of the falls the trail continues down the canyon, close alongside Hedge Creek. Numerous small waterfalls and some interesting waterslides are formed where the creek flows over large, smooth rocks. There are some particularly attractive falls near the end of the trail, which continues only a few hundred yards

A view of Hedge Creek Falls from the trail in the cave.

after passing the waterfall. It concludes at an observation deck hung over the Sacramento River.

Just to the left of the observation deck, an unofficial but well established use trail drops down to the confluence of Hedge Creek and the Sacramento River. Here is a good swimming hole, followed by a shallow area with some easy rapids.

From the observation deck, there are good views looking down on the Sacramento River as well as looking north toward Mount Shasta, which presides majestically over everything. This vista is particularly attractive because it gives a sense of just how deep and dark the forests in this area are. There is an air of density that borders on oppressive but retains a great beauty. Here you can get a sense of what Joaquin Miller meant when he said, "Lonely as God and white as a winter moon, Mount Shasta starts up suddenly from the heart of the great black forests of California."

Miles and Directions

0.0 Start by crossing the road to the small park, and begin hiking down the trail, passing a few switchbacks.

0.3 View Hedge Creek Falls, then follow the trail behind the waterfall.

0.4 Climb onto observation deck with views of the Sacramento River and Mount Shasta. Retrace your steps.

0.8 Arrive back at the trailhead.

5 Elsa Rupp Preserve

This short, easy hike explores a small forest preserve on the outskirts of Mount Shasta City. Though the primeval forest is beautiful, the real draw of this hike is the presence of Big Springs Creek, just downstream from its birth at the large springs at the Mount Shasta City Park. The creek weaves swiftly through the small preserve, giving hikers a chance to enjoy the clear, cold water in a beautiful, relaxing setting.

Total distance: 0.7 mile
Trail type: Lollipop
Elevation gain: None
Difficulty: Easy
Trail surface: Packed dirt
Hiking time: About 0.5 hour
Season: Year-round

Fees and permits: None
Canine compatibility: Dogs are permitted.
Land status: Private forest preserve
Trail contact: None
Other: Water is available in Big Springs Creek. This trail is open to the public but it is on private property. Please be respectful.

Finding the trailhead: From the town of Mount Shasta, head west on West Lake Street, crossing over I-5. At the stop sign, turn right onto Old Stage Road. Drive 0.2 mile and turn right into the small parking lot for the Elsa Rupp Preserve. GPS: N41° 18' 37.12" / W122° 19' 46.20"

The Hike

The small Elsa Rupp Preserve is a little natural oasis on the outskirts of Mount Shasta City. Just a couple short minutes from town, a hike through the little park is a great chance for some quiet solitude, a quick fix for nature lovers, or a wonderful opportunity to just relax and enjoy the beautiful creek. Indeed, it is the presence of Big Springs Creek that makes the preserve such a fantastic resource. The large creek bursts forth fully formed from the large spring at the Mount Shasta City Park, less than 1.5 miles upstream from the preserve.

The trail that winds through the Elsa Rupp Preserve is the best of the few opportunities available to experience the spring-born creeks that emerge at the foot of Mount Shasta. In addition to the hike through the preserve, a short path from the trailhead leads to the Mount Shasta Sisson Museum and the Mount Shasta Trout Hatchery. If you have the time, both of these are worth the visit. The museum and fish hatchery are both free, and combined with the short trail through Elsa Rupp, make a great half-day trip in Mount Shasta.

The short hike through the Elsa Rupp Preserve begins next to a monument in the preserve's small parking area. The area is heavily wooded, predominantly with cedars, ponderosa pines, and oaks. Almost immediately, a narrow spur splits off to the right. This heads back to the west, crosses Old Stage Road, and passes through a gate to Mount Shasta Sisson Museum and the fish hatchery. Continue on the level path for 0.1 mile, crossing a bridge over a small, seasonal stream.

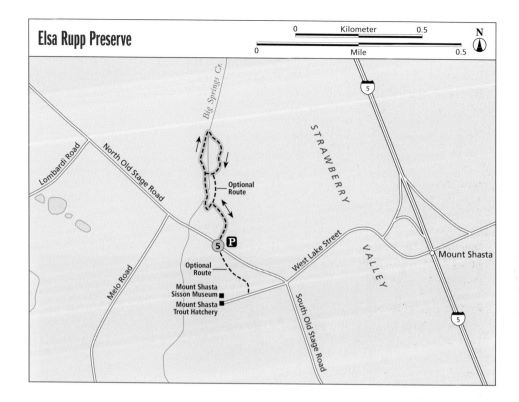

Elsa Rupp Preserve

When you come to a trail junction, turn left and walk a short distance to a bridge over swiftly moving water. This beautiful creek is actually a diversion channel built to funnel water over to the fish hatchery. Cross the split-log bridge and follow the trail alongside the channel. This is one of the nicest sections of the hike. After a couple hundred yards, the creek emerges from a large concrete duct, marking the beginning of the diversion channel. Stay straight and walk toward the sounds of pounding water. A small dam has been built across Big Springs Creek, diverting the water away from its original route. Wooden slats on the dam allow the amount of water that is diverted to be regulated. Usually there is still a small flow in the original creek bed. Past the fish hatchery, the water is restored to its original route and joins Wagon Creek, the northernmost tributary of the Sacramento River, just before it flows into Lake Siskiyou.

At the diversion dam, cross the small bridge and follow the trail through thick underbrush. This is the start of the lollipop. It crosses over a few more small streams, the last of which can have significant flow at times. The trail finally reaches the outer edge of the preserve and turns back to the south, crossing a narrow bridge over Big Springs Creek. This section of the creek is wide and fast-moving. The sound of the joyous water highlights the great beauty of its cold, pure flow.

Once across the bridge, the path widens and passes a few benches set amidst the towering trees. Be sure to stay to the right on the main trail when a short spur veers off to the left. About 0.1 mile from Big Spring Creek, the trail arrives at another junction. Go right and quickly arrive at the diversion dam. From here, retrace your steps back along the diversion channel and then on to the trailhead.

Miles and Directions

0.0 Start the hike at the small parking area.

0.1 At the fork, and cross the bridge over the swift flowing creek.

0.2 At the diversion dam, turn left and walk across the bridge.

0.4 Turn right at the fork and return to the diversion dam. Stay left and retrace your steps back to the trailhead.

0.7 Arrive back at the trailhead.

Big Springs Creek races through the Elsa Rupp Preserve.

6 Spring Hill

This is a surprisingly long trail up Spring Hill, a prominent butte at the north end of Mount Shasta City. Vistas on the summit plateau offer great views of the Trinity Divide, Strawberry Valley, and Mount Shasta.

Total distance: 3.0 miles
Trail type: Lollipop
Elevation gain: 615 feet
Difficulty: Easy
Trail surface: Packed dirt, old dirt road
Hiking time: About 1.5 hours
Season: Year-round

Fees and permits: None
Canine compatibility: Dogs are permitted.
Land status: Private forest preserve
Trail contact: None
Other: There is no water. This trail is open to the public, but it is on private property. Please be respectful.

Finding the trailhead: Head north on Mount Shasta Boulevard to the north end of town. Just beyond the Siskiyou Humane Society, turn right onto Ski Village Drive. The road immediately curves left, and then Ski Village makes a 90-degree turn to the right. Stay straight toward the bulk of Spring Hill, onto a short street. The parking area is at the end of the short street. GPS: N41° 19' 43.77" / W122° 19' 19.39"

The Hike

The Spring Hill Trail is right on the north edge of Mount Shasta City. The hill is visible from most of town, a seemingly younger, shorter sibling to conical Black Butte and mighty Mount Shasta. Despite its prominence above the town, many do not know that a trail meanders up to the summit, offering great views along the way. Looking at the diminutive size of Spring Hill, you would not expect it would take a long trail to reach the summit but, surprisingly, the trail is almost 3 miles round-trip. The length is a result of the long, lazy switchbacks that are used to lessen the trail's grade. The recent addition of a 0.4-mile loop around the summit plateau lengthened it further, and added a great vista. The quick trailhead access and the easy trail are ideal for a swift but enjoyable trip.

The land traveled by most of the Spring Hill Trail belongs to the Coca-Cola Company. Please be respectful of the land; access may be withdrawn if it is misused.

The hike begins at the end of a short residential street. The trail heads west from the roundabout parking area, staying level very briefly before it doubles back to the east and starts the ascent up Spring Hill.

After a short climb, the path enters a small copse of trees and then tops off at a junction with an old dirt road. Turn left onto the road and continue climbing. Make a quick switchback to the right and begin the longest single leg of the whole trail. This 0.3-mile section has no views and is flanked by thick forest. Snow often lingers

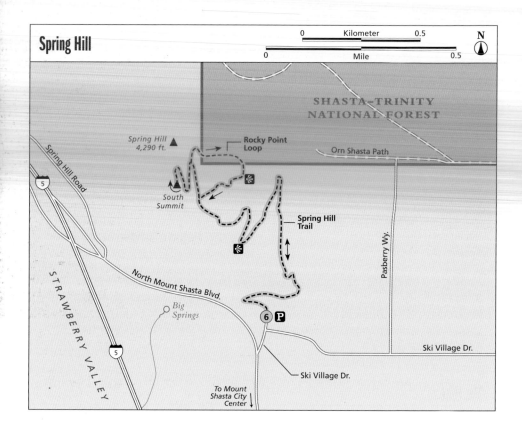

on this section of trail during the spring. As the trail switchbacks to the left, there is a bench with a view of Mount Shasta hidden behind some brush. At the next switchback, there is another bench, this time with a great view of Mount Shasta City and the Strawberry Valley. This is one of the best vistas of the entire trail. After two shorter switchbacks, the road levels off on the summit plateau. The mixed forest of earlier sections of the trail now gives way to ponderosa pine.

Shortly after reaching the summit plateau, the trail arrives at the junction with the Rocky Point Loop. Save the loop for the end, and continue on the main path through open forest for 0.2 mile before switchbacking yet again. Look for the Rocky Point Loop rejoining the main trail here. A short distance away there is another switchback, followed swiftly by a third and final hairpin turn. The end of the trail lies just ahead, where picnic tables dot the top of Spring Hill. The farthest table has the best views, since it is close to the precipice marking the end of the Spring Hill Trail. The views are great, and this is an excellent place to have a picnic.

Heading back, descend the switchbacks to the junction with the Rocky Point Loop, which is at the third switchback. Here the trail heads north, then briefly south, before beginning a long straight leg to the east. This portion of the trail skirts the boundary with Shasta–Trinity National Forest, which owns the northeast corner of

Mount Shasta towers beyond Rocky Point.

Spring Hill. The route was hacked out of the thick brush that looms high along both sides of the trail.

Soon the path turns to the south, and eventually tops out at Rocky Point. A small group of rocks hang precipitously over the sheer east side of Spring Hill. The rocks offer what is possibly the best view on the trail, an unobstructed vantage of Mount Shasta best appreciated in the afternoon. From Rocky Point, the trail heads back to the southwest, where it rejoins the main trail. From here, retrace your steps to the trailhead.

Miles and Directions

0.0   Begin hiking up Spring Hill.

0.25 Turn left and join an old road that climbs the hill.

0.5   Look for a bench with a view at the first of three switchbacks.

0.8   Arrive at another bench with an excellent view of Mount Shasta City.

1.0   Stay left at the first junction with the Rocky Point Loop.

1.1   Stay left at the second junction with the Rocky Point Loop.

1.3   Reach the summit of Spring Hill and enjoy the view.

1.5   Return to the second junction with the Rocky Point Loop. Turn left and follow the loop through dense manzanita.

1.7   Climb onto Rocky Point for a fantastic view of Mount Shasta.

1.9   Complete the Rocky Point Loop, rejoining the main trail and heading back to the trailhead.

3.0   Arrive back at the trailhead.

7 Gateway Trail

Climbing the lower slopes just outside of Mount Shasta City, the Gateway Trail offers beautiful views of Mount Shasta and the surrounding mountains for little effort. Just minutes away from downtown, the trail quickly escapes into the woods at the foot of the mountain and allows hikers to travel deep into the dark recesses that seem a world away from town.

Total distance: 6.9 miles
Trail type: Lollipop or out and back
Elevation gain: 700 feet
Difficulty: Moderate
Trail surface: Packed dirt; rocky
Hiking time: About 4 hours
Season: Year-round
Fees and permits: None

Canine compatibility: Dogs are permitted.
Land status: Shasta-Trinity National Forest
Trail contact: Mount Shasta Ranger District, 204 W. Alma St., Mount Shasta, CA 96067; (530) 926-4511; www.fs.usda.gov/stnf
Other: There is no water. This is a mixed-use trail popular with mountain bikers.

Finding the trailhead: From the beginning of the Everitt Memorial Highway in front of Mount Shasta High School, drive north for 1 mile and turn right into the signed Gateway Trail parking lot. GPS: N41° 20' 4.13" / W122° 18' 30.10"

The Hike

The Gateway Trail is one of the newest trails around Mount Shasta. Developed for hikers, mountain bikers, and equestrians, the easy grade is indicative of the trail's multiple purposes. While it can be inconvenient to deal with other users, the trail does not see too much traffic and is a great opportunity to escape into nature.

The trail has three distinct sections. First comes a gentle climb through open terrain that has great views of Mount Shasta and the surrounding mountains. The second part enters the forest and courses around a few interesting features, including the lowest reaches of long Cascade Gulch and large rock outcroppings. The final part consists of a series of loops that offer several different route options.

The hike begins at a small parking lot just beyond the last few homes of Mount Shasta City, where the city limits and the national forest boundary meet. The trail begins by heading north from the trailhead sign. It quickly makes a tight turn to the east, followed by a few easy switchbacks. The trail climbs throughout the entire first half of the hike, but it is well engineered and never taxing.

The trail soon enters a large clearing with unobstructed views of Mount Shasta and opportunities to observe the other mountains surrounding Mount Shasta City, including the high peaks of the Castle Crags Wilderness, Porcupine Peak, Mount Eddy, and Black Butte. If you are new to Mount Shasta, this is a great opportunity to

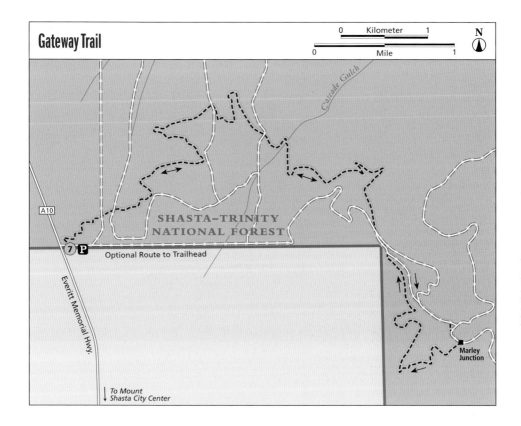

Kilometer

Mile

N

A10

SHASTA–TRINITY
NATIONAL FOREST

7 P
Optional Route to Trailhead

Everitt Memorial Hwy.

Marley
Junction

↓ *To Mount
Shasta City Center*

Cascade Gulch

familiarize yourself with many of the notable landmarks in a natural setting, without man-made intrusions. The open area was clear-cut long ago, which is why the few trees present are small. While you might guess that a clear-cut would not be attractive, enough time has passed that nature has healed the scar. Manzanita covers the ground in many places, and rocks large and small are scattered throughout. The lack of tall trees means that the views are constant and good.

After some long switchbacks through the clearing, the trail crosses a road and enters an uncut area that has larger trees. There are a few road crossings on the hike, but the Gateway Trail is well marked and the route is always obvious. The trail crosses another road a short distance later, before pulling alongside a sandy gully. This is the last vestige of Cascade Gulch, which begins high up on the saddle between Mount Shasta and Shastina. It descends down into Hidden Valley (see Hike 9/Horse Camp), and then plunges down the side of Mount Shasta. The higher sections of the gulch often have water in them, but there is rarely water this far down the mountain. Enjoy the view of Mount Shasta's stately heights. The mountain will not be seen again until you are heading back to the trailhead.

After the trail crosses Cascade Gulch, it cuts across a low ridge and begins a series of short switchbacks. Some nice views appear of Mount Eddy and Black Butte while

Mount Eddy and Black Butte are prominent landmarks on the Gateway Trail.

climbing. This is a particularly appealing perspective because there are few places near town where you get a good opportunity to observe Black Butte without houses or the freeway intruding into the scene.

After the trail straightens out, it passes through shady woods before it skirts the bottom of a large rock outcropping. Past the rock, the trail enters a steep-sided gully choked with thimbleberry, and begins another series of switchbacks. At the top of the climb, the path rounds a corner, and then levels off before reaching the edge of a dirt road, about 2.7 miles from the beginning of the hike.

Once you are on the road, a number of possible options for proceeding appear. The road is the most direct route back to the trailhead. It will take you back to your car in only 1.4 miles. Bikers often ride up the road and then return back to the trailhead via the Gateway Trail. Six trails and a road offer several different loop possibilities. The map at the trailhead shows all the loops and connector trails. One good option is to turn left onto the road and walk 0.4 mile to Marley Junction, staying right at a fork just before the junction. Three different trails intersect the road at Marley Junction, making it a good place to begin other explorations farther into the remote corners of the Gateway network. For just a modest loop, turn right at the first of two trails branching off from the right side of the road at the junction. The sign indicates that this is the way back to the trailhead along the Gateway Trail. Follow the path until it rejoins the road, a few yards away from where the Gateway Trail intersects it. The loop is 1.4 miles. From the junction, hike back to the trailhead on the Gateway Trail, or take the direct route on the dirt road.

Miles and Directions

0.0 Start at the Gateway Trail parking area.

0.3 After crossing a road, leave the forest and enter the large clearing with great views.

1.3 Cross a road and reenter the woods.

1.8 Say goodbye to Mount Shasta as the trail crosses Cascade Gulch.

2.7 Turn left onto the dirt road.

3.1 At Marley Junction, turn right onto the Gateway Trail, and continue hiking through the woods.

4.1 Rejoin the road and turn left. After walking a few yards veer right and resume hiking on the Gateway Trail, retracing your steps.

6.9 Arrive back at the trailhead.

8 Black Butte

Black Butte is one of the iconic landmarks of the Mount Shasta area. As you drive north on I-5, the dark cone looms ominously above the freeway, and it seems unlikely that a hikeable trail could climb to the top. Not only does the trail climb to the very tiptop, it is not a difficult hike and has some nice surprises along the way. From the summit there is a jaw-dropping 360-degree vista. This is one of the classic hikes in the Mount Shasta area.

Total distance: 5.2 miles
Trail type: Out and back
Elevation gain: 1,800 feet
Difficulty: Moderate
Trail surface: Packed dirt, rock scrambling
Hiking time: About 3.5 hours
Season: Year-round
Fees and permits: None

Canine compatibility: Dogs are permitted.
Land status: Shasta-Trinity National Forest
Trail contact: Mount Shasta Ranger District, 204 W. Alma St., Mount Shasta, CA 96067; (530) 926-4511; www.fs.usda.gov/stnf
Other: There is no water. Some sections of the trail have exposure on the edge of cliffs.

Finding the trailhead: From the beginning of the Everitt Memorial Highway in front of Mount Shasta High School, drive north for 2.1 miles to the signed left turn onto a dirt Forest Road 41N18. The sign indicates the "Black Butte Trail." Just past this point, the Everitt Memorial Highway makes a sharp right turn and begins to climb up Mount Shasta. If you reach this turn, you have gone too far.

Once on the dirt forest road, it makes a right-hand turn after 100 yards. The road is easily passable, but it is bumpy. Though there are side roads, the route is obvious to the trailhead. It does make a left turn after 1 mile, and a right turn after another 0.4 mile. Turn left again after 0.8 mile. A short distance from here the road comes to a junction with numerous roads. Follow the obvious road, staying left. The route then makes a quick climb up to the trailhead parking area. GPS: N41° 22' 23.15" / W122° 20' 22.72"

The Hike

Black Butte, the largest of Mount Shasta's satellite volcanic peaks, is one of the most memorable landmarks of the Mount Shasta region. Situated at the north end of the Strawberry Valley, the pyramidal peak is visible from almost everywhere in the Mount Shasta area. A quick examination of the butte reveals that it is essentially a massive pile of rock. In truth, the loose rock is piled up around a few solid volcanic necks. Each neck is the result of a separate eruption. The lower subpeaks of Black Butte are the top of these necks and represent a separate eruption. The butte was once named Muir's Peak, in honor of the great conservationist and the special love that he bore for Mount Shasta.

The Black Butte Trail trailhead is located at a large bulge on the northeast side of the butte, a fortuitous shoulder that cuts 300 feet of elevation gain off of the trail.

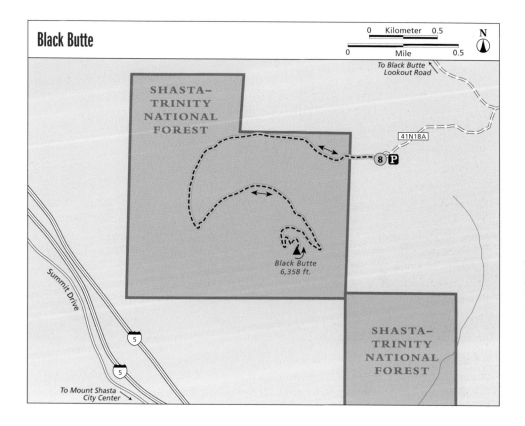

0   Kilometer   0.5

0   Mile   0.5

N

To Black Butte
Lookout Road

SHASTA–
TRINITY
NATIONAL
FOREST

41N18A

8 P

Black Butte
6,358 ft.

Summit Drive

5

5

To Mount Shasta
City Center

SHASTA–
TRINITY
NATIONAL
FOREST

The trail sets off due west from the parking area, and immediately begins to climb at a moderate but steady grade. Though the trail is under forest canopy initially, it does not take long to emerge into the open air with views to the north. Among the many peaks visible are Sheep Rock, the Goosenest, and Willow Creek Mountain. Mount McLoughlin in Oregon is the large, Fuji-like cone in the distance. Epic views of Mount Shasta also bless the early part of the trail.

Coming out of the trees, the trail passes onto a large talus field. The rocks along the path have been arranged to produce a level path amid the scree, while dirt and gravel have been added to create a relatively easy walking surface. As the trail curves to the south, Mount Shasta disappears behind Black Butte and Mount Eddy moves into view. Sprawling Mills Meadow stretches out at the foot of the second highest peak in the region. I-5 is briefly audible before the trail switches back to the east, away from the freeway noise.

Here the Black Butte Trail enters a large rocky canyon that is difficult to perceive from below. It is surprising how many trees have managed to eke out an existence amid the talus that fills the canyon. In terms of footing, this is the most difficult part of the trail. Though the direction of the path is never in doubt, one must often hop from one large rock to the next to traverse this rugged area. When the trail reaches

The Shasta Valley unfolds beyond Black Butte's hidden canyon.

the east end of the canyon, the views to the north return, enhanced by the rim of the canyon in the foreground.

Beyond the canyon the trail arcs southward, and soon the main summit tower comes into view. A short distance later, the trail enters an area where the slope is loose and unstable. A large wire retaining net has been constructed to hold back an immense amount of scree.

Past the retaining net, the trail approaches a rocky outcropping and makes another switchback. From here it is just possible to observe Lassen Peak and Crater Peak to the south. Of course, Mount Shasta is a nearly overpowering presence just a few miles to the east. The trail crosses over the unstable area again. Here the talus is overwhelming the retaining netting and beginning to smother the trail. This is the most unstable part of the entire Black Butte Trail. Caution is necessary while crossing the loose area.

With the trail heading back to the west, it is possible to look north, below the edge of the trail, and observe some of the subordinate peaks formed by the numerous eruptions. Sharp eyes can spot a few pieces of piping and other debris down at their base, remnants of the lookout tower that was removed 40 years ago. With the trail swinging this far to the west, views once again include Mount Eddy, but now take in the area to the southwest, including the Castle Crags Wilderness, the Gray Rocks, and the three canyons of the Upper Sacramento's headwaters.

As the trail doubles back to the east, the summit is within sight, and four more short switchbacks come in quick succession, depositing hikers at the very top of Black Butte. Several clearly defined use trails have been worn into the mountain, making the primary route unclear, but they will all lead to the summit. Finally the trail tops out along a narrow crest with staggering panoramic views. The last 20 feet before the summit lacks a trail completely, and is just a rocky edge that requires careful scrambling. The goal of this endeavor is the square foundation of the old lookout tower situated on the highest point of Black Butte.

The spectacle from the summit of Black Butte is tremendous. The southernmost part of the Cascade Range is visible to the south, including Burney Mountain, Crater Peak, and Lassen Peak. Much of the Upper Sacramento River's watershed is obvious, stretching south from the slopes of Mount Eddy and onward to the Central Valley through its canyon. Aside from Mount Eddy, the high peaks of the river's headwaters, including the Grey Rocks, Boulder Peak, the Castle Crags, Harry Watkins, Gray Rock Dome, and Porcupine Peak, all line the horizon to the west. Mount Shasta City and the Strawberry Valley lie at the foot of Black Butte. To the north is the sprawling high desert of the Shasta Valley, and in the distance, Oregon peaks such as Mount Ashland, Pilot Rock, Soda Mountain, towering Mount McLoughlin, and Browns Mountain can be seen. Other great Cascade peaks, including Willow Creek Mountain and the Goosenest, line the eastern rim of the Shasta Valley. Finally, to the east is majestic Mount Shasta, seemingly so close you can reach out and grab it. It is an unforgettable vista.

Miles and Directions

0.0 Leave the trailhead and begin hiking up the Black Butte Trail.

0.3 Cross a large boulder field with great views of Mount Shasta and the Shasta Valley to the north.

1.3 The trail makes a hairpin turn to the east and enters a large, rocky canyon.

2.0 After traversing the east side of Black Butte, the trail reaches a switchback and begins to climb to the west.

2.3 After crossing an unstable area and rising above a second, smaller canyon, the trail reaches another switchback and completes the last, long traverse of the butte.

2.6 After a series of short, tight switchbacks, arrive at the summit of Black Butte. Retrace your steps.

5.2 Arrive back at the trailhead.

Part II: Mount Shasta Trails

" I consider the evening twilight on Mount Shasta one of the grandest sights I have ever witnessed."

President Theodore Roosevelt uttered these words after witnessing the glorious alpenglow on Mount Shasta. The mountain is indeed a grand sight, and one that beckons to be explored and enjoyed.

Befitting the magnificence of Mount Shasta, the trails on the mountain are among the most spectacular in a state that has an overabundance of incredible trails. If you are looking for hikes amid colossal walls and peaks, mighty glaciers, epic canyons, plunging waterfalls, explosive wildflower displays, or vistas that reach 100 miles to the horizon, you will find them on Mount Shasta. Amazingly, despite these superlative features, the mountain has somehow gone under the radar as a premier hiking destination. What other hikers have missed, you will be able to enjoy on California's mightiest mountain.

The trails on Mount Shasta are divided into two regions. The most heavily used are the six trails that begin on the Everitt Memorial Highway. This is the only paved road on the mountain, and it climbs up to the tree line at 7,850 feet. The road is kept open all year as far as Bunny Flat. The first two trails on Mount Shasta begin there. Past Bunny Flat, the Everitt Memorial Highway continues for 3 miles before ending at the Old Ski Bowl.

Just below the end of the road is Panther Meadow, where there is a great little campground. Trails begin at both the Old Ski Bowl and Panther Meadow. A network of trails connects both trailheads and loops are possible here.

The other four trails are scattered around the east and north sides of Mount Shasta. They are all accessed by long dirt roads, most of which are passable by low-clearance vehicles. These hikes are among the most spectacular, but are lightly used because of their isolation. Don't let this deter you: Mount Shasta's grandeur is often best displayed from the places where few travel.

With the exception of the trail through Panther Meadow, all of the trails on Mount Shasta enter the Mount Shasta Wilderness, where certain things are restricted. Mountain biking is the most notable activity prohibited in the wilderness area.

Lastly, this is a guide to the hiking trails on Mount Shasta, not for climbing the mountain. If you want to make an attempt on the summit, you must get a Summit Pass to climb above 10,000 feet. Be sure to check the conditions on the mountain with rangers. Climbing Mount Shasta is demanding and dangerous. Guiding agencies in Mount Shasta City are good resources for an attempt on the summit.

9 Horse Camp

The trail to Horse Camp is one of the most popular on Mount Shasta, the first stage of the most heavily used route to the top. Climbing up to the Sierra Club's historic Shasta Alpine Lodge, it passes through cool alpine forests before arriving at the cabin. At Horse Camp you will find numerous challenging destinations to explore, including the barren Hidden Valley, tiny Helen Lake, and the summit of nearby Green Butte.

Total distance: 3.2 miles
Trail type: Out and back, or a possible loop with Green Butte Ridge (Hike 10)
Elevation gain: 975 feet
Difficulty: Moderate to difficult, depending on destination
Trail surface: Packed dirt; loose scree
Hiking time: About 4 hours
Season: Summer, fall. This route is popular in winter for summit attempts as well, and may be traveled at that time with snowshoes.

Fees and permits: A Summit Pass is necessary to camp at Helen Lake.
Canine compatibility: No dogs allowed.
Land status: Mount Shasta Wilderness
Trail contact: Mount Shasta Ranger District, 204 W. Alma St., Mount Shasta, CA 96067; (530) 926-4511; www.fs.usda.gov/stnf
Other: Water is typically available at Horse Camp; snow meltwater is usually available at Hidden Valley and Helen Lake.

Finding the trailhead: From I-5, take the Central Mount Shasta exit. Merge onto Lake Street and head east for 1 mile, passing through the intersection with Mount Shasta Boulevard. As the road bends to the north, continue left onto Everett Memorial Highway for 0.1 mile to an intersection by Mount Shasta High School. Pass through the intersection and continue for 11 miles to the Bunny Flat Trailhead. GPS: N41° 21' 15.13" / W122° 13' 59.74"

The Hike

Mount Shasta's craggy countenance looming high above the old Sierra Club cabin at Horse Camp is one of the most iconic images of California's staggering volcano. In addition to simply being a great view, it is often seen because the trail to Horse Camp is possibly the most heavily used on Mount Shasta. This is due to several factors, including ease of access, short distance to tree line, great side trips, and the popularity of the Avalanche Gulch route to the top of Mount Shasta. More than 90 percent of attempts to climb the mountain are made using this route.

The trail has more to offer than just a route to the top. Horse Camp itself, and the lower reaches of Avalanche Gulch, are great destinations for a short hike. However, the longer, more difficult side trips from the cabin are absolutely spectacular. Hidden Valley is a wide depression on the west side of the mountain that cannot be seen until reaching it. The summit of the mountain looms a vertical mile above the valley. Helen Lake is often used as a high camp on the way to the top of the mountain. The lake is

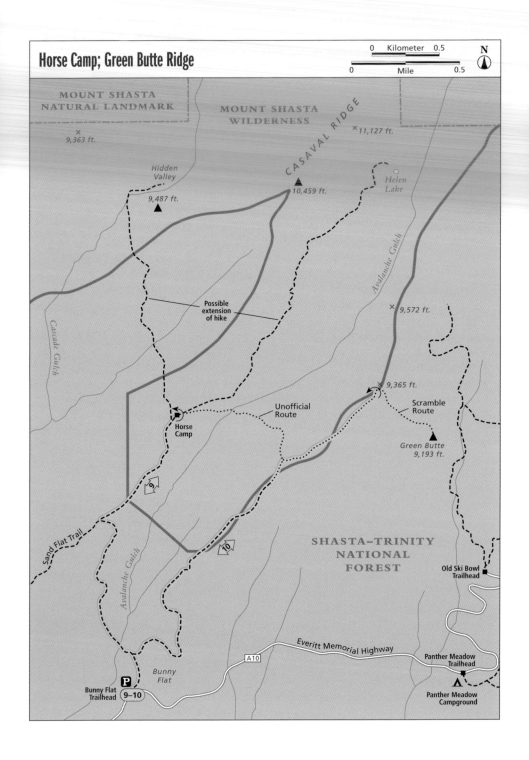

Horse Camp; Green Butte Ridge

0   Kilometer   0.5

0   Mile   0.5

N

MOUNT SHASTA
NATURAL LANDMARK

× 9,363 ft.

MOUNT SHASTA
WILDERNESS

CASAVAL RIDGE

× 11,127 ft.

Hidden
Valley

9,487 ft. ▲

▲ 10,459 ft.

○ Helen
Lake

Cascade Gulch

Avalanche Gulch

Possible
extension
of hike

× 9,572 ft.

Horse
Camp

Unofficial
Route

× 9,365 ft.

Scramble
Route

▲ Green Butte
9,193 ft.

Sand Flat Trail

9

Avalanche Gulch

10

SHASTA–TRINITY
NATIONAL
FOREST

Old Ski Bowl
Trailhead ■

Everitt Memorial Highway

A10

Panther Meadow
Trailhead ■

Bunny
Flat

P
Bunny Flat
Trailhead 9–10

Panther Meadow
Campground

small and difficult to reach, but the spot is incredible. Green Butte is a large peak on the flanks of Mount Shasta. There are a few routes to the top of the butte, including through Avalanche Gulch. This option makes a great loop.

The Horse Camp Trail begins at busy Bunny Flat. The trailhead is a popular destination on its own. It has a spectacular view of Mount Shasta as well as great views to the south, including Lassen Peak. Although a network of paths surround the flat, the official trail begins next to the bathrooms at the trailhead sign. Running along the perimeter of the flat, the path climbs moderately and reaches a junction where it makes a sharp turn to the left. Staying right here leads to the Green Butte Ridge Trail.

Once the path makes its turn away from Bunny Flat, it crosses a small gully, which is, in fact, the smaller, lower remnant of massive Avalanche Gulch. Stay on the main trail when spurs branch off to the left. The trail enters the forest here, and remains in the trees throughout the journey to Horse Camp. In spite of this there are a few points with partially obscured views of the Trinity Divide and Trinity Alps to the west.

About 0.5 mile from the trailhead, stay left at another spur branching off to the left and continue climbing up the rock-strewn trail. After another 0.3 mile, the trail passes a tower that likely houses weather gauges and related equipment. Just beyond the tower the trail crosses a clearing and then reaches a junction with the Sand Flat Trail. This trail is an alternate route to Horse Camp. It is 0.1 mile shorter than the trail from Bunny Flat, but it gains 300 more feet.

Once past the Sand Flat junction, the route makes a long, sustained climb all the way to Horse Camp. Along the way it enters the Mount Shasta Wilderness, and then crosses the boundary of the land owned by the Sierra Club. As it climbs, the trail passes above the gully that eventually widens into gargantuan Avalanche Gulch. After a steep climb, the trail makes a turn to the north and then, 0.8 mile from the junction with the Sand Flat Trail, it reaches Horse Camp.

This is a hub of backcountry activity on Mount Shasta. The cabin itself is occupied by a caretaker who lives there during the summer. Spring water is piped in and cascades down an attractive rock pile. Campsites are available for a small fee, and there are solar toilets available as well. There is also a library inside the cabin.

While Horse Camp is a great destination on its own, consider some of the other options beyond the cabin. Hidden Valley is the best of the three. It combines spectacular scenery with a steep but easy-to-follow route. Helen Lake is a very hard climb and requires a Summit Pass. Green Butte is fairly easy, but there is no official trail and it requires route-finding skills. Other than some portions of the trail to Helen Lake, all of the trails beyond Horse Camp are unofficial and unmaintained.

Hidden Valley

The trail to Hidden Valley is short but steep. It departs Horse Camp to the north. To find the trail, walk to the northeast corner of the cabin. From there, the route

The west face of Mount Shasta soars above Hidden Valley.

heads toward the base of Casaval Ridge, passing a few of the campsites along the way. The trail proceeds through the forest for a short distance, remaining fairly level. It soon makes a short, steep ascent over a small ridge and enters a little bowl that opens up to the west. The bowl is fairly treeless and has good views. Beyond the bowl the trail climbs steeply again, eventually crossing another ridge and entering a larger basin. On the far side of the second bowl it climbs steeply again, and passes through a stunted forest of whitebark and lodgepole pine. A traverse across a final steep talus slope that rises above the lower portions of Cascade Gulch leads to the entrance to Hidden Valley. The views from this section of the hike are great, taking in the entirety of Strawberry Valley, the Trinity Divide, the distant Trinity Alps and Marble Mountains, and the Sacramento Valley far to the south. As it climbs, the trail is angling for an obvious notch. During much of the season water melting high above the valley is funneled through this notch and cascades down the eponymous gulch.

Hidden Valley, at 9,200 feet, is a spectacular basin almost 5,000 feet below the summit of Mount Shasta. The summit itself is not visible from the valley, and the highest point above the area is only 4,000 overhead. On the north side of the valley is Shastina, Mount Shasta's great secondary cone. Campsites are found on both sides of the notch. From here routes up Mount Shasta include Casaval Ridge, West Face Gully, and Cascade Gulch. The primary route up Shastina begins here as well.

Helen Lake

The trip to Helen Lake is more likely to be undertaken as part of an attempt on the summit of Mount Shasta. For much of the season, and depending on the volume of snow that fell during winter, reaching the lake may require crampons and ice axe. The same variables dictate whether the lake itself is covered with snow and not visible.

The trip to the lake begins at the Horse Camp cabin and departs from near the fountain. It consists of a series of large rocks lined up to form stepping-stones. This is known as Olberman's Causeway, built by the lodge's first caretaker, Joseph Olberman. The causeway extends almost 0.5 mile up the mountain and connects to the steep, unmaintained trail that leads to Helen Lake. Past the causeway, the trail climbs over loose sand and rock for much of the hard climb to the lake. At times there are a few alternate routes worn into the mountain, but the most obvious path is easy to discern. Nearer to Lake Helen the trails becomes harder to make out. Snow often covers this area. Helen Lake can often be quite busy, especially on weekends and around holidays.

Green Butte

The final optional destination from Horse Camp is Green Butte. This is a scenic butte that overlooks the Old Ski Bowl, which is on the far side of Green Butte Ridge. The Green Butte Ridge Trail also climbs the butte, and is shorter and steeper than the route from Horse Camp. The Green Butte Ridge Trail also begins at Bunny Flat, so combining the two trails makes a nice loop. If this is the object, the recommended route would be to hike to Horse Camp, climb Green Butte, and then descend down the Green Butte Ridge Trail back to Bunny Flat. In this way the more scenic parts of the trail are hit first and the ascent is more gradual, while the return trip is quick and direct.

To reach Green Butte, proceed from Horse Camp on the unofficial trail that leads to the inner gully of Avalanche Gulch. When the trail hits the gully, look high to a rocky bench hosting a few stunted trees halfway up Green Butte Ridge. Leave the trail, cross the gulch, and scramble up the rocky slope to the bench. From the bench scramble the rest of the way to the top of the ridge. From there it is a steep climb up loose talus to Green Butte.

Miles and Directions

0.0 Start by climbing out of Bunny Flat.

1.0 Turn right at the junction with the Sand Flat Trail.

1.6 Arrive at the Shasta Alpine Lodge at Horse Camp. Retrace your steps. (Options: From here, you can extend your hike with options to Helen Lake, Green Butte, and Hidden Valley.)

3.2 Arrive back at the trailhead.

10 Green Butte Ridge

Forming the eastern wall of massive Avalanche Gulch, Green Butte Ridge rises 5,000 feet from Bunny Flat to where it joins Sargents Ridge at the foot of towering Thumb Rock. Although the upper half of the ridge is far too rugged for a trail, the lower portion is easily climbed via the unofficial Green Butte Ridge Trail. This steep path is a short, direct way to climb above the tree line and get staggering views into Avalanche Gulch. Even after the path fades away amid a sea of loose talus, it is straightforward to scramble over the rock to the top of 9,193-foot Green Butte, where more stunning views await.

See map on page 52
Total distance: 5.2 miles
Trail type: Out and back, or possible loop with Horse Camp (Hike 9)
Elevation gain: 1,900 feet
Difficulty: Strenuous
Trail surface: Packed dirt; loose scree
Hiking time: About 4.5 hours

Season: Summer, fall. This route is popular in winter for summit attempts as well, and may be traveled at that time with snowshoes.
Fees and permits: None
Canine compatibility: No dogs allowed.
Land status: Mount Shasta Wilderness
Trail contact: Mount Shasta Ranger District, 204 W. Alma St., Mount Shasta, CA 96067; (530) 926-4511; www.fs.usda.gov/stnf
Other: No water is available on this route.

Finding the trailhead: From I-5, take the Central Mount Shasta exit. Merge onto Lake Street and head east for 1 mile, passing through the intersection with Mount Shasta Boulevard. As the road bends to the north, continue left onto Everett Memorial Highway for 0.1 mile to an intersection by Mount Shasta High School. Pass through the intersection and continue for 11 miles to the Bunny Flat Trailhead. GPS: N41° 21' 15.13" / W122° 13' 59.74"

The Hike

The Green Butte Ridge Trail is short, steep, and difficult. The grade is severe, the trail is not maintained, and it eventually fades away altogether, leaving hikers to either turn around or continue the climb over loose talus. Despite these drawbacks, it is a spectacular journey up the mountain with unique perspectives on Mount Shasta and the mountains to the south and west.

The highlight of the climb is the opportunity to gaze into the great chasm of Avalanche Gulch, one of the mountain's stupendous canyons. While wonderful views appear as soon as the path arrives at tree line, the vistas from Green Butte and Point 9,365 are unforgettable, and make the hard journey worth it. It is also an ideal trail for solitude, which is something a little harder to find among the trails originating on

Everitt Memorial Highway, and makes a great introduction to the rocky terrain on the higher reaches of the mountain.

To begin, climb up one of the trails that goes from the parking area to a prominently placed bench that has a great view of the mountain. From here a wide path heads north through the treeless clearing of Bunny Flat. At the far end of the clearing is an obvious junction. Turning left connects to the trail to Horse Camp. Stay right, leave the clearing, and enter the forest, which marks the proper beginning of the Green Butte Ridge Trail.

The trail begins at a very comfortable grade. It first heads east, then makes a single, sharp switchback to the west, staying level a little longer. About 0.8 mile from the trailhead, it suddenly makes a steep ascent up the ridge that divides Bunny Flat from the lower section of Avalanche Gulch. Although the trail has been obvious and well graded up to this point, the unofficial nature of the route is made evident here. Rather than a steep trail or a set of switchbacks, multiple scramble routes are worn into the side of the ridge. A pair of tracks run parallel to each other, and of the two, the one on the left is better.

Once the scramble is over, the trail continues to climb steeply. A blue sign high in a tree marks entry into Sierra Club property. (This is the same parcel of land that Horse Camp is on.) Soon you'll reach the foot of another steep scramble. Again, the route is clear even if it is not well maintained. Lupine and other alpine plants hint at the change in terrain that waits at the top of the ascent, where the trees suddenly give way and an open alpine expanse unfolds beyond the path. Lofty Mount Shasta holds sway in the distance, and the summit pinnacle of Green Butte thrusts upward to the east. Loose, rocky talus suddenly replaces the soil of the lower parts of the ridge.

The trail stays near the top of the ridge, following its contour north, then turning east. Along most of the climb to this point the trees, mostly Shasta red fir, are all large and old. More exposed to the elements here, the trees are suddenly shrunken and gnarled. The small, twisted condition is referred to as *krummholz*, an indication that the tree line is at hand. The small trees cling precariously to the crest of the ridge, forming a green band coursing to the east. The path follows them closely.

After a short, level section the trail climbs steeply again, toward an obvious false summit composed of gray scree and capped by a small cluster of *krummholz*. As the trail climbs, it begins to grow more indistinct, finally fading away at the top of the false summit. Along the southern edge of the ridge one can look down into Sun Bowl, one of two popular backcountry skiing areas between Bunny Flat and Green Butte. Past the false summit there is a short, level area, and then another hard climb up the loose rock. This time the destination is the trail's zenith on Point 9,365. The rock in this area changes from a flat gray color to a distinctive reddish hue.

Staying near the southern edge, peer down into another backcountry ski area. This is the immense Powder Bowl, which seems to be twice the size of companion Sun Bowl to the west. From this spot, turn back to the north and traverse the final,

A spectacular view of Mount Shasta from Point 9,365.

steep talus field below Point 9,365. On the point are fantastic views of Mount Shasta, Avalanche Gulch, Shastina, the Old Ski Bowl, Sargents Ridge, Thumb Rock, Shastarama Point, and Green Butte. To the west, across the Strawberry Valley, rise Mount Eddy and the high peaks of the Trinity Divide. Beyond the divide, the Trinity Alps are arrayed like dragon's teeth.

Reaching the top of Green Butte is a simple matter from here. Cross a short, shallow saddle to another prominent point. From here a narrow neck descends down to the summit plateau of Green Butte. The neck, dividing Powder Bowl and the Old Ski Bowl, is narrow, but does not present much serious danger as long as you proceed with caution. Beyond the neck, it is a short, level hike to the base of Green Butte's summit pinnacle.

A difficult loop can be made by connecting the Green Butte Ridge Trail with the Horse Camp trail, which is best done by beginning on the Horse Camp Trail and returning via Green Butte Ridge. (See the description in Horse Camp/Hike 9 for details on the loop.)

Miles and Directions

0.0 Start by hiking through Bunny Flat. Begin climbing up the trail at the north end of the clearing.

1.3 The trail reaches tree line and the views of Mount Shasta open up.

1.7 The last remnants of the trail fade away, making it necessary to scramble over loose talus to reach the top of the ridge.

2.2 Reach the top of Point 9,365 for excellent views.

2.6 Complete the exposed traverse to the top of Green Butte. Retrace your steps.

5.2 Arrive back at the trailhead.

11 Panther Meadow

This short, easy trail, located high on Mount Shasta, explores delicate Panther Meadow. The hike has great views of Mount Shasta itself, as well as views of the surrounding mountains to the south and west, plus beautiful springs and lush meadows loaded with wildflowers. It is a great introductory trail to California's best peak.

Total distance: 1.4 miles
Trail type: Lollipop
Elevation gain: 350 feet
Difficulty: Easy
Trail surface: Packed dirt
Hiking time: About 1 hour
Season: Summer, fall

Fees and permits: None
Canine compatibility: No dogs allowed.
Land status: Mount Shasta Wilderness
Trail contact: Mount Shasta Ranger District, 204 W. Alma St., Mount Shasta, CA 96067; (530) 926-4511; www.fs.usda.gov/stnf
Other: No water is available on this route.

Finding the trailhead: From I-5, take the Central Mount Shasta exit. Merge onto Lake Street and head east for 1 mile, passing through the intersection with Mount Shasta Boulevard. As the road bends to the north, continue left onto Everett Memorial Highway for 0.1 mile to an intersection by Mount Shasta High School. Pass through the intersection and continue for 12.5 miles to the Panther Meadow Campground and the Panther Meadow trailhead. GPS: N41° 21' 17.78" / W122° 12' 11.62"

The Hike

Mount Shasta is indisputably one of the most spectacular hiking destinations in Northern California. Highlights of its mountain trails include exploration of the rugged terrain near the timberline, beautiful rocks and cliffs, staggering vistas of the volcanic peak, fantastic views of the surrounding mountain ranges, rushing creeks, and delicate meadows.

While most of these features are present in varying degrees on many of Mount Shasta's hikes, none offer all of them in such a complete, easily accessible package as the trail through Panther Meadow. Though it is a diminutive trail in terms of length and difficulty, the hike is a giant when it comes to scenery. Boasting constant views of Mount Shasta and Green Butte, the hike includes plenty of chances to observe the stark cliffs of Gray Butte, as well as view the Trinity Divide and the distant Trinity Alps. This is all available while looping around a small but gorgeous alpine meadow.

Panther Meadow is divided into an upper and lower section separated by a band of hemlock trees. Both sections have wonderful views of Mount Shasta, but while the lower meadow lies in the shadow of Gray Butte and has a good perspective on that scenic mountain, the upper meadow is a great vantage from which to look to the south and see the craggy peaks of the Trinity Divide and Trinity Alps.

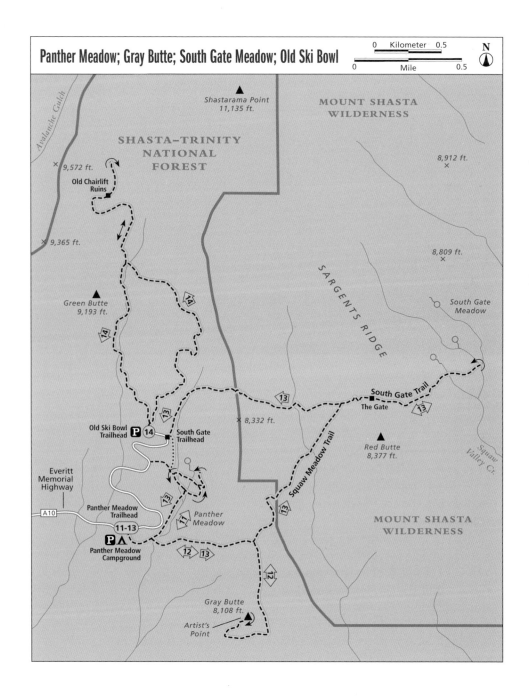

Panther Meadow; Gray Butte; South Gate Meadow; Old Ski Bowl

The meadow is fragile, and the forest service has made efforts to keep hikers on the trail to prevent further marring of the grasses. The area around the meadow is typical of high elevation environments on Mount Shasta. Rocks are plentiful and the soil is poor, providing a remarkable contrast between the meadow and the area

Panther Meadow frames an awesome view of Mount Shasta.

around it. Many people hold Panther Meadow to be a sacred place. It is not uncommon to come upon people meditating or performing other rituals and ceremonies. Whatever your beliefs, please show everyone in the meadow respect and consideration, and enjoy this incredible place.

From the parking lot at the Panther Meadow Campground, follow the wide, dusty path to the east. Much of the trail through here is lined with rocks, which form definitive borders for the trail and minimize hikers' off-trail exploration and impact on the delicate landscape. The trail quickly leaves the campground behind and arrives at the lower section of Panther Meadow. A little over 0.1 mile from the trailhead the path splits. Going to the right crosses the lower meadow and leads to trails destined for Gray Butte and the exquisite South Gate Meadow. Even if these are not the intended destinations, it is worth the time to stroll this section of trail and enjoy the excellent views of Mount Shasta, Green Butte, and Gray Butte. To hike the Panther Meadow Trail, stay to the left and skirt the edge of the grassy field. The sounds of water running get louder as the trail nears the northern end of the meadow.

At the northern edge of lower Panther Meadow, the trail runs parallel to the creek and soon enters a dense copse of mountain hemlock as it begins to climb moderately. After climbing over 100 feet in a little over 0.1 mile, the path finally emerges at the edge of the upper meadow, an exceptionally scenic spot with Mount Shasta and Green Butte towering powerfully over the rock-strewn green grass.

At the edge of the meadow the trail arrives at another fork, the beginning of the Panther Meadow Loop. Stay to the right and cross the spring-fed creek before reentering the forest. The path climbs very moderately for 0.1 mile before coming to another trail junction. Follow the path to the right and skirt the uppermost section of the meadow before arriving at the spring that feeds Panther Meadow. Quarried rock lines the small pool from which the water wells up. The water runs off as a creek, carrying the life-sustaining moisture into the grassy paradise that is the upper meadow. From the spring, the views to the south are tremendous—taking in the Castle Crags, Grey Rocks, much of the Trinity Divide, and a significant portion of the distant Trinity Alps.

Returning to the main trail, the path soon arrives at the edge of the meadow again. Cross the lush grass via a series of large stones that have been arrayed to facilitate the crossing of the meadow without damaging the fragile grasses. On the far side of the meadow the trail continues to the west, entering an area choked with small boulders. The trees here are smaller and farther apart, as timberline draws near. The path heads west through the boulders for just short of 0.1 mile before reaching a junction. Proceeding straight ahead leads to the parking lot that accesses the short trail to upper Panther Meadow. Turn left at the junction and make a short descent through the boulders back to the beginning of the loop at the southern end of the upper meadow. Enjoy the view briefly before heading back down the trail to the lower meadow and the campground parking lot.

Miles and Directions

0.0 Start by hiking through the Panther Meadow campground to the meadow.
0.1 Stay left to begin the trail that leads to the upper meadow.
0.4 Turn right and cross over the creek to begin the loop around the upper meadow.
0.5 Turn right onto the spur trail that leads to the Panther Meadow spring.
0.8 Return to the upper meadow loop and turn right.
0.9 At a junction, turn left to complete the upper meadow loop.
1.0 Rejoin the main trail and retrace your steps.
1.4 Arrive back at the trailhead.

12 Gray Butte

This moderate trail to the top of Gray Butte has awesome scenery as it journeys through beautiful meadows and old-growth red fir and hemlock groves. Here are opportunities to observe some of Mount Shasta's stunning backcountry geography before reaching Artist's Point, one of the finest vistas in the Mount Shasta area.

See map on page 61
Total distance: 3.2 miles
Trail type: Out and back
Elevation gain: 650 feet
Difficulty: Easy
Trail surface: Packed dirt
Hiking time: About 1.5 hours
Season: Summer, fall

Fees and permits: None
Canine compatibility: No dogs allowed.
Land status: Mount Shasta Wilderness
Trail contact: Mount Shasta Ranger District, 204 W. Alma St., Mount Shasta, CA 96067; (530) 926-4511; www.fs.usda.gov/stnf
Other: No water is available on the route.

Finding the trailhead: From I-5, take the Central Mount Shasta exit. Merge onto Lake Street and head east for 1 mile, passing through the intersection with Mount Shasta Boulevard. As the road bends to the north, continue left onto Everett Memorial Highway for 0.1 mile to an intersection by Mount Shasta High School. Pass through the intersection and continue for 12.5 miles to the Panther Meadow Campground for the Panther Meadow trailhead. GPS: N41° 21' 17.78" / W122° 12' 11.62"

The Hike

The view of Mount Shasta at sunset from the summit of Gray Butte is unforgettable. The mountain, in all its hulking glory, overshadows everything on the horizon. Gray Butte itself is a fine peak, rising like the prow of an old dreadnought from the dark forests that surround it. The trail to the summit of Gray Butte is one of the shortest and easiest trails on Mount Shasta. Despite its relative ease, it is not without charm and great scenery. The brevity of the trail actually works in its favor, making it easy to catch the sunset on Mount Shasta and then race down to Panther Meadow before it is totally dark.

The trail begins at the Panther Meadow campground, about a mile before the highway ends at the Old Ski Bowl. After passing through the campground, the route cuts across Panther Meadow. Stay right at the fork where a trail leaves to the left, climbing to the upper meadow. A couple of small stream crossings later, the trail plunges into a forest of old-growth Shasta red fir. After 0.7 miles, the gradually climbing trail reaches a wooded saddle. Here the trail splits, with the route to the summit of Gray Butte turning right and heading off to the south. The Squaw Meadow Trail goes left at the fork, continuing to the northeast.

The staggering vista from the summit of Gray Butte.

Beyond the junction, the Gray Butte Trail goes through a sparse forest of red fir as it begins to traverse the east side of Gray Butte. The trees transition from red fir to a large grove of mountain hemlock. Around 0.4 mile from the trail junction, the path crosses a large talus slope that falls away to the east. This is a great opportunity to observe the large dome of Red Butte. On the far side of the talus, the trail once again enters the forest, where it reaches a sharp right-hand turn. The trail curves onto the south side of Gray Butte about 1 mile from the trailhead.

Once on the south side of the butte, a long, switchbacking road that climbs to the communication facility on Gray Butte's southern end becomes visible. The final leg of the road is only 40 or 50 feet below the trail and the two parallel each other for a few hundred yards. Eventually the hemlock forest begins to recede as the path makes another sharp right turn, this time to the north. Here the forest thins even more and the hemlocks become stunted as a result of elevation and exposure. The trail narrows but is never faint. It climbs moderately with ever-improving views of Mount Shasta, and finally ends at the summit of Gray Butte, known as Artist's Point. Here, the grand, climactic view of Mount Shasta opens up and you can survey the monumental mountain and much of Northern California.

Miles and Directions

0.0 Start by leaving the Panther Meadow campground and hiking to the meadow.

0.2 Reach the far end of Panther Meadow and begin climbing through red fir forest.

0.7 At the junction, turn right onto the trail signed for Gray Butte.

1.0 Cross over a large talus slope with good views of Red Butte.

1.2 Round a shoulder and traverse the south side of Gray Butte.

1.5 Turn back to the north and begin the final ascent to the summit.

1.6 Reach the top of Gray Butte for a magnificent vista. Retrace your steps.

3.2 Arrive back at the trailhead.

13 South Gate Meadow

This hike is a fantastic trip through Mount Shasta's barren volcanic landscape, leading to the largest and most beautiful meadow on the mountain. This trail has everything: distant views, towering crags, scenic valleys, beautiful creeks, and explosive wildflower displays. A wonderful loop is possible, which is quite possibly the best trip on the volcano.

See map on page 61
Total distance: 4.0 miles via Panther Meadow; 4.0 miles via Old Ski Bowl; 4.8 miles via loop
Trail type: Out and back or lollipop
Elevation gain: 875 feet (Panther Meadow); 400 feet (Old Ski Bowl); 1,275 feet (loop)
Difficulty: Moderate
Trail surface: Packed dirt (rocky); loose scree; cross-country

Hiking time: About 3 hours
Season: Summer, fall
Fees and permits: None
Canine compatibility: No dogs allowed.
Land status: Mount Shasta Wilderness
Trail contact: Mount Shasta Ranger District, 204 W. Alma St., Mount Shasta, CA 96067; (530) 926-4511; www.fs.usda.gov/stnf
Other: Water is available at South Gate Meadow.

Finding the trailhead:

Panther Meadow: From I-5, take the Central Mount Shasta exit. Merge onto Lake Street and head east for 1 mile, passing through the intersection with Mount Shasta Boulevard. As the road bends to the north, continue left onto Everett Memorial Highway for 0.1 mile to an intersection by Mount Shasta High School. Pass through the intersection and continue for 12.5 miles to the Panther Meadow Campground and the Panther Meadow trailhead. GPS: N41° 21' 17.78" / W122° 12' 11.62"

Old Ski Bowl: Follow the directions above to Panther Meadow, but continue on Everitt Memorial Highway about 1 mile past the Panther Meadow Campground to the end of the road, which terminates at the Old Ski Bowl Trailhead. The trail to South Gate Meadows departs from the lower (far east) end of the parking lot. GPS: N41° 21' 40.46" / W122° 11' 58.71"

The Hike

South Gate Meadow is a lush garden tucked away in the barren folds of Mount Shasta's volcanic flanks. The hike's highlights are a long list of superlatives, revealing some of the best scenery anywhere on the mountain.

South Gate Meadow can be accessed by two different trailheads, one at Panther Meadow and the other at the Old Ski Bowl. Both trails are excellent and both see a fair amount of use, though the Panther Meadow route seems to be a bit more popular. While either of the two routes makes a high quality hike on its own, the two trails can be connected to form a reverse (traveling counterclockwise) lollipop loop. This is the ideal way to hike to South Gate Meadow. This description describes the hike from both trailheads, as well as the loop option.

Old Ski Bowl Route

The trail departs to the north from the Old Ski Bowl, toward the summit of Mount Shasta. The area is riddled with unofficial use trails, but the main path is easy to follow. It climbs north and then curves toward a gap in Sargents Ridge, the long, ragged rib of Mount Shasta that climbs up to the crags around Thumb Rock. At the gap the views are excellent, particularly to the west. The top of the ridge marks the boundary of the Mount Shasta Wilderness. Once on the east side, the trail descends toward the Gate, a gap between the south end of Sargents Ridge and Red Butte, a large volcanic dome composed of reddish-colored andesite. Descending from the top of the ridge, follow a delicate, narrow creek with small fringes of meadow on either side. This is sometimes referred to as Hummingbird Meadow. The creek may dry up toward the end of summer. After rounding a large rock outcropping, the trail from the Old Ski Bowl joins the route coming from Panther Meadow at the beginning of the South Gate.

Panther Meadow Route

The trail begins by passing through the Panther Meadow campground, then cuts across Panther Meadow. Upon entering the meadow, a signed trail splits off to the north, heading toward the upper section of Panther Meadow. This track connects to the Old Ski Bowl trailhead, completing the loop, should you decide to follow that route.

Continuing across the meadow, there are great views of Mount Shasta and a couple of small stream crossings before the trail enters a forest of old-growth Shasta red fir. After 0.7 miles of climbing, the trail reaches a saddle, where there is a junction. To the right is the way to Gray Butte. The route to South Gate Meadow stays left, going to the northeast. The trail nears a band of cliffs and goes north, through a rocky gully.

Near the top of the gully the trail climbs out and turns back to the northeast. From here, it is only a short distance through the woods before you reach the first scenic vista since departing Panther Meadow. Red Butte rises steeply on the far side of a moonscape valley. Only isolated clumps of grass and western pasqueflower grow here. The trail drops quickly, is graced with a nice view of Mount Shasta, and then cuts through the center of the valley. With the cliffs of Red Butte on the right and Mount Shasta and Green Butte looming on the other side of the valley, it is a barren but memorable scene. On the far side of the valley, the trail climbs briefly to join the trail from the Old Ski Bowl at the mouth of the South Gate.

South Gate Trail

Once the two trails have converged, the combined route descends a short distance into the South Gate, a narrow defile between the southern end of Sargents Ridge and Red Butte. At first passing through more moonscape terrain, the trail soon enters

Squaw Valley Creek cascades through South Gate Meadow.

a large boulder field cascading off the side of Red Butte. Meandering through the rocks, the path begins to gradually descend again. Views to the east are good, and include Black Fox and Buck Mountains, seldom-traveled peaks in a subdued part of the Cascade Range.

Beyond the boulders, the route journeys into another Shasta red fir forest. It maintains a fairly level grade for a short distance before finally coming to an end at the edge of South Gate Meadow. It is a scene that is at once spectacular and idyllic. Where much of the landscape traveled on the way to South Gate Meadow was barren and harsh, here lush grass carpets the ground and numerous spring-fed creeks course through the loamy channels. It is a testimony to the life-giving importance of water. Above the pastoral scene looms awesome Sargents Ridge, topped by Shastarama Point, Thumb Rock, and the Konwakiton Glacier.

The official trail ends at the edge of the meadow. There are a couple of unofficial trails that head north toward the upper section of South Gate Meadow. Please stay on these trails to avoid impacting the fragile meadow environment. Follow the right-hand trail along the main branch of the creek through the meadow to a large cascade that descends from the upper meadow. Climb up the trail, paralleling the cascade. At the upper meadow, the creeks emerge from a large complex of springs bursting from the rock and lined with thick grass, as Shastarama Point looms dramatically above.

A great loop can be formed by connecting the two trailheads. Although you can start at either trailhead, Panther Meadow is probably the best place to begin because it allows the loop to finish with a long downhill section with climactic views to the west. There is a fairly well-established use trail that descends from the Old Ski Bowl parking lot to Panther Meadow. On the east side of the parking lot, look for a trail about 10 feet down an embankment. The trail, inside a shallow, dry gulch, is well established at first, but eventually becomes faint. At this point, follow the dry gulch all the way to the four-way intersection with the upper Panther Meadow trail. The trail to the left leads to the spring that supplies the water that sustains the meadow. The trail to the right leads to a small parking area on the road leading to the Old Ski Bowl. Stay straight through the intersection, passing through a small glade alongside the spring-fed creek flowing from the upper part of Panther Meadow before arriving at its lower section. The path joins with the main trail. Turn right to return to the parking lot.

Miles and Directions

Note: **Miles and directions are provided for the loop option.**

0.0 Leave the Panther Meadow campground and hike to the meadow.

0.2 Reach the far end of Panther Meadow and begin climbing through old-growth red fir forest.

0.7 At the junction, turn left onto the trail signed for South Gate Meadow.

0.9 Come out of the forest to a great view of a moonscape valley. Begin to hike down into the valley.

1.3 On the far side of the valley, arrive at the junction with the trail coming from the Old Ski Bowl. Hike through the narrow gap of the South Gate.

1.7 Leave the South Gate and reenter the forest.

2.2 Arrive at the edge of gorgeous South Gate Meadow.

2.9 Return through the South Gate and go right onto the trail that leads to the Old Ski Bowl.

3.2 Climb alongside small, delicate Hummingbird Meadow.

3.5 Reach the top of a ridge at the boundary of the Mount Shasta Wilderness. Begin the descent down into the Old Ski Bowl.

4.0 Arrive at the Old Ski Bowl trailhead. Drop down the embankment at the east end of the parking area and follow the faint track through the rocks and sand.

4.2 At a three-way junction, stay straight and continue to the south.

4.3 Stay to the right and hike down to lower Panther Meadow.

4.6 Turn right to return to the trailhead.

4.8 Arrive at the trailhead at the Panther Meadow Campground.

14 Old Ski Bowl

This is a spectacular loop above tree line in Mount Shasta's historic Old Ski Bowl, where a ski park once operated. The trail climbs high over rocky slopes and through a secluded valley on the way to the ruins of the ski park's chairlift, where staggering views await. From there, the trail explores a vast talus slope before fading out at the head of the dizzyingly large bowl. On the return leg of the loop, the trail skirts the edge of Green Butte before passing a hidden spring.

See map on page 61
Total distance: 4.0 miles
Trail type: Reverse lollipop
Elevation gain: 1,800 feet
Difficulty: Moderate
Trail surface: Loose scree; rocky
Hiking time: About 2.5 hours
Season: Summer, fall

Fees and permits: None
Canine compatibility: Dogs are permitted.
Land status: Shasta-Trinity National Forest
Trail contact: Mount Shasta Ranger District, 204 W. Alma St., Mount Shasta, CA 96067; (530) 926-4511; www.fs.usda.gov/stnf
Other: Water is available seasonally at a small spring just above the trailhead.

Finding the trailhead: From I-5, take the Central Mount Shasta exit. Merge onto Lake Street and head east for 1 mile, passing through the intersection with Mount Shasta Boulevard. As the road bends to the north, continue left onto Everett Memorial Highway for 0.1 mile to an intersection by Mount Shasta High School. Pass through the intersection and continue for 14 miles to the end of the road, which terminates at the Old Ski Bowl Trailhead. GPS: N41° 21' 41.92" / W122° 12' 3.68"

The Hike

The Old Ski Bowl Trail climbs high up the mountain, yielding great views of some Mount Shasta's craggiest terrain. This is complemented by excellent vistas to the south, including the McCloud area, the Sacramento River canyon and the Castle Crags. The hike is also an opportunity to visit some of the mountain's bygone days.

As the name implies, the remnants of an old ski park occupy what is now referred to as the Old Ski Bowl. Skiing was a popular activity here from the mid–1950s until 1978, when an avalanche wiped out several of the chairlift towers. Indeed, the ski park is the reason that there is both a trail in the Old Ski Bowl and a paved road leading all the way to the trailhead.

The path itself was originally constructed as a service road that led all the way to the top of the chairlift and to a nearby radio tower. The old road has decayed since the ski park closed, and is now nothing more than a wide, rocky trail running across the ubiquitous scree that fills the bowl. Exploring the decaying ruins of the ski park is one of the highlights of hiking the Old Ski Bowl Trail. Of course, it also

Alpenglow on Sargents Ridge.

happens to have tremendous scenery. With the towering crags of Mount Shasta and the trio of Gray Butte, Red Butte, and Green Butte visible nearly every step of the way, the trail is a feast for the eyes.

The Old Ski Bowl Trail begins at the picnic area just to the west of the parking lot located at the west end of the Everitt Memorial Highway. This is a different trailhead from the one that climbs to South Gate Meadow, which is located at the east end of the parking lot. The trailhead is close to the tree line, the sparse trees yielding spectacular vistas.

The trail is wide and sandy as it sets out to the north. The entirety of the bowl spreads out before the trail, so the whole route is visible at the outset. Looking north toward the mountain, four notable landmarks can be identified. First is the vertical wall of Green Butte on the left. Next, on the far right, is the massive turret of Shastarama Point. Moving left from there, the craggy cluster of spires topped by Thumb Rock is higher and foreboding. On the horizon between all these landmarks is the serrated crest of Casaval Ridge, climbing inexorably toward the top of Mount Shasta. The summit itself is not visible from here.

The sandy terrain lasts for 100 yards or so before the trail gets rocky. Stay right when a wide trail splits off to the left; this is the west side of the Old Ski Bowl Trail's loop. The main trail soon begins to angle to the east. About 0.3 mile from the trailhead, another trail branches off to the right. At 0.7 mile, stay right at a large fork. The path to the left cuts across the Old Ski Bowl and connects to far side of the loop. If you are looking for a shorter hike, this is a good option, creating a nice 1.5-mile loop through the lower half of the bowl.

The trail makes a wide arc, first to the east side of the Old Ski Bowl, then back to west, traversing the entire width of the bowl. Climbing steadily along the traverse, the track passes a seep that sustains a small, lush, grassy area above the trail. Although there is no running water, it is a refreshing respite from the barren and rocky terrain. When the trail nears the west side of the bowl, stay on the main path as a few use trails descend to the south. These link up to the western trail that functions as the descent leg of the loop.

Finally, after climbing nearly 1.25 miles from the trailhead, the trail rounds a corner and arrives at a bench near the base of Green Butte. This is where the route connects to the western leg of the loop, which is the way to return to the trailhead.

This spot is a fine destination for those who want to skip the climb to the higher reaches of the Old Ski Bowl. The imposing Green Butte towers overhead and the view to the south is terrific. Red Butte and Gray Butte are also visible. Far to the south are the Sacramento River canyon, the Castle Crags, and the awesome spires of the Grey Rocks.

From the intersection of the two trails, the Old Ski Bowl Trail proceeds north. While the main trail is obvious, several unofficial paths spread out in other directions, and still more run parallel to the main route. All of these are viable options, but the main trail avoids potential route-finding. As the trail climbs north, a hidden bowl is revealed to the west, below the north side of Green Butte, but the main destination is the top of an obvious bluff directly ahead. The trail makes a sharp swing to the west and crosses the base of the bluff. The detritus of the old ski operation makes its first significant appearance here, mostly in the form of scattered concrete chunks and huge wooden beams. On the west side of the bluff, the trail turns to the north again and rounds to a plateau on the backside of the bluff, where substantial ruins are found.

Although the ski outfit is now a mess of concrete, wooden beams, steel cable, and rebar, it is obvious that a substantial structure once occupied this spot. This was the end of the chairlift that used to ferry skiers to the top of the run, where they could begin the 1,400-foot descent to the base of the slopes. Note the small cluster of *krummholz* (whitebark pine) clinging to the rim of the plateau. At just over 9,200 feet, these are the highest trees in the Old Ski Bowl.

The main trail continues beyond this point for another 0.3 mile, passing the remains of an old radio tower. This is the end of the old roadbed. Beyond this point a use trail climbs up into the vast talus slope below Thumb Rock.

On the return, head back to the junction of the main route and the western leg of the loop. This section of the hike is steeper than the ascent. It skirts the base of Green Butte, offering more great vistas as it descends. This side of the trail, beneath the cliffs of the massive butte, tends to get less usage, and it can feel quite secluded, even lonely.

About halfway down to the trailhead, the western leg of the loop reaches one of the prettiest spots on the whole hike. An old pipe stuck into the ground funnels a healthy flow of spring water, even late into the season. The water sustains a fair-size meadow amid the desolate rocks and pumice of Mount Shasta. This is the only point on the hike that has running water. The sound of the cascade is quite welcoming. The water does not last long; it disappears into the thirsty soils of the mountain. This point marks the end of the meadow too. Beyond this point, the trip down to the trailhead is a quick one.

Miles and Directions

0.0 Start hiking from the Old Ski Bowl trailhead, and climb up some wide, lazy switchbacks through old-growth red fir forest.

0.7 Stay right to hike the entire Old Ski Bowl Trail. Go left for 0.4 mile, and then left again, to hike a shorter but still scenic loop through the bowl.

1.3 Stay right at the high junction, at the foot of Green Butte.

1.5 The trail splits into many different paths, many of them user-created. The three trails on the north side of the junction are the ones to take. They rejoin quickly.

1.9 Arrive at the ruins of the old chair lift.

2.3 The trail fades out at the foot of a vast boulder field. Tracks wind through the boulders for a while before fading out too.

3.0 Return to the junction at the foot of Green Butte and stay right, beginning the return portion of the loop through the Old Ski Bowl.

3.5 Stay right at a fork, and continue to descend toward the trailhead.

4.0 Arrive back at the Old Ski Bowl trailhead.

15 Clear Creek

The trail to the Clear Creek Springs is a wildflower-strewn journey along the rim of spectacular Mud Creek Canyon. With staggering views of Mount Shasta's soaring towers, the deep canyon, and mighty Mud Creek Falls, it offers some of the most fantastic scenery of any of the mountain's trails. This hike provides a chance to explore verdant Clear Creek Springs in a stunning volcanic basin. Furthermore, it is the base camp for the only non-technical route to the top of Mount Shasta. Simply put, this is one of the best outings on the great volcano.

Total distance: 6.0 miles
Trail type: Out and back
Elevation gain: 2,000 feet
Difficulty: Strenuous
Trail surface: Packed dirt, rocky
Hiking time: About 5 hours or overnight
Season: Summer, fall
Fees and permits: None

Canine compatibility: No dogs allowed.
Land status: Mount Shasta Wilderness
Trail contact: McCloud Ranger Station, 2019 Forest Rd., McCloud, CA 96057; (530) 964-2184; www.fs.usda.gov/stnf
Other: Water is available at the Clear Creek Springs.

Finding the trailhead: From Mount Shasta, head east on CA 89 to McCloud. Continue past the main McCloud intersection on CA 89 for 3 miles. Turn left onto Pilgrim Creek Road and proceed for 5.3 miles. Turn left on FR 41N15, staying straight for 4.9 miles to where it intersects FR 31. Stay straight, crossing over FR 31 and continuing onto FR 41N61. Go 0.1 mile and then stay left. Continue another 0.5 mile, then turn left onto FR 41N25. Stay on this road for 2.2 miles to the trailhead. This road is passable for low-clearance vehicles and is well signed. GPS: N41° 21' 55.79" / W122° 7' 32.94"

The Hike

Ascending a large rib that emerges out of the dense forest of the McCloud River flats, the Clear Creek Trail is as close to a straight line as a trail on Mount Shasta is likely to be. Despite the simple course, it boasts epic, jaw-dropping scenery with a variety of vistas.

A sense of monumental vastness permeates the trail, especially at the springs, which are tucked away in the bosom of the mighty volcano's hinterland. Although the hike begins subtly, the vistas soon explode, as Mud Creek Canyon, Mud Creek Falls, and Mount Shasta itself and its attendant glaciers loom high above. This scene alone would make a worthy destination, but the trail continues, passing through expansive fields of rabbitbrush. Finally, the trail enters an expansive basin where great cliffs and turrets rise like citadels above the barren, volcanic terrain, marching inexorably toward the summit. In the midst of this arid landscape, the gushing springs of Clear Creek create a verdant oasis.

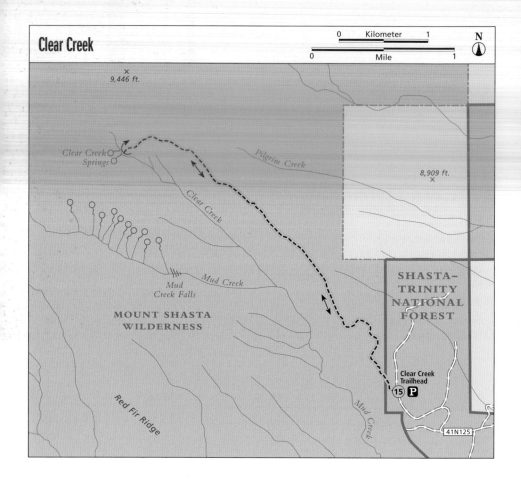

The Clear Creek Trail begins its journey in an old-growth Shasta red fir forest. This tree, which blankets most of the mountain's mid-elevation regions, is distinct from the red firs found in the Sierra Nevada farther to the south. The variety found on Mount Shasta also grows in the eastern portions of the Klamath Mountains and farther to the north, in parts of the southern Oregon Cascades.

Initially following a series of lazy switchbacks, the Clear Creek Trail rounds a couple of low bluffs and climbs through some wide gullies. At the top of the switchbacks the path finally reaches a clearing as it pulls close to the Mud Creek Canyon rim.

From the clearing, a short jaunt to the rim reveals an astounding spectacle. Spreading out below is Mud Creek Canyon. This massive trough, the largest on Mount Shasta, is believed to be the remnants of an earlier buildup on the volcano, before more recent eruptions gave the mountain its present shape. This vantage is just downstream from the confluence of Mud Creek and Clear Creek. The latter is composed of a long series of cataracts tumbling about 1,350 feet. However, it is the thundering

Mount Shasta gazes down on wildflowers lining the Clear Creek Trail.

torrent of Mud Creek Falls that dominates the aural landscape. The falls, Mount Shasta's largest, are nearly 200 feet high. Even though they are a mile across the canyon from the vista, they still look large and impressive. Above this great pageant presides the upper reaches of Mount Shasta.

Numerous towers, including Shastarama Point and Thumb Rock, line tall Sargents Ridge. Three glaciers, the Konwakiton, the small Watkins, and the massive Wintun, are all visible.

After tearing yourself away from this stupendous panorama, begin hiking the long, linear trail, which has plenty more to offer. The climbing is steady as the trail parallels the rim of Mud Creek Canyon, about 40 or 50 feet from the precipice. As you climb higher, the ground is blanketed with rabbitbrush and lupine, adding a lot of color to the scene in July and August. Looking north toward the horizon, Mount Shasta looms imposingly, the ice-clad cone constantly beckoning the hiker forward. The Watkins and Wintun Glaciers are always visible, and at times the Konwakiton Glacier makes an appearance.

After climbing straight and steady for 1.8 miles, the open trail finally arrives at the base of a rocky bluff, at about 8,300 feet, and levels off for the first time. This marks the beginning of Wintun Ridge, which leads to the summit. The track now enters a small copse of whitebark pine. Passing through the trees reveals another stunning spectacle: Mount Shasta, in all of its mighty glory, spreads out above the trail. To the left, Sargents Ridge completes its climb to the summit, crowned by the spires of Shastarama Point, Point 11,267 (a tiny sliver of the hidden Mud Creek Glacier is just visible clinging to the base of the spire), and Thumb Rock, which cradles the Konwakiton Glacier. Overhead to the right, Wintun Ridge forms the divide between the tiny Watkins Glacier and the enormous Wintun Glacier. The upper cliffs lining Mud Creek Canyon disrupt the broad, barren plain extending to the west. Closer at hand, the large Clear Creek Meadow complex fills a shallow valley. It is a dazzling panoply of alpine splendor.

To reach the Clear Creek Springs, continue on the trail as it begins to arc across the enormous basin. Thankfully, after the relentless climb to this point, the trail is reasonably level, gaining only 150 feet in the 0.5 mile to the meadows. The green grass stands out against the barren volcanic land as the trail approaches the banks of Clear Creek, which has recently emerged from a beautiful spring.

Here, the upper slopes of Mount Shasta are a desolate volcanic wasteland, inhabited only by rock, ice, and *krummholz*. In the midst of this, a complex of springs produces clear, cold water that nourishes the lush Clear Creek Meadows. The water's clarity stands in contrast to the opaque water of nearby Mud Creek, which is filled with glacial flour. High over the meadows, Mount Shasta overshadows everything else, drawing the eye inevitably to the summit. It is easy to lose yourself in such a spectacular setting.

Miles and Directions

0.0 Start at the Clear Creek trailhead and hike up some wide, lazy switchbacks through old-growth red fir forest.

0.8 Arrive at a clearing for the first good views of Mount Shasta, Mud Creek Canyon, and Mud Creek Falls.

1.2 Above a collapsed part of the canyon is the best view of the Mud Creek area.

2.5 Pass through the last band of trees and enter the large basin containing the Clear Creek Springs.

3.0 Reach the edge of verdant Clear Creek Springs, set beneath the spectacular towers of Mount Shasta. Retrace your steps.

6.0 Arrive back at the trailhead.

16 Brewer Creek

This fairly easy trail on the rarely seen east side of Mount Shasta offers staggering views of the mountain, two of its largest glaciers, and a beautiful alpine creek. A cross-country excursion from the end of the trail leads to majestic Ash Creek Falls, reportedly John Muir's favorite spot on Mount Shasta.

Total distance: 3.0 miles to Brewer Creek; 6.2 miles to Ash Creek Falls
Trail type: Out and back
Elevation gain: 500 feet
Difficulty: Easy to Brewer Creek; difficult to Ash Creek Falls
Trail surface: Packed dirt, rocky; loose scree; cross-country
Hiking time: 2 to 5 hours

Season: Summer, fall
Fees and permits: None
Canine compatibility: No dogs allowed.
Land status: Mount Shasta Wilderness
Trail contact: McCloud Ranger Station, 2019 Forest Rd., McCloud, CA 96057; (530) 964-2184; www.fs.usda.gov/stnf
Other: Water is available at Brewer Creek.

Finding the trailhead: From Mount Shasta, drive east on CA 89 to McCloud. Continue past the main McCloud intersection on CA 89 for 3 miles. Turn left onto Pilgrim Creek Road and proceed for 7.4 miles. This road will remain paved until it intersects FR 19, which is Military Pass Road. This intersection is signed for Northgate and Brewer Creek. Stay on FR 19 for 7 miles as it twists around the base of Sugar Pine Butte. Though it's a dirt road, it is fairly well maintained. After 7 miles on FR 19, turn left onto FR 42N02. This road is a lot bumpier, but still quite passable by a low-clearance vehicle. Stay right at 2 miles, then continue 0.8 miles farther to the intersection with FR 42N10. Turn left onto FR 42N10 and climb 3 miles up to the trailhead. Numerous side roads branch off, but the main road is obvious. There are a few signs indicating the way to the Brewer Creek Trailhead. GPS: N41° 26' 6.68" / W122° 7' 58.98"

The Hike

The east side of Mount Shasta is the lonely side of the great mountain. No communities gaze upward at its glaciated cliffs, and no paved roads access its slopes. This should not be taken as a discouragement, for the east side of Mount Shasta is perhaps its most majestic. Cloaked in the massive sheets of the Hotlum and Wintun Glaciers, this is the wildest side of an extremely wild mountain.

Indicative of how forsaken it is, one lone trail, the Brewer Creek Trail, provides access to the east side of California's monumental volcano. In this case, lone most definitely does not mean lame. The Brewer Creek Trail is an absolutely stunning path with epic views of Mount Shasta and two of its largest glaciers, the Hotlum (California's largest) and the Wintun (California's third largest). In addition to fantastic views and the chance to explore the delicate, alpine, riparian world of Brewer Creek, the

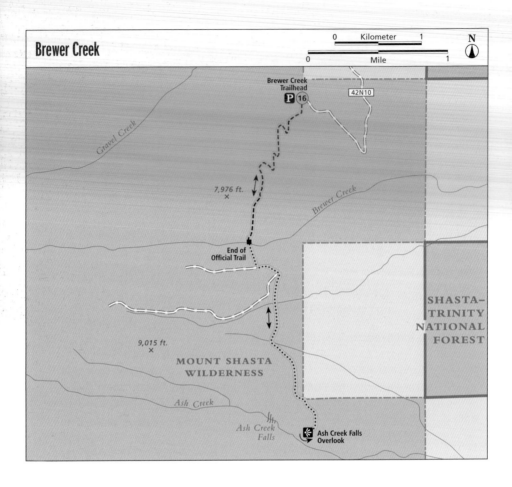

0   Kilometer   1

0   Mile   1

N

Brewer Creek
Trailhead
P (16)   42N10

Gravel Creek

7,976 ft.
×

Brewer Creek

End of
Official Trail

SHASTA–
TRINITY
NATIONAL
FOREST

9,015 ft.
×

MOUNT SHASTA
WILDERNESS

Ash Creek

Ash Creek
Falls

Ash Creek Falls
Overlook

trail leads to a cross-country route to Ash Creek Falls, Mount Shasta's most sublime waterfall. The vista of the falls, with Mount Shasta and the Wintun Glacier looming high overhead, is purported to have been John Muir's favorite view on the volcano.

The Brewer Creek Trail departs the trailhead in a southerly direction, crossing the boundary of the Mount Shasta Wilderness fairly quickly. At almost 7,300 feet, the trailhead is the second highest on Mount Shasta, after the Old Ski Bowl Trailhead. The first mile of the trail is through continuous tree cover, mostly consisting of red fir and whitebark pine. There are occasional views of the peak through the trees, but they are never particularly good, just teasing of the grandeur to come. Patience will be rewarded. The trail makes several switchbacks, always climbing at a very moderate grade, never too steeply. Nonetheless, the path eats away at the elevation, ultimately gaining 300 feet in about 0.8 mile. Finally, the trail makes one last turn to the south before it levels off and leaves the switchbacks behind.

As the trail nears the tree line, it gains unobstructed views of the snowy giant to the west. The trail continues south for about 0.5 mile, where it finally reaches Brewer

Ash Creek Falls.

Creek. This is the end of the officially maintained trail, and an attractive destination for those out for a short hike.

Here Mount Shasta soars into the clouds, filling the horizon as only a mountain of its monumental girth can. Both the Wintun and Hotlum Glaciers are clearly visible. Several of the Hotlum Glacier's large icefalls are apparent, as the grinding ice cascades over hidden cliffs in slow motion. The Hotlum Glacier's headwall rises above the glacier, a sheer cliff just below the summit. Brewer Creek itself is a noisy, clear stream, free of the glacial flour that colors some of Mount Shasta's other creeks. The water flows through a wide, rocky, U-shaped trough. Narrow ribbons of alpine grass hug the shores of the creek, and small cataracts enhance the song of the water. With the mountain presiding over everything, Brewer Creek is a beautiful and memorable spot.

A well-established use trail continues south past the creek for 0.2 mile through flat, open terrain. Eventually the trail reaches the base of a small ridge. Here it forks, as it meets old four-wheel-drive tracks, built before the establishment of the wilderness, which have evolved into trails used by climbers headed for the summit. The track to the right heads along the base of the ridge to the west before fading away in the sandy dirt. The other road goes straight, to the south, but briefly becomes difficult to follow. It rounds the end of the rise and climbs onto the ridge, now heading west up the side of the mountain. Once on the ridge, this road is much easier to follow. It climbs above 9,000 feet and eventually fades out along the edge of a canyon.

Rather than climbing higher on the mountain, a cross-country route leads to one of Mount Shasta's most awe-inspiring spectacles: Ash Creek Falls. There is no trail to the waterfall's overlook, but the route is not too difficult. To reach the falls, climb past Brewer Creek to the beginning of the second old road. When you reach the top of the low ridge and the trail turns to the west and begins to climb, stay straight and walk across open terrain to the south. This area is dotted with only a few, scattered, stunted trees. As always, Mount Shasta towers to the west. After staying in a straight line for about 0.4 mile, you will reach the edge of a deep, dry gulch. The far side has a steep, nearly treeless slope that suddenly levels off onto a flat, heavily wooded bench. Aim for this bench while crossing the gulch. Climbing the far side can be a bit challenging because of the loose scree. Watch for loose rocks and try to find stable footholds where possible.

Once on the far side of the gulch, continue south across the wooded bench. Though the forest canopy is thick, the ground is open and cross-country travel is easy. As you proceed, look for a shallow, dry gully, one that's only a few feet deep. Enter the shallow gully and head in a southeasterly direction. The gully gets rockier and a little deeper. It soon drops off precipitously, at times almost vertically. However, lots of large boulders in the gully make the going much easier.

Once at the bottom, a short jaunt to the south brings you to the edge of the canyon, where you behold magnificent Ash Creek Falls, Mount Shasta's most beautiful waterfall. The falls are about 0.3 mile away from the overlook, and the 330-foot drop is dramatic against the rugged, tortured cliff. Like other waterfalls on Mount Shasta, the falls have developed where a band of hard rock crosses one of the mountain's deep canyons. Unable to erode away the rock, the creek must fall over it instead. Making the view of the falls especially grand is the looming majesty of Mount Shasta and the upper reaches of the Wintun Glacier clinging to the higher slopes. The wondrous vista, with its canyon, waterfall, mountain, and glacier suggest that Muir very well may have been right to count it as his favorite.

Miles and Directions

Note: This is the beginning of a cross-country route to Ash Creek Falls.

0.0   Start at the Brewer Creek trailhead and begin climbing gradually. The trail crosses the boundary into the Mount Shasta Wilderness almost immediately.

1.0   The trail reaches the top of a series of switchbacks near the tree line. Awesome views of Mount Shasta open up along the trail.

1.5   Reach Brewer Creek and the end of the official trail. An obvious but unofficial trail continues to the south, leading to a pair of old roads that climb high onto Mount Shasta, and a cross-country route to Ash Creek Falls. You can retrace your steps, or continue cross-country to Ash Creek Falls.

1.7   The unofficial trail connects to the first old road in a washed-out area. The old road climbs west, up the mountain.

1.8   A quick walk to the south across open terrain leads to the beginning of the second old road climbing up Mount Shasta. This is the beginning of the cross-country route to Ash Creek Falls or a climb up the side of the mountain on the old road.

3.0   Arrive back at the trailhead.

17 North Gate

Exploring the isolated northern flank of Mount Shasta, the North Gate Trail climbs to tree line and offers great views of the mountain and areas to the north, including the Cascade Range, the Marble Mountains, and the wide Shasta Valley. There is potential for additional exploration by following routes used by mountaineers, as well as visiting hidden canyons and the North Gate Plug's highest point.

Total distance: 6.8 miles
Trail type: Out and back
Elevation gain: 1,835 feet
Difficulty: Moderate
Trail surface: Packed dirt, rocky
Hiking time: About 5 hours
Season: Summer, fall

Fees and permits: None
Canine compatibility: No dogs allowed.
Land status: Mount Shasta Wilderness
Trail contact: Mount Shasta Ranger District, 204 W. Alma St., Mount Shasta, CA 96067; (530) 926-4511; www.fs.usda.gov/stnf
Other: No water is available on this route.

Finding the trailhead: From I-5, drive east on US 97 for 14.8 miles. Turn right onto Military Pass Road. Proceed along this dirt road for 4.5 miles to the junction with Andesite Logging Road, where signs indicate the North Gate Trailhead. Turn right onto Andesite Logging Road and follow the signs to the trailhead for almost 4 more miles. The road gets rougher as you near the trailhead. Low-clearance vehicles are not recommended on this section of the road. Once off Military Pass Road en route to the trailhead there are numerous junctions, but the signs are well situated and will successfully guide drivers to the trailhead. GPS: N41° 28' 5.80" / W122° 10' 25.92"

The Hike

The North Gate Trail accesses Mount Shasta's isolated north side. The trail takes its name from a pass traveling between the main bulk of the mountain and a series of volcanic plugs that pushed up out of the Mount Shasta's slope. Used primarily by climbers to access mountaineering routes to the summit, the trail is worthwhile for the spectacular panoramas and solitude. It is also a great opportunity to observe the fantastic north side of Mount Shasta from a trail. The only drawback is the difficult drive to the trailhead.

Setting out to the southeast from the trailhead, the path climbs at a moderate grade passing through an open red fir forest. There is little underbrush on the forest floor, giving the area an unenclosed feeling, despite being beneath a high forest canopy. Shortly, the path crosses a dry gulch. The original North Gate Trail traveled directly up this drainage to the North Gate area, but this route was abandoned due to the trail being perpetually washed out by occasional flash floods. A faint track still leads up the gulch. For those who want to reach the climbing routes in haste, this is the way to go.

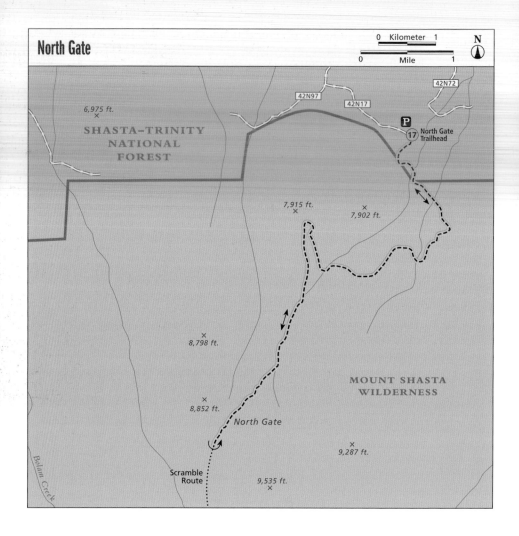

0 Kilometer 1

0 Mile 1

N

42N72

42N97

42N17

6,975 ft.
×

SHASTA–TRINITY
NATIONAL
FOREST

P

North Gate
Trailhead
17

7,915 ft.
×

7,902 ft.
×

8,798 ft.
×

MOUNT SHASTA
WILDERNESS

8,852 ft.
×

North Gate

9,287 ft.
×

Scramble
Route

9,535 ft.
×

Bolam Creek

If you want a more leisurely climb, continue on the main trail. Rather than heading steeply up the gulch, the trail laterals to the southeast. It begins to climb up the side of the mountain, following a few switchbacks while maintaining a reasonable gradient. After 0.8 mile, the trail turns south, continuing for another 0.3 mile before making a sharp turn to the west and recrossing the dry gulch. For the first time the forest canopy begins to recede and the views open up. Note the small summits to the north, which are the lower two summits of the North Gate plugs. The trail makes one long switchback, coming within close proximity of Plug 7,915 as it angles back to the south.

The trail rides the crest of a forested ridge, and pulls alongside the dry gulch again 0.5 mile from the switchback. Now the forest is thinner and the trees are smaller, an indication that the trail is approaching timberline. Mount Shasta, with the striking

Looking north from the summit of North Gate Plug 8,852.

headwall above the massive Hotlum Glacier, California's largest, comes into view for the first time. The vista to the north also improves as you climb.

Eventually the scree-covered domes of North Gate Plugs 8,852 and 8,798 become visible. The trail continues to the southwest as the area begins to constrict, squeezed between the walls of North Gate Plug 8,852 and the broad base of the Hotlum–Bolam Ridge. This is the North Gate, similar to South Gate, the narrow gap between Red Butte and Sargents Ridge on the south side of Mount Shasta. The trail crosses a small creek that originates from snowmelt in this area and flows to the north. The official trail begins to fade out here, as the trees continue to shrink and an epic view of Mount Shasta really opens up to the south.

A number of possible hiking options are available from this point, all of which require some cross-country hiking. The summit of North Gate Plug 8,852, the rocky tower on the north side of the trail, is a great destination, though it demands great caution in climbing up loose rock. To climb the plug, continue west from the narrowest point of the North Gate, angling toward the base of the plug. There is a broad, talus-filled chute down the south face of the plug. While this looks like a quick way to the top, the talus is very loose. Rather than attempting this, continue west just a little farther to a makeshift campsite surrounded by whitebark pines. Here a large rib of solid rock leads up the plug. Climb the large rocks on the left side of this rib. The rock along here is larger and more stable, and the rib is solid and provides a sound base for climbing to the summit.

From the top, the northern Eddys, the Scott Mountains, the Russian Mountains, the Marble Mountains, the Red Buttes, the Siskiyous, and southern Oregon Cascades are all visible. Mount McLoughlin is visible for the first time, situated right above the Goosenest. Far below, Lake Shastina, the Haystack, Yellow Butte, and Grass Lake can all be observed.

Other options from the end of the North Gate Trail include exploring the rim of Bolam Creek Canyon, which lies to the west, or following the mountaineer's trail farther up the mountain. This trail fades out around 10,000 feet and is a steep climb, with great views all the way.

Miles and Directions

0.0 Depart the North Gate trailhead.

0.3 Cross a gully and enter the Mount Shasta Wilderness.

1.9 The trail makes a hairpin turn and begins to traverse a long ridge.

2.5 At the end of the long ridge, the trail enters the North Gate, a narrow gap between the main bulk of Mount Shasta and some small volcanic plug domes.

3.4 The trail exits the North Gate, officially ending. A climber's trail continues up the side of Mount Shasta. It is also possible to climb the highest of the plugs, Peak 8,852, for excellent views. Retrace your steps.

6.8 Arrive back at the trailhead.

18 Whitney Falls

The hike to Whitney Falls was once one of the classic trails on Mount Shasta. The falls are the obvious highlight, yet even before you get to the main attraction, magnificent views, a wild creek through volcanic country, lava flows, and dramatic examples of nature's ability to reshape the landscape all combine to make this a beautiful, memorable journey on Mount Shasta's lonely north side.

Total distance: 3.0 miles
Trail type: Out and back
Elevation gain: 800 feet
Difficulty: Moderate due to some challenging creek crossings and a little bushwhacking
Trail surface: Packed dirt; loose scree; rocky
Hiking time: About 2 hours
Season: Spring, summer, fall
Fees and permits: None

Canine compatibility: No dogs allowed.
Land status: Mount Shasta Wilderness
Trail contact: Mount Shasta Ranger District, 204 West Alma S., Mount Shasta, CA 96067; (530) 926-4511; www.fs.usda.gov/stnf
Other: No potable water is available on this route. As of spring 2015, the trail presents some difficulties, particularly a short stretch where the route is washed out.

Finding the trailhead: From the beginning of US 97 in Weed, drive northeast for 11.8 miles. Turn right onto Bolam Road, which is also FR 43N21. This is the last major turn to the right before US 97 intersects CR A12 on the left. Once on Bolam Road, proceed 0.3 mile to an intersection, staying to the right on FR 43N21. Continue 3.7 miles to the road's end at the trailhead. GPS: N41° 28' 56.64" / W122° 14' 31.79"

The Hike

Whitney Falls is a gorgeous waterfall on Mount Shasta's north side. At an elevation of about 6,700 feet, it is the lowest of the mountain's major waterfalls and the only one that has a trail dedicated to it. The hike to the falls has fantastic scenery, fascinating geology, and great potential for solitude. Unfortunately, Whitney Creek tends to be fickle about its volume, and it is possible to hike to the overlook and find no water falling.

Whatever the state of the falls, the hike is still a great outing with many other features to recommend it. Views of the Bolam and Whitney Glaciers on Mount Shasta, as well as the Shasta Valley to the north, plus lava flows and creeks running white with glacial debris, combine to make a terrific hike through unusual terrain. Of course, if you are determined to see Whitney Falls, be sure to watch for water in Whitney Creek as it flows under US 97. It is a safe bet that if water is visible from the highway, there will be water at the falls.

Unfortunately, the hike to Whitney Falls is not without its challenges. The most pressing is the condition of the trail itself. A short but critical part of the trail was

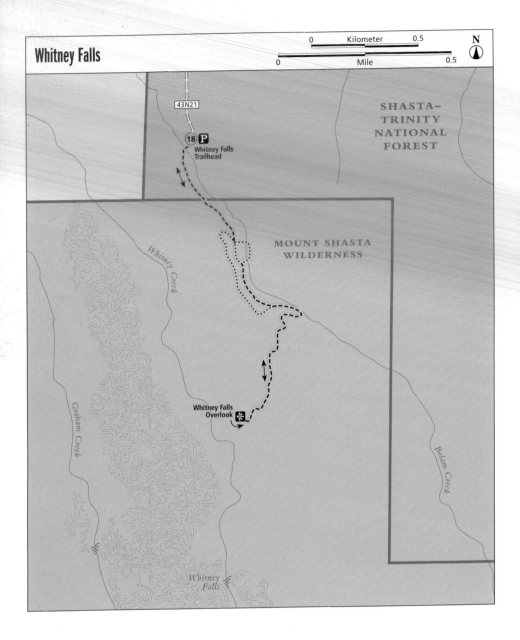

0   Kilometer   0.5

0   Mile   0.5

N

43N21

SHASTA-
TRINITY
NATIONAL
FOREST

18 P
Whitney Falls
Trailhead

Whitney Creek

MOUNT SHASTA
WILDERNESS

Whitney Falls
Overlook

Graham Creek

Bolam Creek

Whitney
Falls

wiped out by a glacial outburst flood in 1997. The hot weather late in the summer caused the Whitney Glacier to release an enormous amount of water and debris, causing a torrential flash flood. The debris flow reached all the way down to US 97 and buried the area under vast quantities of silt and rocks. The entire area was reshaped by the debris. Most of the trail was high enough above the creek that it escaped damage, but one short section was wiped out entirely. Not to be deterred, hikers blazed new

Whitney Falls.

trails through the brush and along sandy slopes to get to the Whitney Falls overlook. The trail was eventually reconstructed and some sections rerouted, but the creek's channel continues to be altered. Now one crossing is completely obliterated, rendering some of the new trail work useless. While this is an inconvenience, the trail can still be hiked and the waterfall is still worth the effort, assuming it is flowing.

The trailhead for the Whitney Falls Trail is quite small, with room for only a couple of cars. Just beyond the parking area, Bolam Creek flows through a large clearing littered with rocks. The clearing was created by the debris flow, which spread several feet of rock, silt, and ash over the area. The creek has carved a deep channel through the remnants of the debris flow. Like the large rivers coming off of great, glaciated volcanoes like Mounts Hood and Rainier, the creek runs white with glacial detritus. The Whitney Falls Trail actually begins on the far side of the creek, making it necessary to cross the gully. Unfortunately, there is no established route through the loose, constantly eroding soil. But the trail is easy to pick up on the far side, marked by frequent cairns.

Now that you are on the main trail, proceed south along a dry gulch that runs parallel to Bolam Creek. About 0.2 mile from the creek crossing, cross the boundary of the Mount Shasta Wilderness. The trail soon exits the dry gulch and crosses a sandy, rock-strewn wash. It passes through a grove of ponderosa pines, then narrows and climbs across the steepening slopes of Bolam Creek's canyon. After 0.5 mile the obvious path comes to an abrupt halt at a precipice above the creek. Here confusion ensues, making this the hardest part of the entire hike.

In the past, three route options began at this point. The original Whitney Falls Trail made a switchback here and climbed out of the canyon to a broad slope lying between Bolam and Whitney Creeks. Remnants of this route are still visible climbing north, up the sandy slope. The trail passed through an expansive manzanita field with majestic views of Mount Shasta and the Bolam and Whitney Glaciers. This was once one of the best views of the mountain from a hiking trail. Sadly, this section of trail has inexplicably been abandoned and is getting overgrown, making it a difficult option. Unless maintenance is undertaken soon, this great section of trail faces an uncertain future.

Back at the precipice, the most popular option was blazed by hikers after the debris flow. It descended down into the gully and climbed back up the other side. The trail then continued on the east side of the creek for 0.1 mile before recrossing the creek on some large boulders. This route was incorporated into the main trail when it was reconstructed. However, Bolam Creek continues to transform its surroundings. Where the channel was once only 10 feet deep and a manageable crossing, now it is 20 feet deep with vertical sides.

The best option to proceed is to climb the sandy slope to the right of the precipice for about 15 feet to a narrow track that continues upstream, high above the creek. This requires some light bushwhacking and shifting sands for 0.1 mile before the track reconnects to the main, easily followed trail. Once the routes have reconnected, the trail turns away from the creek to the west, and climbs onto the broad divide that separates Bolam and Whitney Creeks. Here the trail turns back to the south, and enters a thick manzanita brush field. The trail is wide and views of the Shasta Valley spreading out to the north are excellent.

After another 0.4 mile through the manzanita, the route begins to curve toward the west. It finally leaves the manzanita behind and enters a dense forest. With a short climb up a sandy slope you find yourself on the treeless rim of Whitney Creek Canyon. Whitney Falls is visible (when it is flowing), thundering about 250 feet over a gray cliff. The constant clatter of boulders rocketing over the falls is distinctly audible, evidence that the contours of the mountain are ever in flux. Mount Shasta and Shastina peer over the top of a tree-covered rise beyond the falls. Below Whitney Falls, Whitney Creek races through its deep gorge.

The sides of the canyon are generally loose scree, still in search of its ultimate angle of repose. The west side of the canyon is capped by a thick layer of dark, jagged lava flows, the black rock a striking contrast to the sandy canyon below. Beyond the lava flows, the Shasta Valley and Klamath Mountains are clearly visible. However, it is the waterfall that unfailingly draws attention southward.

Miles and Directions

0.0   Begin hiking from the small trailhead. Immediately cross Bolam Creek.

0.3   Enter the Mount Shasta Wilderness.

0.5 The trail narrows as it comes alongside Bolam Creek. It continues another 100 yards and then reaches a precipice overlooking the creek's channel. This is the washed-out creek crossing. The best option is to follow the narrow track that continues upstream just above the end of the trail. This route requires a little bushwhacking.

0.6 Beyond the sandy, narrow connecting track, descend to the original trail.

0.9 The trail makes a hairpin turn and begins to climb up onto the brushy divide between Bolam and Whitney Creeks.

1.5 The trail ends at a fantastic overlook above Whitney Creek's canyon, where there is a great view of Whitney Falls plunging off of a tall cliff. Retrace your steps.

3.0 Arrive back at the trailhead.

Part III: Shasta Valley and Cascade Crest Trails

The two dominant features north of Mount Shasta are the expansive Shasta Valley and the crest of the Cascade Range as it continues north toward Oregon. Although these areas are quite different from each other, they are united by two characteristics: Both were created and shaped by volcanism, and the entire area is generally overlooked by hikers, meaning that it is likely you will have all the trails here to yourself. However, even though they are neglected, these trails still boast exceptional beauty, with the added bonus of observing the north side of Mount Shasta, possibly the mountain's most stunning profile.

The Shasta Valley is a broad expanse extending nearly 35 miles north from the base of Mount Shasta. The mountain is tall and large enough to wring significant quantities of moisture out of passing storms. This results in a rain shadow, where little precipitation falls and the land is arid.

Most of the land in the valley is given over to ranching and agriculture, and utilizes water from Lake Shastina, the Shasta River, and large springs. Despite this, a few blocks of public land remain. One is along US 97, where the Klamath National Forest has significant holdings. The other is the Shasta Valley Wildlife Refuge, near the town of Montague at the north end of the valley. Hikes in this area offer the experience of traveling through a desert landscape while gazing up at the glacier-clad heights of Mount Shasta.

While the valley is a thirsty land, the mountains of the Cascades are high enough to claim more moisture from storms. The Cascade high country is blanketed in vast forests, punctuated by occasional meadows. Despite extensive logging over the years, these mountains still have some vast old-growth forests. Not all of the Cascades are high enough to enjoy increased precipitation; however, the terrain immediately to the south of US 97 is gentler and the peaks lower. Like the Shasta Valley, this falls within Mount Shasta's rain shadow and is a high desert landscape.

Trails in Shasta Valley and the high desert parts of the Cascade Range are typically open for hiking in the winter: There is little snow or rain and skies are often clear. It may get cold, but a crisp winter morning in the high desert with Mount Shasta towering overhead is certainly not a bad thing.

19 Black Lava Trail

This hike follows a short, obscure trail through an old-growth forest at the foot of Mount Shasta. The path encounters numerous areas of black, exposed lava rock, remains of an ancient lava flow.

Total distance: 1.4 miles
Trail type: Out and back
Elevation gain: 200 feet
Difficulty: Moderate
Trail surface: Packed dirt; loose scree; rocky
Hiking time: About 1 hour
Season: Spring, summer, fall

Fees and permits: None
Canine compatibility: Dogs are permitted.
Land status: Mount Shasta Wilderness
Trail contact: Mount Shasta Ranger District, 204 W. Alma St., Mount Shasta, CA 96067; (530) 926-4511; www.fs.usda.gov/stnf
Other: There is no water.

Finding the trailhead: From downtown Weed at the beginning of US 97, drive east on US 97 for 5.2 miles. Turn right onto FR 42N15. There is no sign identifying the road, but there is a stop sign marking the spot. FR 42N15 is a dirt road and requires a high-clearance vehicle in a couple of places. Proceed down the road for 1.7 miles to the railroad crossing. There are no gates, so be sure to check before crossing that no trains are approaching. Once across, continue for another 0.1 mile to FR 42N14. Turn right and climb steeply for a short, rough pitch. If you continue 20 yards up FR 42N15, there is a second opportunity to turn onto 42N14 that is not quite as rough a climb. Once on FR 42N14, proceed about 0.3 mile to the trailhead. The last section of the road is not particularly difficult, but it is a bit bumpy. Park in the clearing near the trailhead sign. GPS: N41° 27' 44.70" / W122° 18' 43.39"

The Hike

Lying at the border between the Shasta Valley and the great black forests of Mount Shasta, the Black Lava Trail is a relic from an earlier age. Initially a rugged four-wheel-drive road, in 1984 it fell into the newly created Mount Shasta Wilderness and vehicular travel was prohibited. Consequently, the old road was officially reclassified as a trail.

Although the route is short, it penetrates dark, primeval forests that blanket the northwestern foot of the mountain. After the logging operations of the early twentieth century cleared much of the low-elevation timber off of Mount Shasta, there were few old-growth forests left at the mountain's feet. However, the trees on the northwest side, despite their proximity to the lumber mills in Weed, were preserved because these forests had grown out of a harsh, rugged lava flow. The appropriately named Black Lava Trail explores these ancient forests and offers interesting opportunities to examine the remains of the lava flows. It should be noted that this trail is neither long nor difficult. At one time there was a narrow footpath extending beyond

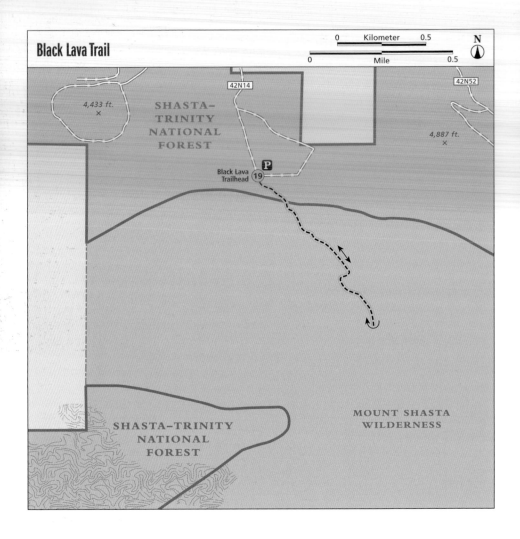

0   Kilometer   0.5

0   Mile   0.5

N

42N14

42N52

4,433 ft.
×

SHASTA–
TRINITY
NATIONAL
FOREST

4,887 ft.
×

Black Lava
Trailhead ⑲

P

MOUNT SHASTA
WILDERNESS

SHASTA–TRINITY
NATIONAL
FOREST

the end of the main trail. This was used for training by the Siskiyou County Sheriff's Department. All but the first few dozen yards of this route have been obliterated by time and nature.

Unfortunately, unless you are willing to do some bushwhacking, there are no great views of the mountain beyond the trailhead. Despite this, if you are looking for a lonely stroll through an isolated, ancient forest with interesting lava features, it is hard to go wrong with the Black Lava Trail. This is a particularly good option in late winter and early spring.

To start the hike, walk over the large earthen hump at the south end of the parking area, intended to block motorized vehicles from using the trail. Beyond the mound, the trail ascends moderately up the flanks of forested lava flow. Black basalt is obvious along the entire length of the climb. After a couple hundred yards of climbing the trail

A lava flow seen from the Black Lava Trail.

levels off. This marks the unsigned passage into the Mount Shasta Wilderness. From here the trail continues to the southeast. Note the large ponderosa pines and the big basalt boulders. The trail occasionally passes small treeless lava fields. The encroaching forest has not yet managed to take root in these concentrations of dark rocks.

As the trail proceeds there is a brief, filtered view of Mount Shasta, 10,000 feet overhead. This is the only view of the mountain on the hike. Eventually the path makes another short, steep climb as it bends around the low end of a long lava ridge that extends to the south. If you are willing to bushwhack, an unusual perspective of Mount Shasta presents itself from this ridge. To make the short trek, look for an obvious worn spot climbing up the low ridge immediately after the trail has completed the switchback and parallels the ridge. A fairly obvious route leads through the brush for about 40 yards or so until the thicket finally encloses the top of the ridge and the view opens up.

Back on the trail, the forest opens up along this level section, where there is a fine collection of gorgeous old-growth ponderosas. The trail goes a little farther until it comes to a sudden halt where the forest gets thicker. A very faint path continues through the brush, and a short distance later the track emerges on the edge of a small sink filled with lava rock. It seems as though the old route may have continued up the rocky gully, on top of which is a fairly extensive treeless section and lots of exposed black lava. If you don't want to make the push past the sink, a nice section of the lava flow sits immediately south of where the trail ends, only about a dozen yards or so off the trail. It makes a good place to stop and enjoy the unusual terrain in the forest. Unless you are willing to endure the bushwhack atop the lava ridge, this marks the end of the hike.

Miles and Directions

0.0 Start by hiking by crossing earthen mounds blocking the end of the road.

0.5 Round the ridge that offers a rough bushwhack to an interesting view of Mount Shasta.

0.7 The trail fades out in a large flat area. Some nice lava flows are just south of the trail. Retrace your steps.

1.4 Arrive back at the trailhead.

20 The Goosenest

The hike to the summit of the Goosenest, a large volcanic peak that towers above the Shasta Valley, yields one of the best panoramas in the Mount Shasta area. The hike is short, moderately steep, and has lots of solitude and interesting geology. The drive to the trailhead may take longer than the hike, but both are very scenic.

Total distance: 3.8 miles
Trail type: Out and back
Elevation gain: 1,154 feet
Difficulty: Moderate
Trail surface: Packed dirt; loose scree; rocky
Hiking time: About 3 hours
Season: Summer, fall

Fees and permits: None
Canine compatibility: Dogs are permitted.
Land status: Klamath National Forest
Trail contact: Goosenest Ranger District, 37805 Highway 97, Macdoel, CA 96058; (530) 398-4391; www.fs.usda.gov/klamath
Other: There is no water.

Finding the trailhead: From the beginning of US 97 in central Weed, head east on US 97 for 19.6 miles. Turn left onto FR 45N22. At 0.5 mile from US 97, stay to the right. At 2.9 miles, stay to the right, continuing on FR 45N22. Brown signs indicating a hiking trail are occasionally placed along the route, so watch for these to mark the correct path. Stay on the well-graded and maintained dirt road for 7.2 miles from US 97. At a logging clear-cut, turn left onto an unsigned dirt road. Another 0.4 mile leads to another fork. Stay left and proceed on the decent dirt road. Stay left again 1.2 miles from the previous junction, merging onto FR 45N72. The road switchbacks into another clear-cut before reentering the dense forest. Once back under the forest canopy, watch for the trailhead on the left, a total of 11.9 miles from the US 97. GPS: N41° 43' 35.42" / W122° 13' 13.09"

The Hike

Lying to the north of Mount Shasta, the Goosenest is one of the tallest, most scenic, and most interesting peaks in the California Cascades. Yet, for all the superlatives, it is not a particularly well-known mountain. While this is surprising considering how prominently visible the summit is from I-5, it is in an area that sees very little recreational use and requires a fair amount of travel to reach. For those few who venture into these mountains, a great feast of natural beauty awaits, especially around the Goosenest.

The lower flanks of the peak, an old shield volcano, are blanketed in magnificent forests of red fir, white pine, and hemlock. The higher portions consist of a large cinder cone. The entire western side of the mountain is covered by a massive lava flow. As dramatic as the mountain is, it is exceeded by the transcendent view from the summit. Most of the prominent features of Siskiyou County are visible from the top, including distant peaks such as Preston Peak and the Red Buttes, far to the west in the Siskiyou Mountains. Needless to say the view of Mount Shasta alone is worth the hike.

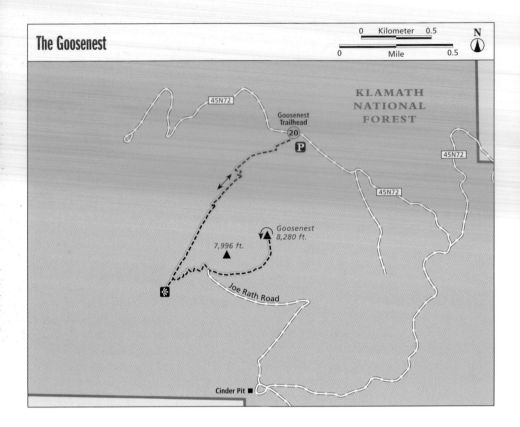

0   Kilometer 0.5

N

0   Mile   0.5

45N72

Goosenest
Trailhead

20

P

KLAMATH
NATIONAL
FOREST

45N72

45N72

Goosenest
8,280 ft.

7,996 ft.

Joe Rath Road

Cinder Pit

From the trailhead, the Goosenest Trail sets out to the west through an old-growth forest. The ground is littered with forest detritus, with downed trees and broken branches scattered about. The old trees themselves are excellent specimens, and are quite a departure from the logged-out areas you drove through to reach the remote trailhead. The path begins to climb right away, and the grade does not let up until the very top of the mountain. Still, the attractive forest makes the climb more enjoyable.

Roughly 0.1 mile from the trailhead, the trail climbs a short series of switchbacks before straightening out and continuing the westward trajectory. Breaks in the forest become more frequent and it soon becomes possible to appreciate spectacular views to the north. It comes as a bit of a surprise how high up the trail is already, and you get a sense that the flanks of the Goosenest fall away very steeply to the floor of the Shasta Valley, more than 5,000 feet below. To the north, Willow Creek Mountain, one of the volcanic summits prominently visible from I-5, rises on the far side of a deep canyon. The chasm is drained by the Little Shasta River, the largest tributary of the Shasta River.

As the trail climbs, it reaches another, larger series of switchbacks about 0.3 mile from the trailhead. Having surmounted them, the path resumes its ascent to the west.

The Shasta Valley spreads out beneath the Goosenest.

A few more sporadically placed, short switchbacks eventually deposit hikers on a level bench 1.1 miles from the beginning of the hike. Here the trail turns to the south. To the right there is an obvious pile of large boulders just beyond some trees. A short scramble out onto these boulders leads to a prominent point at the top of the lava flow that smothered the Goosenest's entire western side. This vantage point has a tremendous view of Mount Shasta, the Shasta Valley, and the many peaks of the Klamath Mountains to the west. This view is a worthy destination on its own, but considering how close to the summit you are, it is worth the effort to finish the climb.

Back on the trail, the path soon begins to climb again, more steeply than ever. Switchbacks quickly resume as the trail makes its final push up the side of the mountain. As you get higher, the soil gets looser and the tree cover much thinner. The Goosenest's cinder composition becomes more obvious and it is quickly apparent that the trail is not climbing to the summit of the mountain, but rather to the rim of a massive crater.

When the path finally levels off, after climbing 0.2 mile from the vista point, the interior of the crater comes into view. Follow the trail to the right, to a junction where Joe Rath Road leads back down the slope. This is the former route to the top of the peak, beginning at a cinder pit on the south side. Stay left, passing a pile of rocks that forms a wind barrier. The trail climbs again, but the grade is a lot easier. It is still 0.4 mile up to the summit, but it is all vistas the entire way.

From the top a grand view unfolds, with Mount Shasta taking center stage. The Trinity Divide, including Mount Eddy, the Gray Rocks, and the Castle Crags, also demands attention. Many Oregon peaks, including fantastic Mount McLoughlin, the Mountain Lakes caldera, the Crater Lake rim, and Pilot Rock are all prominently visible. As at the lower vista, the great Klamath Mountains also vie for the hiker's eye. It is a marvelous spectacle and one of the finest vantages in the North State. It is possible to return to the trail by completing the loop around the crater rim: Though the path dissipates on the summit, travel is easy and the route is obvious. Once back on the main trail, retrace your steps to the trailhead.

Miles and Directions

0.0 Start by passing through a beautiful, old-growth red fir forest.

0.4 Climb a major series of switchbacks.

1.1 The trail briefly levels off, and there is a grand view just west of the trail.

1.3 Reach the rim of the crater after another series of switchbacks. Stay left at a junction on the rim.

1.9 Arrive at the summit of the Goosenest and enjoy the amazing vista. Retrace your steps.

3.8 Arrive back at the trailhead.

21 Orr Lake

This gorgeous hike leads through the high desert and oasislike meadows, with great views of wildlife, surprising Orr Lake, the Cascade Crest, and majestic Mount Shasta.

Total distance: 3.4 miles
Trail type: Out and back
Elevation gain: Level
Difficulty: Moderate
Trail surface: Packed dirt, gravel, old dirt road
Hiking time: About 2.5 hours
Season: Year-round; the southern portion of the trail is closed in spring (through July 15)

Fees and permits: None
Canine compatibility: Dogs are permitted.
Land status: Klamath National Forest
Trail contact: Goosenest Ranger District, 37805 Highway 97, Macdoel, CA 96058; (530) 398-4391; www.fs.usda.gov/klamath
Other: There is no drinking water on the trail.

Finding the trailhead: From the beginning of US 97 in central Weed, head east on US 97 for 28.5 miles. Turn right onto Tennant Road, which is signed for Tennant and Bray. Follow this paved road for 5.1 miles, then turn left onto Old State Highway, a well-maintained gravel road. Continue down this road for 2.2 miles. Turn left onto Orr Mountain Lookout Road, which is signed for Orr Lake. Cross over the railroad tracks, and then cross a bridge over Butte Creek. Proceed for another 1.8 miles, staying left at the fork shortly after crossing Butte Creek. Park at the day use area at the Orr Lake campground. GPS: N41° 39' 47.91" / W121° 59' 20.98"

The Hike

Remote Orr Lake is a wonderfully lonely and scenic corner of the Mount Shasta region. Flanked by a pleasant mix of pine forest and high desert landscape filled with sagebrush and juniper, the lake is a surprising oasis amid a thirsty land that lies in the rain shadow of mighty Mount Shasta.

This is a world that lives at two extremes. On one hand, it is essentially a desert. Little precipitation falls out here, most of the moisture having been wrung from the clouds by the great volcano. Yet, in the midst of the arid earth, the life-giving waters of nearby Butte Creek have created a lush riparian area. Between these two poles lies Orr Lake. It is situated in a notch created by a ridge running south from nearby Mount Hebron and the western flank of dome-shaped Orr Mountain. The notch seems to have captured water supplied by adjacent Butte Creek, possibly when the creek overflows during the spring thaw. Since there is no constant flow from a creek flushing the plant life out of the lake, it has a significant lily pad presence. The thriving plant life in the lake makes it an excellent destination for anglers.

For whatever reason, the area to the north of Mount Shasta is mostly overlooked by hikers. While it is not close to any of the area's population centers, it is still easily accessible and close enough to make a convenient trip from Weed or Mount Shasta,

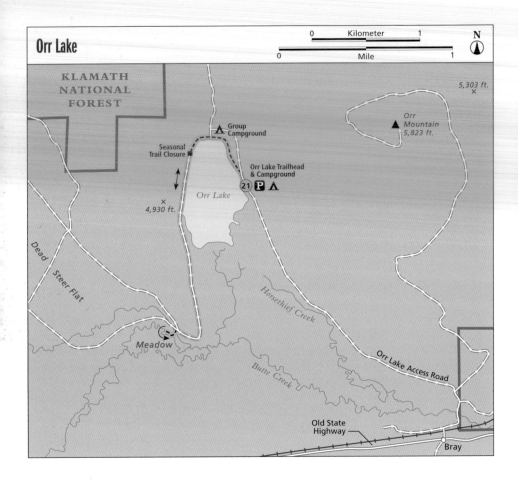

even for only a few hours. The Orr Lake Trail, in particular, makes a great outing for both serious hikers and families looking to enjoy some easy hiking with great scenery and abundant wildlife.

Skirting the edge of the lake, the trail also extends farther to the south, and provides easy access to Butte Creek. This creek rises in the high, remote mountains immediately east of Mount Shasta and flows north through some broad valleys until it reaches large Butte Valley. Butte Creek is endorheic: It is a closed system that does not connect to any other river or creek, and its waters never reach the sea. Instead, what water is not used for agriculture collects in large, shallow, marshy Meiss Lake and evaporates. Whatever its fate, Butte Creek is a very scenic destination and boasts awesome views from its banks.

From the day use parking area on the edge of the Orr Lake campground, follow the dirt road down to the small boat launch. A floating dock is adjacent to the launch and offers great views of the lake and Mount Shasta. When it is time to begin the hike, go north on the wide path, following the lakeshore. The views

Mount Shasta seen from the shore of Orr Lake.

of Mount Shasta continue for a little while before the mountain is hidden behind the ridge on the west side of the lake. After walking around the lake for 0.25 mile, pass another floating dock. This enables anglers to reach out to the deeper sections of the water. Beyond the dock, the trail begins to arc to the west, passing a third floating platform before the path goes through the Orr Lake group campground, about 0.5 mile from the trailhead. From here you can view the mountains to the south beyond the lake, notably the rounded summits of Haight Mountain and West Haight Mountain.

Past the campground, the trail begins to turn to the south, encountering two more floating docks as it does. Just beyond the last dock a pair of rock columns support a tall log fence blocking the trail. This is 0.7 mile from the trailhead. The path beyond the fence is closed from spring through July 15 to protect nesting fowl. If you are hiking within that time frame, return to the trailhead, enjoying the increasingly good views of Mount Shasta during the walk back.

If you are there when the trail is open, hop over the fence and continue along the wide path, which was once an old road. This section of the trail has a fair amount of shade, and is hemmed in by the steep ridge on the right and Orr Lake immediately to the left. A band of trees filters the view of the lake for 0.5 mile, before the trail finally emerges from the forest cover. There are good odds of seeing numerous types of birds along this section of the hike, including eagles, pelicans, and great horned owls.

The views improve significantly once the trail is in the open. By this point the trail has moved beyond the south end of Orr Lake and the area to the left is now a vast, marshy meadow, with the juniper-cloaked dome of Orr Mountain rising above. Continue south on the level path, avoiding randomly placed sagebrush growing out of the old roadway.

About 0.9 mile from the fence blocking the trail, the path turns to the west, rounding the end of the long ridge on the western edge of Orr Lake's basin. Mount Shasta finally comes back into view, towering above the rounded hump of the Whaleback, one of the tallest peaks in the Mount Shasta area. At this point Butte Creek flows just a few yards south of the trail, and it is an easy matter to bushwhack out to it. However, pressing on just a little farther leads to some better views of Mount Shasta and the opportunity to enjoy some oxbows on Butte Creek.

To reach this point, follow the trail a bit more to the west. While going down a slight grade, veer left at a junction onto a signed forest "road." Immediately beyond the junction, the old road crosses a seasonal creek that is usually dry. Right after the crossing, turn off the road to the left and walk cross-country for a couple dozen yards, picking an easy route through the sagebrush. This leads to some lovely meadows along the banks of Butte Creek as it twists lazily around convoluted oxbows. Some of the oxbow necks are less than 10 feet wide and Butte Creek almost makes complete circles.

The towering cinder cone summit of the Goosenest rises to the west, while Orr Mountain lines the eastern horizon. However, it is the soaring, icy cone of Mount Shasta looming to the south that inevitably draws attention. It is a crowning sight to an already splendid setting.

Miles and Directions

0.0 Start from the Orr Lake day use area.

0.5 Pass through the wooded Orr Lake group camp.

0.7 If it is the time of year when the trail is open, climb over the fence and continue down the road. Otherwise, this is the turnaround.

1.6 Round the south end of the long ridge above Orr Lake.

1.7 Veer left onto a rough dirt road, cross a seasonal stream, and go off-trail to the south for a few dozen yards to reach Butte Creek. Retrace your steps.

3.4 Arrive back at the trailhead.

22 Juanita Lake

The trail around little-known Juanita Lake is an enjoyable little amble around a quiet lake that's hidden away in remote mountains. On the outer fringe of the Mount Shasta area, the lake is one of the few developed recreation areas in the California section of the Cascade Range north of Mount Shasta. Despite having picnic areas and a campground, Juanita Lake still manages to fly under the radar. This may be because it lacks the jaw-dropping scenery of other lakes and campgrounds in the Mount Shasta area. However, if you are looking for a peaceful, secluded place for solitude and beautiful forests, Juanita Lake may just fit the bill.

Total distance: 1.6 miles
Trail type: Loop
Elevation gain: Level
Difficulty: Easy
Trail surface: Paved
Hiking time: About 1 hour
Season: Spring, summer, fall
Fees and permits: None

Canine compatibility: Dogs are permitted.
Land status: Klamath National Forest
Trail contact: Goosenest Ranger District, 37805 Highway 97, Macdoel, CA 96058; (530) 398-4391; www.fs.usda.gov/klamath
Other: Water is available. The trail is ADA-compatible.

Finding the trailhead: From the beginning of US 97 in central Weed, head east on US 97 for 36 miles. After leaving the mountains for the agricultural fields of Butte Valley, turn left onto West Ball Mountain-Little Shasta Road. Drive 2.7 miles, then veer right onto paved FR 46N04. Continue 3.6 miles to the campground and trailhead. GPS: N41° 49' 6.27" / W122° 7' 34.35"

The Hike

Between Mount Shasta and the Oregon border, the Cascade Range gets very little attention from hikers or campers. Despite the Cascade Crest stretching more than 35 miles, there are only three developed trails in the entire area. Those that have been developed are forgotten or ignored, as is the case with the modest loop around Juanita Lake.

The lake, a small reservoir occupying a depression between a low knoll and towering Ball Mountain, is a quiet mountain getaway in an out-of-the-way mountain range. Most of the use comes from the small population of the Butte Valley. The lonely spot makes a serene place to camp or simply relax and enjoy the forests and mountains.

The trail begins at the campground by the boat ramp. Head south along the paved trail that parallels the shore. The Juanita Lake campground is spread in the woods to the left of the trail. Large trees line the lakeshore, but periodic openings offer nice views across the water toward a low shoulder of tall Ball Mountain. While the

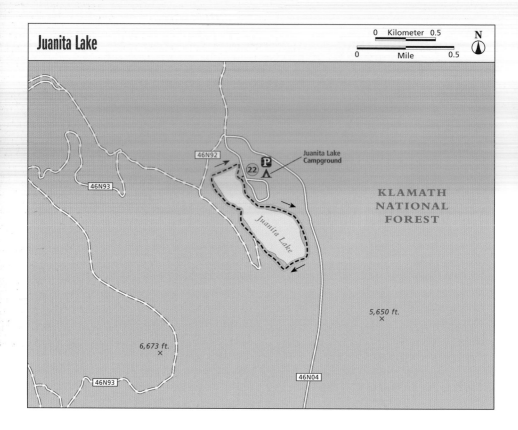

Juanita Lake

0   Kilometer   0.5

0   Mile   0.5

N

46N92

46N93

22   P   A

Juanita Lake Campground

Juanita Lake

KLAMATH NATIONAL FOREST

5,650 ft.

6,673 ft.

46N93

46N04

shoulder is only 1,000 feet above the water, the summit of Ball Mountain climbs a lofty 3,000 feet overhead, though it is not visible from the trail.

After 0.4 mile the trail leaves the campground behind and makes its way toward the south end of the lake. The path turns to the right and crosses the long earth dam.

On the west side of Juanita Lake, the trail turns north and enters a dark forest. Although the woods are thick, there are nice grassy fringes along the lake where you can sit, relax, and enjoy the view of the pleasing forest across the water. The trail continues along the west side of the lake for 0.7 mile.

As the trail approaches the north end of the small reservoir, look for water flowing under the path through a diversion channel that supplies the water for Juanita Lake. The source of the water is nearby spring-fed Musgrave Creek. Just past the diversion channel the trail reaches the north dam. Cross over the dam, which has some of the best views of the hike, and then return to the trailhead by the boat launch. Below the north dam are some nice meadows that offer a chance for some relaxing exploration.

Miles and Directions

0.0   Begin the hike around Juanita Lake at the boat launch.

0.6   Cross over the south dam.

Looking north across Junaita Lake.

1.3 Pass the diversion channel that supplies water to the lake.

1.4 Cross over the north dam.

1.6 Arrive back at the trailhead.

23 Pluto's Cave

The hike at Pluto's Cave makes a loop through beautiful high desert terrain with great views of Mount Shasta, the Trinity Divide, and the Cascade Range's crest. Belowground, mysterious Pluto's Cave, a long lava tube, beckons to be explored.

Total distance: 1.0 mile (aboveground loop) to 3.0 miles (including hike through Pluto's Cave)
Trail type: Loop
Elevation gain: None
Difficulty: Moderate due to challenging conditions inside Pluto's Cave
Trail surface: Packed dirt, rocky; cave
Hiking time: About 3 hours
Season: Year-round
Fees and permits: None

Canine compatibility: Dogs are permitted.
Land status: Klamath National Forest
Trail contact: Goosenest Ranger District, 37805 Highway 97, Macdoel, CA 96058; (530) 398-4391; www.fs.usda.gov/klamath
Other: There is no water. If you go into Pluto's Cave, bring a couple of flashlights for each person and some warm clothes. Even when it is hot aboveground, the cave maintains temperatures in the mid-40s.

Finding the trailhead: From the beginning of US 97 in downtown Weed, proceed north on US 97 for 12 miles. Turn left onto CR A12. Continue north on CR A12 for 3.2 miles. Turn left onto a poorly signed dirt road and proceed to the trailhead. The dirt road is shortly after the well-signed turnoff for the Juniper Valley OHV area. Metallic letters spelling out "Pluto's Cave" are nailed to the telephone pole by the dirt road. GPS: N41° 34' 14.61" / W122° 16' 44.90"

The Hike

Being in such proximity to one of the largest volcanoes in North America, it comes as no surprise to find lava flows, cinder cones, and volcanic buttes in the high desert Shasta Valley. One of the most dramatic features is the classic lava tube known as Pluto's Cave. Lava tubes form when lava cools and hardens around lava channels that are still moving. When the flow has depleted, the hardened lava remains, leaving the hollow tube. The north side of Mount Shasta experienced the most recent lava flows, and more than a half-dozen flows are scattered around the north flank. The flow around Pluto's Cave is one of the older ones, and is largely hidden from view by the proliferation of juniper and sagebrush.

The hike at Pluto's Cave allows investigation of worlds both above- and belowground. The open-air section leads to the cave entrance and then winds alongside holes in the ground, which are collapsed sections of the tube. From there the trail becomes a narrow, unofficial track through high desert terrain. It climbs over uplifted lava sections and boasts many great views of the surrounding mountains before returning to the trailhead. Belowground, the cave extends for a mile. The collapsed

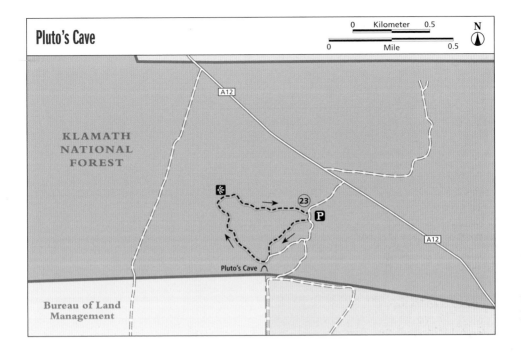

Pluto's Cave

KLAMATH
NATIONAL
FOREST

Bureau of Land
Management

roof sections admit some light in the first 0.2 mile of the cave, but after that it is pitch-black.

The route to Pluto's Cave departs on a wide trail through juniper, heading west. The presence of Mount Shasta, towering majestically to the south, is inescapable. The Cascade Crest, including the Whaleback, Herd Peak, and the Sheep Rock, all line the horizon to the east, but tall, gnarled junipers often obscure the views. A short distance along, the trail passes over a rocky stretch, where the old lava flow is exposed. Shortly after, the path arrives at the entrance to Pluto's Cave, about 0.3 mile from the trailhead.

The cave is only apparent to hikers because portions of the roof have collapsed and exposed the subterranean channel. Within the collapsed section high desert plants have taken root, and the exposed sections of the cave now look like the terrain has simply sunk. However, the caverns opening up in the rocky walls quickly reveal that this is not an ordinary sink.

When the trail finally reaches the edge of the collapsed area, a trail marker indicates the rocky route that drops down to the cave's entrance. As you climb down, a wide cavern yawns only a few feet away. In addition to abundant graffiti, you notice the unusual smell. The odor indicates the presence of guano, the calling card of the bat community.

This cave only extends about 70 or 80 feet before it is blocked off by a large cave-in. After taking a few minutes to explore the cave, exit and follow the trail to

Mount Shasta towers above Pluto's Cave.

the north. The rock walls are about 30 feet high and quickly close in toward a natural arch spanning the sink. The arch is a section of the lava tube that did not collapse. Go under the arch and walk through more collapsed lava tube debris before finally arriving at the dark, foreboding entrance to Pluto's Cave, the hellish reference seemingly appropriate.

The entrance to Pluto's Cave is massive—a dark, gaping hole close to 40 feet high leading underground. The downward angle of the cave makes the opening seem even larger. Be sure to bring warm clothes and a couple of flashlights. After the first 0.2 mile in the cave, there is absolutely no light, so it is important to have a flashlight and a backup. The temperature inside is fairly constant, staying in the upper 40s whether the outside temperature is blazing hot or frigid. Even if you do not want to follow the cave to its end, the first 0.2 mile is worth exploring. A few more collapsed sections flood the cave with daylight, and make exploration easier.

Once in the cave, the trail descends through a large pile of rocks, then reaches the sandy floor. A small section of the cave's rough roof has caved in just ahead, allowing a bright beam of daylight to illuminate the cave. Wherever the light shines is an extensive collection of graffiti. While much of it is recent, some prominent markings were made by explorers in the twentieth century.

Walk past the skylight collapse and follow the cave a little farther. Light ahead indicates another caved-in section, this one much larger. The open area is choked

Light from a collapsed section of ceiling illuminates Pluto's Cave.

with small trees, but the trail is obvious. On the far side, the trail once again enters Pluto's Cave, this time for good. From this point on, there is no light and the cave extends another mile underground. It is possible to follow the cave to its end, a dark and fascinating journey.

After exploring Pluto's Cave, return to the aboveground trail. Rather than returning to the trailhead the way you came, look for the unofficial loop, which explores surface features on the lava flow and offers some great views of the peaks around the Shasta Valley.

To take the loop, follow the narrow track north from the trail marker indicating the route down into the cave. When passing the natural arch, be sure to climb up onto it for a great view of part of the cave and Mount Shasta. Back on the trail, continue north, passing the main entrance to the cave. The path soon passes the skylight collapse and then the second, final caved-in section.

Roughly 0.2 mile farther, the route arrives at a large, fractured lava uplift. Looping around to the backside of the pile of broken lava, the trail now climbs to the top and follows a narrow cleft in the rock for a couple hundred yards. It seems like you are hiking along the broken rampart of an ancient castle. To the southwest is a great view of China Mountain and Mount Eddy, giants of the Trinity Divide. Though tall and standing nearly a mile above the surrounding valley, they are dwarfed by the awesome bulk of Mount Shasta.

Soon the trail drops off the lava wall and returns to the dusty high desert. It continues only a short distance to the south before ascending a second, shorter lava wall. This section can be easy to miss and is at times marked by rock cairns. After climbing off the second rampart the trail goes east, with views of Herd Peak and Sheep Rock. After another 0.3 mile the track becomes vague. When this happens, turn south and walk toward Mount Shasta for 40 yards or so. This will bring you to the road, within a stone's throw of the trailhead parking lot, and completes the Pluto's Cave loop.

Miles and Directions

Note: Miles and directions are only provided for the above-ground hike.

0.0 Walk west on the dusty trail to Pluto's Cave.

0.3 Arrive at the collapsed area at the beginning of the cave.

0.5 Pass the final collapse in cave ceiling.

0.6 Climb up onto the fractured lava uplift.

0.7 Climb onto second, smaller lava uplift.

1.0 Arrive back at the trailhead.

24 Trout Lake

The hike along the banks of Trout Lake in the Shasta Valley Wildlife Refuge is a short but incredibly scenic outing. The area around the lake is classic high desert but beautiful. With views of mountains in all directions, the scene is crowned by the glacier-clad glory of Mount Shasta. The hike at Trout Lake is great any time of year but especially in the winter, when the high country is still buried under snow.

Total distance: 2.1 miles
Trail type: Out and back
Elevation gain: Minimal
Difficulty: Moderate
Trail surface: Old dirt road; packed dirt
Hiking time: About 2 hours
Season: Year-round
Fees and permits: None
Canine compatibility: Dogs are permitted.
Land status: Shasta Valley Wildlife Refuge

Trail contact: Shasta Valley Wildlife Refuge, 1724 Ball Mountain Little Shasta Rd., Montague, CA 96064; (530) 459-3926; www.wildlife.ca.gov/Lands/Places-to-Visit/Shasta-Valley-WA
Other: There is no water. The refuge may be closed from Nov to Jan. Be sure to check postings for closures in the refuge during hunting seasons.

Finding the trailhead: From Mount Shasta, drive north on I-5 for 27 miles to the Grenada exit. From the off-ramp, turn right onto CR A12 and proceed for 0.7 mile, then turn left onto Montague-Grenada Road. Continue north for 5.8 miles. In downtown Montague, turn right onto Webb Road, which becomes Ball Mountain–Little Shasta Road as it leaves town. Proceed a total of 1.5 miles from Montague-Grenada Road, then turn right onto the paved road at the sign indicating the "Shasta Valley Wildlife Refuge." Stay south on the paved road for about 0.5 mile. Upon arrival at the refuge offices, follow signs to the refuge. The road will turn east and become a well-maintained gravel road, passable to all vehicles. From the offices, follow the gravel road for 2 miles to a fork in the road. Note the crossing of the Little Shasta River about halfway to the fork. At the fork, stay right and continue another 0.8 mile to the end of the road at the parking lot for Trout Lake. GPS: N41° 41' 26.17" / W122° 28' 51.24"

The Hike

The Shasta Valley stands in remarkable contrast to the high, alpine regions immediately to its east, west, and south. The valley is a classic high desert. Sparsely covered with junipers in lieu of pines and firs, the gold hues of the Shasta Valley give notice that this is a very different landscape.

Hemmed in on the east and west by the Cascade and Klamath ranges, the valley is crowned on its southern end by the snowy pyramid of Mount Shasta, presiding regally over its domain. The high desert terrain is a result of the valley's position within Mount Shasta's rain shadow. When storms move through the area, the mountain forces the turbulent currents upward and wrings moisture from the clouds,

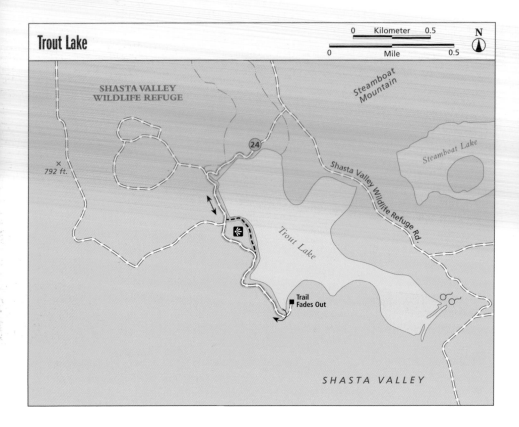

Trout Lake

SHASTA VALLEY
WILDLIFE REFUGE

Steamboat
Mountain

× 792 ft.

24

Shasta Valley

Shasta Valley Wildlife Refuge Rd.

Steamboat Lake

Trout Lake

Trail
Fades Out

SHASTA VALLEY

0   Kilometer   0.5

0   Mile   0.5

N

nourishing its dense forests. Consequently, there is little precipitation to the north, and the desert holds sway. Unfortunately for hikers, most of the Shasta Valley is a productive ranching area and there is limited opportunity to enjoy the dry climate. The little public land available is found in the southeast corner, hugging the foot of Mount Shasta.

The rest of the valley is privately owned, except for one little-known exception. At the north end of the valley, just east of the town of Montague, is the Shasta Valley Wildlife Refuge, administered by the California Department of Fish and Game. This 4,657-acre slice of the Shasta Valley is a diamond in the rough. What little development there is, aside from old agricultural infrastructure, is oriented toward hunters and anglers. Nonetheless, the refuge is blessed with gorgeous scenery and absolutely spectacular views of Mount Shasta and the rest of the peaks that ring the Shasta Valley.

Hiking in the Shasta Valley Wildlife Refuge is a bit different from other destinations around Mount Shasta. For the most part, the hiking is on roads or cross-country. The most significant exception to this is the Trout Lake Trail. Surprisingly large and deep, Trout Lake is a closely guarded secret among anglers. Loaded with its namesake fish, the lake is spectacularly situated amid grassy plains and rocky, juniper-covered

Trout Lake and Mount Shasta.

mounds. It is particularly noteworthy for its staggering view of Mount Shasta, and anyone lucky enough to arrive at the lake when the wind is calm is guaranteed to enjoy a fantastic reflection on the water. The Trout Lake Trail is not an officially sanctioned route, but it is the closest thing the refuge has to an actual hiking trail.

The journey through the high desert is a great change of pace from other hikes in the Mount Shasta area. Although it is not long, there is excellent potential for exploration all around Trout Lake. During the winter months, when the mountains are cloaked in snow, a hike along Trout Lake is an ideal opportunity to get outside and enjoy terrific scenery.

Like nearly anywhere in the Shasta Valley, the trailhead has fantastic views of Mount Shasta. Highlighted against the large lake and golden hills, Mount Shasta is an amazing sight. The trip to Trout Lake is worth it just to enjoy this spot.

To begin the hike, head east and cross the levee. Views northward include Cottonwood Peak to the northwest, Paradise Craggy and Black Mountain directly to the north, with Soda Mountain and Fuji-like Mount McLoughlin far to the northeast, in Oregon. Even though farms and ranches surround the refuge, little of this development is visible.

On the far side of the levee the road drops lower and makes a long loop back to climb up a prominent rocky point. Note the quarry at the top, where rock was blasted out of the knoll to construct the levee. The road continues south across another levee.

Trout Creek Lake is visible to the right the original route of the spring-fed creek that forms the lake, passing through a marshy area on its way to another small pond.

On the far side of the levee, the road turns west. Where it does, note a large, man-made bird's nest on a pole that's protected by shields that prevent predators from climbing up it. Look for a path splitting off the road just below the nest. The trail continues southeasterly, just above Trout Lake's high-water mark. The singletrack trail is easy to follow and stays fairly close to the water. Views are great, particularly to the east, where Steamboat Mountain (the refuge's highest point) and distant Willow Creek Mountain and the Goosenest are all visible. The path is tucked between the water and the rocky slope of a high hill.

Weaving through the broadly scattered junipers, the trail remains distinct the entire way except for one spot, where large rocks obscure the route to some degree. It is not difficult to find the trail beyond this point. The path proceeds south for about 0.2 mile from the end of the levee before it joins an old road and continues along the level shoreline. Passing occasional junipers, it skirts the base of yet another small hill. A small valley opens up at the south end of the second hill. Trout Lake extends a narrow finger into the valley, and the trail arcs wide to the west to avoid it. Views of Mount Shasta, good elsewhere along the trail, are now even better.

The road rounds the narrow finger of the lake and continues on the far side. Dense reeds, which turn gold in the fall and winter, line the shore throughout this section of the trail. At the southern end of the lake another broad, level valley opens up. This generally marks the end of the Trout Lake Trail, as it becomes increasingly faint. Thankfully, the ground is level and travel is easy.

For those looking to extend the hike, it is possible to walk along the southern end of the lake for another 0.5 mile. Unfortunately it is not possible to completely circumnavigate Trout Lake. A series of marshes that are hard to cross make up the southeast corner of the lake, and the southern property line is so close at this point that there usually is no dry land in this corner of the refuge. Retrace your steps.

On the return trip, when the old road arrives at its junction with the singletrack trail that branched off at the end of the levee, take the old road up the hill. This path climbs over the shoulder of the hill and offers a great opportunity to scramble up to its summit. Views from the top are stupendous, and are certainly among the most memorable vistas in the area. To the east the Cascade Crest towers above the Shasta Valley, topped by Willow Creek Mountain, Ball Mountain, and the Goosenest. Looking north, all of the aforementioned peaks can be observed, as can much of the eastern bulwark of the Klamath Mountains, including China Mountain and Mount Eddy. To the south, the great bulk of Mount Shasta, looming above the valley, and Trout Lake, dominates the entire scene.

When you are able to tear away from this incredible spot, continue south on the old road as it climbs over the hill and descends to a junction. Turn right onto the road just as it's about to cross the levee. From there, it is an easy hike across the levees to the trailhead.

Miles and Directions

0.0 Enjoy the awesome sights at the trailhead. To start the hike, walk west toward the levee.

0.4 At the end of the second levee, turn left onto a narrow footpath that parallels the lakeshore.

0.6 Stay straight when the footpath and an old road merge.

1.0 The trail fades away at the south end of Trout Lake. It is possible to follow the lakeshore for another 0.5 mile before the property line blocks further progress.

1.4 On the way back, turn left onto the old road and climb up the hill.

1.5 At the top of the rise, veer right off the road and scramble to the top of the hill for one of the best views of the Mount Shasta region.

1.7 Turn right onto the road and cross the levee.

2.1 Arrive back at the trailhead.

Part IV. Scott Mountains Trails

A part of the larger Klamath Mountains, the Scott Mountains are a forgotten range loaded with craggy peaks and beautiful lakes. The Scotts are classic Klamath terrain. Composed of peridotite, they have a distinctive bright red or orange color, while their poor soil results in stunted trees and thin forests.

The Scotts are ignored for several reasons. They are overshadowed by the neighboring Trinity Divide, where high peaks like Mount Eddy and spectacular destinations like Castle Lake pull attention away from other alpine areas. The Scotts are also arranged to ensure that they are underappreciated. Running east to west, the mountains are bisected by CA 3, and the half of the range lying west of the highway is included in the vast Trinity Alps Wilderness. The eastern half of the range, nearer Mount Shasta, is left to its own devices and, subsequently, ignored.

This is unfortunate. The Scott Mountains have most of the qualities hikers look for in alpine landscapes: tall, craggy peaks and cliffs, beautiful lakes, vast pine forests, lush meadows, sweeping vistas, and a sense of boundlessness that makes you feel like you could hike these mountains for days. This, of course, is exactly what some people do. Most of the use the Scott Mountains get is from backpackers on the Pacific Crest Trail. Over 20 miles of the PCT meander through the Scotts, and two of the three hikes that explore the range travel along the long trail. If you time your hike to avoid the gaggle of thru-hikers, you will likely have the trails in these beautiful mountains to yourself.

25 Kangaroo Fen and Bull Lake

This beautiful hike travels a lightly used section of the Pacific Crest Trail in the remote Scott Mountains. Passing though beautiful meadows and boasting great views, the hike ends at the edge of lonely Bull Lake, scenic but underappreciated.

Total distance: 8.0 miles
Trail type: Out and back
Elevation gain: 1,100 feet
Difficulty: Moderate due to length
Trail surface: Packed dirt, rocky
Hiking time: About 6 hours or overnight
Season: Summer, fall
Fees and permits: None

Canine compatibility: Dogs are permitted.
Land status: Klamath and Shasta-Trinity National Forests
Trail contact: Salmon/Scott River Ranger District, 11263 N. Highway 3, Fort Jones, CA 96032; (530) 468-5351; www.fs.usda.gov/klamath
Other: Water is available at Bull Lake.

Finding the trailhead: From Mount Shasta City, travel north on I-5. Take exit 751 for Edgewood. Turn left, passing under the freeway. Immediately turn right onto Stewart Springs Road for 0.5 mile, until it becomes Old Highway 99. Continue north on Old Highway 99 for 7.0 miles. Turn left onto Gazelle–Callahan Road and follow it for 16.5 miles, crossing over the crest of the mountains and entering the Scott River watershed. At the signed turnoff for Kangaroo Lake, turn left onto Rail Creek Road and stay on it for 7.0 miles, until it ends at Kangaroo Lake. Park in the campground's ample parking lot. The trailhead is on the south (right) side of the road. GPS: N41° 20' 4.63" / W122° 38' 31.27"

The Hike

Kangaroo Lake comes as a bit of a relief after driving up from the high desert valley of the East Fork of the Scott River. After climbing through the ponderosa and fir trees, the road suddenly ends at the lake, a glimmering, sapphire gem set amid pink and gray cliffs. Considering how remote it is, the lake itself receives its fair share of attention. Most who come here are anglers. Since it is not generally regarded as a hiking destination, the exceptional scenery just above the lake is usually ignored. The majority of those who explore the area beyond Kangaroo Lake are thru-hikers on the Pacific Crest Trail (PCT).

When the flurry of hikers heading north toward Oregon is not on the PCT, the area is essentially forsaken, left waiting for the motivated handful who come here for spectacular scenery and excellent solitude. The destination is Bull Lake, a large lake set in a barren bowl. On the way there, the PCT passes rugged peaks, small tarns, and large, beautiful Robbers Meadow. Views of the surrounding mountains are fantastic. The first part of the hike climbs up the Kangaroo Fen Trail, a scenic path that connects Kangaroo Lake to the PCT. The trailhead is located just down the road from

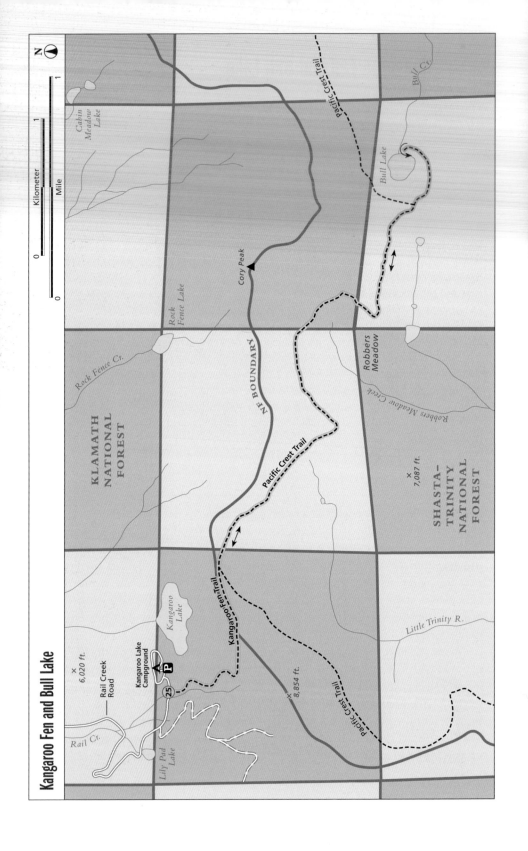

Kangaroo Fen and Bull Lake

KLAMATH NATIONAL FOREST

SHASTA–TRINITY NATIONAL FOREST

Cabin Meadow Lake

Bull Ck.

Bull Lake

Pacific Crest Trail

Cory Peak

Rock Fence Lake

Rock Fence Cr.

NF BOUNDARY

Robbers Meadow

Robbers Meadow Creek

× 7,087 ft.

Pacific Crest Trail

Kangaroo Fen Trail

Little Trinity R.

Kangaroo Lake

Kangaroo Lake Campground

P

25

× 6,020 ft.

Rail Creek Road

Rail Cr.

Lily Pad Lake

× 8,854 ft.

Pacific Crest Trail

N

Kilometer
0   1
Mile
0   1

Bull Lake and Mount Eddy.

the campground parking lot and is marked with an obvious sign. Even though the trail switchbacks constantly, it is still a fairly steep climb, rising more than 500 feet in about 0.5 mile.

The trail crosses many small creeks, and the carnivorous *Darlingtonia* pitcher plant is common. The path initially angles away from the lake, then arcs back toward it midway up the climb. A faint use trail goes out to a rocky ledge for one of the best views of Kangaroo Lake. The route again angles away from the lake as it continues to switchback upward. Eventually it turns back to the east, toward the lake, as it nears the crest of the Scott Mountains. This final traverse, just below the crest, often holds snow into July.

The trail continues east, descending gradually toward the PCT. While numerous pines and firs cover the area on the north side of the crest, this section of the trail travels through a barren landscape with lots of oddly colored rocks. After dropping only 100 feet in 0.3 mile, the Kangaroo Fen Trail ends at a junction with the PCT. Turn left here.

The trail heads southeast, rounding the head of a small basin that contains a small lake and some meadows. These are the headwaters of the Little Trinity River, which flows from here south for 6 miles before joining the main fork of the Trinity River. As the trail reaches the east end of the basin, it passes through a gap between the main crest of the Scott Mountains and craggy Peak 7,087. This rugged little peak is an unusual tan color, a departure from the red to russet found on most of the rocks in this area, which is made up of serpentine and peridotite.

Beyond the saddle that separates the Scott crest from Peak 7,087, the trail enters the larger basin that contains Robbers Meadow, an attractive patchwork of lush grassy areas watered by springs. Unfortunately, the trail never passes through the meadow, but stays high above. Nevertheless, the sounds of Robbers Meadow Creek are audible.

On the far side of the basin, the trail crosses the brushy foot of a large boulder field composed of bright red rocks. This is the place to begin climbing if you wish to attempt the summit of Cory Peak above.

Past the boulder field, the trail continues to the south for 0.2 mile before making a sharp turn to the left as it rounds another low shoulder. Look for a trail splitting off to the right here. While this too was once part of the old Sisson–Callahan Trail, it is now the main route that leads down to Bull Lake, which is visible below the trail. Here are amazing views of the upper headwaters of the Trinity River, including the great, hulking massif that is Mount Eddy. The west side of Bull Lake is barren, which means it has great views. You will usually have this fantastic place to yourself.

Miles and Directions

0.0 Start at the Kangaroo Lake parking area. Walk back along the road a short distance and begin climbing up the Kangaroo Fen Trail.

0.3 Pass a great overlook above Kangaroo Lake.

0.9 Reach the crest of the Scott Mountains, where there is a fantastic panorama.

1.2 The Kangaroo Fen Trail intersects the Pacific Crest Trail. Turn left onto the PCT.

2.1 Pass through a saddle and enter the Robbers Meadow basin.

3.7 Turn right onto the spur trail that drops down to Bull Lake.

4.0 Arrive at Bull Lake. Retrace your steps.

8.0 Arrive back at the trailhead.

26 Caldwell Lakes

The Caldwell Lakes are a rarely visited cluster of small tarns in the high country at the east end of the Scott Mountains. The hike travels through lush meadows filled with carnivorous plants, alongside racing creeks, through lovely forests, and below high cliffs. Great views of Mount Shasta and Mount Eddy are frequent along the entire length of the hike. The three lakes, though small, are very scenic. The upper two lakes are in a large, craggy basin just below the summit of China Mountain.

Total distance: 4.0 miles
Trail type: Out and back
Elevation gain: 1,300 feet
Difficulty: Moderate
Trail surface: Packed dirt, rocky
Hiking time: About 3 hours
Season: Summer, fall
Fees and permits: None

Canine compatibility: Dogs are permitted.
Land status: Shasta-Trinity National Forest
Trail contact: Mount Shasta Ranger District, 204 W. Alma St., Mount Shasta, CA 96067; (530) 926-4511; www.fs.usda.gov/stnf
Other: Water is usually available in Parks Creek and at the Caldwell Lakes.

Finding the trailhead: From Mount Shasta City, drive north on I-5 through the town of Weed. Exit at the Edgewood/Stewart Springs exit. Turn left and drive under the freeway, then turn right onto Old Highway 99. Continue north for a couple hundred yards, and then turn left onto Stewart Springs Road. After 4 miles, FR 17 splits off to the right. Follow FR 17 for 5.4 miles, and park at the beginning of FR 41N74. GPS: N41° 22' 55.89" / W122° 32' 6.18"

The Hike

Almost completely forgotten, the Caldwell Lakes Trail is a hidden gem on China Mountain, the fourth highest peak in the Mount Shasta region. Like the trail and the lakes, China Mountain itself is seemingly a forgotten giant. From most places where the mountain is visible, it appears to be a forested hump just north of the naked, rocky grandeur of Mount Eddy. However, what is hidden from below makes fantastic scenery for the few hikers who venture here.

The great views, rugged terrain, meadows, pretty lakes, and rushing creeks are all arranged in a pleasing order. The route's east- and south-facing orientation is a bonus, since the trail is often clear earlier in the season, when other hikes in the area may still be snowbound, affording the mountain-starved a chance to get into the high country a bit ahead of schedule.

The trail to the Caldwell Lakes begins 0.5 mile up a dirt road off FR 17. Although a high-clearance vehicle could cover that half-mile, it is advisable to just park off FR 17 and hike the 0.5 mile up the road. Parks Creek runs alongside the road here, making this section more enjoyable. Parks Creek is one of the largest tributaries of the Shasta River, which drains the large Shasta Valley.

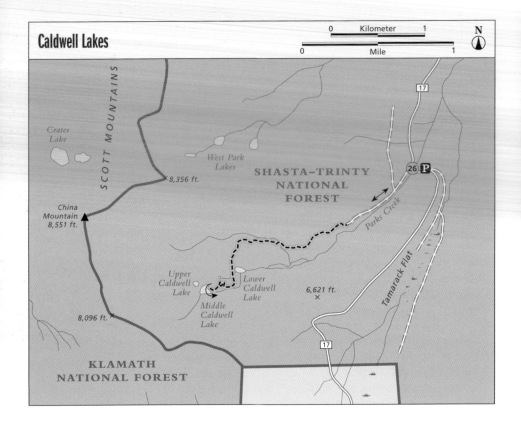

Kilometer

Mile

N

SCOTT MOUNTAINS

Crater
Lake

West Park
Lakes

8,356 ft.

SHASTA–TRINITY
NATIONAL
FOREST

17

26 P

Parks Creek

China
Mountain
8,551 ft.

Upper
Caldwell
Lake

Lower
Caldwell
Lake

6,621 ft.

Tamarack Flat

Middle
Caldwell
Lake

8,096 ft.

17

KLAMATH
NATIONAL FOREST

After climbing at a moderate grade for 0.5 mile, the road comes to an end. This is the most confusing part of the trail to the Caldwell Lakes. At the end of the road, there is a large pile of rocks, behind which is a dirt mound. Beyond these two landmarks is a large meadow, and Parks Creek courses around its southern perimeter. About 30 yards before the rock pile, a trail branches off to the right and climbs above the meadow. If you miss this turnoff, it is still easy to connect to the trail by passing through the meadow and climbing the bluff on the northwest side.

Once on the trail proper, you will climb moderately in a westerly direction. Views of Mount Shasta are good. The trees thin out and the route is generally open. The rocky crags of the Caldwell Lakes' cirque rise overhead to the west. Although Parks Creek can be heard, it is no longer visible. About 0.5 mile after departing the road, the trail crosses one of the forks of Parks Creek, coming from an extensive network of meadows in a canyon about 200 feet below Upper Caldwell Lake.

The trail enters thicker forest cover and continues climbing for 0.4 mile through rockier terrain. Soon it turns to the south and passes below a rocky cliff. Look for a cairn next to the path, marking the easiest way to descend 100 feet to Lower Caldwell Lake. The lake itself is tree-bound and does not have great views. The

Lower Caldwell Lake and Mount Shasta.

creek enters from the south and can be heard from the trail. Scrambling up the cliffs above the lake provides the best view of the hike. From here you can observe Lower Caldwell Lake, Mount Eddy, and Mount Shasta, as well as much of the northern Eddy Range.

After passing Lower Caldwell Lake, the path swings west and closes in on Parks Creek again. The water fans out along this section of trail, coursing through numerous small channels as it tumbles down a steep slope. After following the creek briefly, the route begins to switchback tightly through an open, rocky area, with views of Mount Shasta to the east. At the top of the switchbacks you arrive at the mouth of Middle Caldwell Lake. The rocky cirque comes as a bit of a surprise, with stark gray cliffs climbing up to the summit of China Mountain, which presides 1,400 feet above the basin. Small Upper Caldwell Lake is just beyond the larger, middle lake. When the water level is high, the distinction between the two lakes may be imperceptible. The edge of the lake is a great place to relax and enjoy your own alpine haven.

Miles and Directions

0.0 Begin by hiking up the old road off FR 17.

0.5 At the road's end, turn right and continue hiking up a wide path.

1.2 Cross over Parks Creek.

China Mountain forms a dramatic backdrop to Upper Caldwell Lake.

1.6 The spur trail leading down to Lower Caldwell Lake splits off to the left. It is 0.1 mile down to the water.

1.8 Begin climbing the switchbacks just below Middle and Upper Caldwell Lakes.

2.0 Reach the edge of Middle Caldwell Lake. The tiny upper lake is just across the water. China Mountain rises to the west of the lakes. Retrace your steps.

4.0 Arrive back at the trailhead.

27 Bluff Lake and Cement Bluff

The trip to Bluff Lake is a lonely hike on a rarely traveled section of the Pacific Crest Trail. The easy, level trail curves around a remote high mountain basin below a shoulder of underappreciated China Mountain, the fourth highest peak in the Mount Shasta area. After enjoying great views, remote forests, and bright red talus slopes, the journey ends at the pretty little Bluff Lake and the bizarre formation called the Cement Bluff.

Total distance: 9.2 miles
Trail type: Out and back
Elevation gain: 250 feet
Difficulty: Moderate due to length
Trail surface: Packed dirt; rocky; rough scrambling
Hiking time: About 6 hours or overnight
Season: Summer, fall

Fees and permits: None
Canine compatibility: Dogs are permitted.
Land status: Shasta-Trinity National Forest
Trail contact: Mount Shasta Ranger District, 204 W. Alma St., Mount Shasta, CA 96067; (530) 926-4511; www.fs.usda.gov/stnf
Other: Water is available at Bluff Lake.

Finding the trailhead: From Mount Shasta City, drive north on I-5 through the town of Weed. Exit at the Edgewood/Stewart Springs exit. Turn left and drive under the freeway, then turn right onto Old Highway 99. Continue north for a couple hundred yards, and then turn left onto Stewart Springs Road. After 4 miles, FR 17 splits off to the right. Follow this road 9.1 miles to the Parks Creek trailhead. GPS: N41° 20' 35.13" / W122° 32' 15.14"

The Hike

Parks Creek Pass is a high saddle between giant Mount Eddy and China Mountain. The pass, which is crossed by the Pacific Crest Trail, is a popular trailhead for hikers heading south to the Deadfall Lakes and the ascent of Mount Eddy, among the most heavily used trails in the Mount Shasta area. In striking contrast, the section of the PCT that departs Parks Creek Pass to the north is almost completely unused, except for the brief period when the flurry of PCT thru-hikers travels through the area. Despite its anonymity, this part of the PCT is very scenic, maintains an easy and level grade, and leads to a fine mountain lake and a bizarre geological feature. For those who yearn for beautiful backcountry that is deeply isolated, the hike on the PCT to Bluff Lake and the Cement Bluff is sure to satisfy.

Depart north from the PCT trailhead at Parks Creek. Though the trailhead may have many parked cars, it is almost a surety that they are all there for the hike south toward the Deadfall Lakes and Mount Eddy.

The trail passes an old quarry on the left before dropping below the crest of the mountains. The route maintains a level grade, slung high on cliffs as it makes a

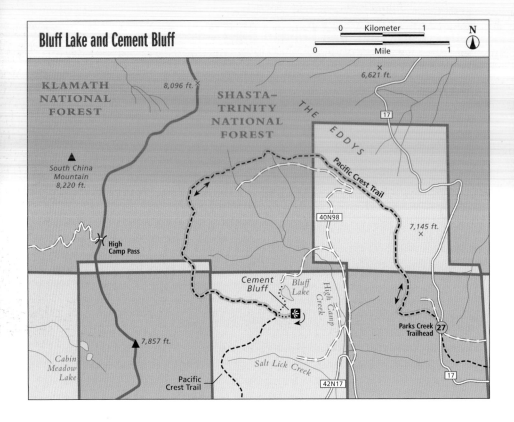

sweeping arc along the edge of High Camp Basin. The basin is almost completely enclosed; High Camp Creek escapes the giant bowl through a fairly narrow gap at the basin's southern end, and is joined just downstream by Eddy Creek flowing out of Deadfall Basin. The confluence of the two creeks marks the beginning of the mighty Trinity River. Early in the season the rushing water can be heard far below.

The Cement Bluff is visible on the far side of the basin. This is due to the very wide arc the trail makes circling the basin. The trail soon rounds a large rocky bluff, turning west and then north. A large red peak flanked by a long, rocky ridge, unofficially named High Camp Peak, is another prominent landmark across the canyon. A sliver of meadow-rimmed Bluff Lake, at the foot of the Cement Bluff, is briefly visible. China Mountain towers above the end of the canyon.

The PCT continues north. After 1 mile of level hiking, the path passes through a small meadow, which lies only 40 feet or so below the crest of the mountains. The area around the trail is sparsely forested and the views to the west remain good. Soon the PCT begins to angle toward the northwest. About 1.8 miles from the trailhead, it nears a rocky draw on the right. This is the point at which you would depart the PCT to begin an ascent of China Mountain.

Looking down on Bluff Lake from the top of the Cement Bluff.

Staying on the trail, the route now heads due west, rounding the uppermost part of High Camp Basin. The forest thickens for the first time. The terrain is much more moderate here, the slope more gentle, and there is room for the forest to grow. Though the views all but disappear when the trail enters the woods, it is still pleasant hiking through open forest with a parklike feel. Continuing west, the PCT crosses a few small creeks, which may be dry later in the season.

After traversing the northern perimeter of High Camp Basin for 1 mile the PCT begins to turn south. The forest is still relatively thick, but the ground is alternately covered with grass or small rock fields. The area is not very brushy. Many of the trees are beautiful, old-growth giants. Occasional views of Mount Shasta to the southeast filter through the trees, and at times the rocky ridge that lines the western side of the basin can be seen climbing up toward High Camp Peak.

The trail crosses another, larger creek with a dense fringe of grass. About 50 yards away is another small meadow. Here the trail crosses a seep that has turned the path into a thick bog. Steer to the right of the bog to bypass the mud. The trail continues south as the trees begin to thin out and the views of the cliffs overhead improve.

Look for a striking series of white slabs to appear just above the trail. Though these smooth-surfaced slabs appear to be sandstone, they are probably one of the rock types related to serpentine or peridotite, which makes up the majority of mountains in this area. The slabs seem out of place, like they are some lost fragment from the cliffs around Zion, Sedona, or Moab. However they came to be, they mark a distinct transition in the nature of the PCT. Prior to the white slabs the trail passed through forest, but beyond them the trees come to an end and the trail crosses onto a steep talus slope composed of bright red rocks. The shift is as dramatic as the scenery is breathtaking.

Off to the east, the uppermost portion of Mount Shasta is visible rising above the far side of the basin, near where the trail started. Mount Eddy is visible at times as well. Below the trail the talus drops away steeply toward the bottom of High Camp Basin, which spreads out like a sea of trees. To the north, China Mountain and neighboring, dome-shaped South China Mountain rise high above the basin.

The trail continues south along the slope. At times large, rocky outcroppings poke through the loose rock above the trail. Finally, after having circled all the way around High Camp Basin, Bluff Lake and the Cement Bluff creep into view.

Just before reaching the top of the Cement Bluff, the PCT enters a thin cluster of trees, then reemerges into the open. Here the trail makes a sharp turn to the right, where it continues west, down the length of the Scott Mountains before crossing over to the Trinity Alps.

Rather than following the PCT, take the obvious spur to the left and hike onto the broad summit of the Cement Bluff. Sweeping views of High Camp Basin greet hikers, while eroded gullies in the cliff lead the eye down to Bluff Lake, nestled 300 feet below. To the south the enormous bulk of Mount Eddy rises like a giant sienna bubble from a sea of green. It is a fine place to sit and enjoy the mighty view.

Unfortunately, there is no maintained route down to Bluff Lake, and the hillside is steep. The quickest way down is to proceed back down the PCT a few yards from the spur. There is a prominent gully through the aggregate-rich rock that has observable signs of use. Climbing down this gully leads to an obvious path worn into the hillside. This route is quite steep and not for the faint of heart. An easier, though less direct or apparent, route is a little farther back down the trail. Nothing marks the spot, but there is a point back up the trail about 0.2 mile or so where the brush has crept nearly up to the PCT for the first time. From here, climb down and pick a route through the brush. The way gets more obvious as you descend, and it should not be necessary to do any bushwhacking. If the route has been negotiated correctly, you will reach level ground near a large stack of cut tree trunks. The north edge of the lake is about 70 yards to the right.

Though most of Bluff Lake is ringed by trees, the northern end has a small, lush meadow. There are a few great campsites here, with memorable views of the great cliff of the Cement Bluff. The scale is a bit difficult to appreciate, but the rocks protruding from the cliffs are several feet across. Bluff Lake and the Cement Bluff are certainly among the more unusual destinations in the Mount Shasta area.

Miles and Directions

0.0   Start by heading north on the Pacific Crest Trail from the parking lot at Parks Creek Pass.

1.2   The PCT passes just beneath a saddle. Climb up the ridge directly above the trail for a view of Mount Shasta.

2.4 As the trail traverses the north side of High Camp Basin, it enters dense forest for the first time.

3.8 The forest thins as the PCT skirts the western edge of the basin.

4.1 Pass the large white rock with red streaks as the PCT begins to traverse a large, red talus slope.

4.3 Veer left off the trail for the gentler descent down to Bluff Lake. There is no path, and it is necessary to scramble down the slope to reach the lake.

4.5 From the PCT, look for a narrow slot in the aggregate cliff just below, which shows signs of wear. This is the steep, direct route to the lake. Follow the narrow track below the slot. To get to the top of the Cement Bluff, turn left just after the slot onto a spur trail.

4.6 Reach the end of the Cement Bluff and enjoy the incredible views of the headwaters of the mighty Trinity River. Retrace your steps.

9.2 Arrive back at the trailhead.

Part V. Trinity Divide Trails

The Trinity Divide is the vast Klamath Mountains' answer to the Cascades' Mount Shasta. Forming the Klamath's tall, eastern bulwark, the divide rises prominently to the west of Mount Shasta. Unlike the giant mountain, which is uniformly volcanic, the Trinity Divide is a range of contrasts.

The varied terrain includes soaring glacier-carved cliffs, barren wastes where meager vegetation manages to eke out an existence, and gorgeous alpine lakes in deep glacial cirques. Expansive forests cover much of the mountain range, but some areas have such poor soil that the sparse trees are stunted because they lack important nutrients. Yet, for all of the rocky cliffs and barren ridges, the Trinity Divide gives birth to two of California's largest rivers. The west side of the divide gives rise to the mighty Trinity River, which flows 165 miles to its confluence with the Klamath River. The east side births the Sacramento River, California's longest and largest river, which flows south 447 miles before discharging into San Francisco Bay.

Aside from the rivers that rise in the Trinity Divide, water remains one of its defining characteristics. It contains 40 named lakes, several unnamed smaller lakes, and dozens of creeks and streams. Even though it may lack the overwhelming glory and magnitude of Mount Shasta and the alpine grandeur of the nearby Klamath subranges like the Trinity Alps, the Trinity Divide boasts a rugged mountain beauty of its own that demands to be appreciated on its unique terms.

Geologically, the different parts of the Trinity Divide are strikingly diverse. It has a complex composition, with numerous different types of rock seemingly thrust together with little explanation. Most of the range is composed of either gabbroic rock or ultramafic rock. Gabbro is a plutonic rock similar to granite, but with a different chemical composition. Ultramafic rock is metamorphic rock that is uplifted from the earth's mantle. In the Trinity Divide, most of the ultramafic rock is either serpentine or peridotite. The former is common in California, so much so that it is the state rock. Peridotite, in contrast, is not common in high concentrations on land. Much of the earth's mantle beneath the surface of the ocean is composed of peridotite. Both types of ultramafic rock produce very poor soils. This is why some parts of the divide, especially around Mount Eddy, seem like arid deserts.

The contrasts of the Trinity Divide extend to human use as well. Some portions of the range see extensive activity, while other areas are essentially abandoned by humans and exist in a primeval state. Even though large stretches of the range are wild domains, other parts have extensive road networks and have been logged. However, past road-making yields great bounty for hikers. Three paved roads climb into the high country of the Trinity Divide. Every trail in the Trinity Divide in this guide is accessed by means of these roads. Most of the routes begin at trailheads right on the paved section, while a few require drives on dirt roads.

No matter what draws you into the Trinity Divide, you are sure to be satisfied by the trails that roam these superb mountains. The peaks, lakes, creeks, and meadows are exceptional. Yet, as is so often the case, Mount Shasta still commands attention, and the views of the giant volcano from the Trinity Divide are among the best you will find. Here you can enjoy the best of both worlds: classic alpine terrain and commanding vistas of California's greatest mountain.

28 Deadfall Lakes and Mount Eddy

Mount Eddy is the second highest peak in the Mount Shasta area. At 9,025 feet, it is a lofty summit that overlooks much of the region. Indeed, the view from the top may be the finest vista in Northern California. The view takes in most of the Klamath Mountains and the southern portion of the Cascades, far into southern Oregon. Along the way to the top, the trail journeys through spectacular Deadfall Basin, where a trio of lakes and numerous small ponds are highlights of the trip.

Total distance: 8.2 miles via Deadfall Meadow; 11 miles via the PCT
Trail type: Out and back
Elevation gain: 2,580 feet via Deadfall Meadow; 2,150 via the PCT
Difficulty: Moderate to strenuous
Trail surface: Packed dirt, rocky
Hiking time: 4–6 hours
Season: Summer, fall

Fees and permits: None
Canine compatibility: Dogs are permitted.
Land status: Shasta-Trinity National Forest
Trail contact: Mount Shasta Ranger District, 204 W. Alma St., Mount Shasta, CA 96067; (530) 926-4511; www.fs.usda.gov/stnf
Other: Water is available in Deadfall Meadow and from the Deadfall Lakes.

Finding the trailhead: From Mount Shasta City, drive north on I-5 through the town of Weed. Exit at the Edgewood/Stewart Springs exit. Turn left and drive under the freeway, then turn right onto Old Highway 99. Continue north for a couple hundred yards and then turn left onto Stewart Springs Road. After 4 miles, FR 17 splits off to the right. Follow FR 17 to the Parks Creek trailhead. To reach the Deadfall Meadow trailhead, continue on FR 17 for another 1.3 mile, descending swiftly. At a sharp, hairpin turn, there will be a small parking lot on the right. The trail is across the road. GPS: N41° 20' 6.13" / W122° 31' 15.33"

The Hike

Though often languishing in the shadow of formidable Mount Shasta, Mount Eddy is one of the great mountains of Northern California. Rising high above the Strawberry Valley, it looms ominously over the surrounding landscape. If it were not for Mount Shasta, Mount Eddy would be a major attraction on its own. The mountain is the highest point in the Klamath Mountains, the great, unsung mountain range of Northern California. The Klamath Mountains contain spectacular subranges that include the awesome Trinity Alps and the beautiful Marble Mountains, among many others.

No peak in any of those ranges is taller or larger than Mount Eddy. As much a major massif as it is a solitary peak, the mountain is miles wide and stands more than 1,000 feet above the surrounding ridges. Only China Mountain, nearly 7 miles to the north, comes close to the heights of Mount Eddy, and it still falls 500 feet short. Six

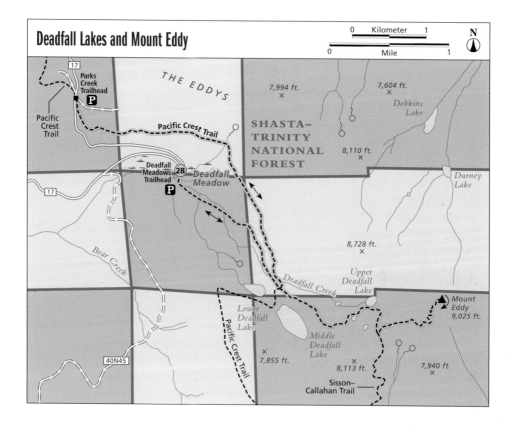

Kilometer

Mile

N

Parks Creek Trailhead

17

P

Pacific Crest Trail

THE EDDYS

7,994 ft. ×

7,604 ft. ×

Dobkins Lake

SHASTA–
TRINITY
NATIONAL
FOREST

8,110 ft. ×

Durney Lake

Deadfall Meadows Trailhead 28 *Deadfall Meadow*

17

P

8,728 ft. ×

Bear Creek

Deadfall Creek

Upper Deadfall Lake

Mount Eddy 9,025 ft.

Lower Deadfall Lake

Pacific Crest Trail

Middle Deadfall Lake

7,855 ft. ×

8,113 ft. ×

7,940 ft. ×

40N45

Sisson–
Callahan Trail

alpine lakes are scattered around three lakes basins below the summit. Of these, the largest and most beautiful are the Deadfall Lakes. Lower, Middle, and Upper Deadfall Lakes are among the prettiest bodies of water in the Trinity Divide.

The hike through the Deadfall Lakes to the summit of Mount Eddy is one of the premier hikes in the Trinity Divide. Beautiful meadows, alpine lakes, soaring cliffs, and breathtaking vistas are plentiful on the hike. All are arranged for maximum scenic effect, revealing each highlight as if being conducted for the sole benefit of the hiker.

Although the trail boasts more than its share of superlative qualities, they do not come at a heavy price. The hike has two trailheads, offering different routes to the Deadfall Lakes, where the two paths converge. The more popular route is to begin on the Pacific Crest Trail and travel it south for 2.9 miles, while gaining 350 feet. This option has good views of the Scott Mountains to the north, and passes a couple of small springs. The other option is to begin at the Deadfall Meadow trailhead and hike through the meadow and along Deadfall Creek, gaining 750 feet in 1.5 miles. Both options have their virtues, but the Deadfall Meadow route, with its rushing creek and explosive wildflower displays, is the prettier of the two. Both options are described below.

Parks Creek Trailhead

Beginning at the Pacific Crest Trail trailhead at the summit of Parks Creek Road, the PCT travels southeast in a long traverse across one of Mount Eddy's long shoulders. An old road leads east from the trailhead, which is sometimes mistaken as the trail. Be sure to find the trailhead sign next to the PCT to ensure starting out on the proper route.

The trail passes through shaded stretches initially, punctuated occasionally by grassy areas. When the forest cover clears, views to the west are good. Approximately 1.5 miles from the trailhead, the PCT crosses a spring-fed creek. Once across, the trail turns sharply south. Although Mount Eddy is not yet visible, the walls of Deadfall Basin can be made out. Soon Deadfall Meadow, rapidly climbing up the Deadfall Creek drainage, begins to approach the same elevation as the PCT. About 2.9 miles from the trailhead, the PCT finally intersects the Sisson–Callahan Trail, and the trail climbing up from Deadfall Meadow.

Deadfall Meadows Trailhead

From the parking area at the Deadfall Meadows trailhead, cross the street and take a few steps down into the meadow. Depending on the time of year and the amount of precipitation during the winter, this first part of the trail can be very muddy. After 0.1 mile, the trail crosses Deadfall Creek and angles to the southeast. The route temporarily leaves the meadow and passes through some open forest, though the meadow and creek are still visible and audible. About 0.3 mile beyond the first crossing, the trail crosses another creek, this one coming from Lower Deadfall Lake. This creek's flow is much less than the main branch of Deadfall Creek. A third crossing, over the main branch of Deadfall Creek again, comes in another 0.3 mile.

At this point the trail begins to climb steeply, skirting the outer edge of the meadow. Small, spring-fed streams cross the trail intermittently, causing the trail to get muddy at times. The creek, at times visible, can always be heard. Eventually the trail levels out as it enters a sparse forest and intersects the PCT, 1.5 miles from the trailhead.

Sisson–Callahan Trail

At the junction with the Pacific Crest Trail, it is possible to head west on the PCT, then cross-country for about 0.1 mile to get to Lower Deadfall Lake. The PCT also crosses above the lake, but it requires climbing 60 feet down a talus slope to reach the water.

To continue toward the other Deadfall Lakes and Mount Eddy, head east from the junction with the PCT, which is the beginning of the Sisson–Callahan Trail, an old route from the nineteenth century that connected the Mount Shasta area with the town of Callahan, at the south end of the Scott Valley. This small community was on the old stage line between Weaverville and the Scott Valley, and was the major north–south route through this region until the railroad was built up the Sacramento

Mount Eddy pierces the sky above Upper Deadfall Lake.

River valley. Today, the Sisson–Callahan Trail (Hike 29) is a National Recreation Trail stretching from the Deadfall Basin to the north shore of Lake Siskiyou, just outside of the town of Mount Shasta.

As the trail enters Deadfall Basin, a spur branches off to the right and leads to Middle Deadfall Lake. At 25 acres, Middle Deadfall is the largest in the basin and one of the largest in the Trinity Divide. The forest in the area is sparse, evidence of the poor, highly mineralized soil. Mount Eddy is composed of serpentine and peridotite, neither of which is particularly hospitable to most plants. Views of the high cliffs, over 1,000 feet above the basin, improve.

Back on the main trail, the route climbs gradually through the heart of the basin. Nearly 0.6 mile past the junction with the PCT, the trail begins a short, sudden, steep climb. This is one of the steepest parts of the trail, though it does not last long. At the top of the steep grade is a small lake, one of many minor, unnamed tarns in the basin. Here, the true summit of Mount Eddy finally comes into view. From most perspectives, Mount Eddy appears to be a high red lump, hardly as impressive as some of its statistics might indicate. However, when viewed from inside Deadfall Basin, with its red-and-white-streaked, 1,200-foot face plainly visible, Mount Eddy seems a much more formidable mountain.

Beyond the small lake, the trail winds its way along the south shore of meadow-fringed Upper Deadfall Lake, the prettiest of the lakes in the basin. The lake is fed by a cold stream that meanders slowly through a luxuriant meadow perched at the base of Mount Eddy's sheer west face. If making the steep climb to the top of the mountain is too much for one hike, Upper Deadfall Lake makes a great place to turn around.

Rather than passing through the meadow, the Sisson–Callahan Trail makes a sharp turn to the south, and climbs steadily out of Deadfall Basin onto the south shoulder of Mount Eddy. Once on top of the ridge, the Sisson–Callahan Trail descends into the canyon of the North Fork of the Sacramento River, ultimately ending at Lake Siskiyou. The route to the summit of Mount Eddy departs to the east, beginning the final ascent of the mountain.

Mount Eddy Ascent

After leaving the Sisson–Callahan Trail, the route to the summit of Mount Eddy continues along the crest of the ridge for nearly 0.4 mile before it begins a long series of switchbacks up the mountain. Once the switchbacks commence, it is another 0.6 mile to the summit. Views get continually better as you climb, particularly to the south and to the west. The final push to the summit is filled with drama.

When you near the top, the views get better and better as Mount Eddy fills less and less of the vista. Finally, just as the trail arrives at the summit, Mount Shasta, heretofore obscured, bursts into view and dominates the panoramic, 360-degree vista. Though magnificent, don't let Mount Shasta lead to neglect of the rest of the panorama. To the north, the Whaleback, the Goosenest, and Willow Creek Mountain all lead your attention to distant Mount McLoughlin in Oregon. To the northwest, the Scott Valley, Marble Mountains, Russian Mountains, and Scott Mountains are all discernable. To the west is an arresting view of the Trinity Alps, with nearly every major summit of the eastern, higher part of the range visible. To the south the rest of the Trinity Divide is readily apparent.

All of the major peaks, including the Grey Rocks, the Castle Crags, Castle Peak, Grey Rock Dome, and Soapstone Peak, can be seen. Far to the south, Lassen Peak and the rest of the Mount Tehama rabble line the horizon.

On the summit, the ruins of an old lookout are in the latter stages of decay. From this point, a use trail leads to the east, crossing a saddle to Peak 8,881. While crossing the saddle, the impressive bowl beneath the summit of Mount Eddy drops off to the north. The bowl often holds snow well into the later parts of the summer, and often lasts all the way through to the next winter. From Peak 8,881, a much more rewarding view of Mount Shasta, Black Butte, and the Strawberry Valley can be had. The bowl directly below Peak 8,881, which is often referred to as Eddy Bowl, is the uttermost beginning of the Sacramento River.

Miles and Directions

Parks Creek Trailhead via PCT

0.0 Begin hiking on the Pacific Crest Trail.

0.8 Cross over a dirt road and continue on the PCT.

1.5 Pass a spring just above the trail.

2.9 Arrive at the junction with the trail from Deadfall Meadow.

Deadfall Meadow Trail

0.0 From the parking area, cross the road and drop down the embankment to begin hiking across the meadow.

0.1 Reach the far side of the meadow and cross over Deadfall Creek.

0.6 Cross Deadfall Creek a second time.

1.5 Arrive at the junction with the Pacific Crest Trail.

Mount Eddy Ascent (mileage reset)

0.0 To reach Lower Deadfall Lake, hike 0.4 mile south on the Pacific Crest Trail. To reach Mount Eddy, begin hiking east on the Sisson–Callahan Trail.

0.1 Spur trails descend down to large Middle Deadfall Lake.

1.0 Climb up to Upper Deadfall Lake.

1.4 Reach the top of the Deadfall Basin rim. Turn left at the junction to climb Mount Eddy.

2.6 Arrive at the summit of Mount Eddy and enjoy the finest view in Northern California! Retrace your steps.

29 Sisson–Callahan Trail

A long trail (most of which is rarely traveled) that passes through one of the best lake basins in the area, visits gorgeous, little-appreciated meadows, and descends through a largely abandoned canyon alongside the North Fork of the Sacramento River.

Total distance: 12.2 miles
Trail type: Shuttle
Elevation gain: 1,160 feet (4,500 feet in elevation loss)
Difficulty: Strenuous due to length
Trail surface: Packed dirt, rocky, rock scrambling
Hiking time: 6.5 hours
Season: Summer, fall

Fees and permits: None
Canine compatibility: Dogs are permitted.
Land status: Shasta-Trinity National Forest
Trail contact: Mount Shasta Ranger District, 204 W. Alma St., Mount Shasta, CA 96067; (530) 926-4511; www.fs.usda.gov/stnf
Other: Water is available from lakes along the route.

Finding the trailhead: *To reach the Parks Creek Trailhead on the Pacific Crest Trail (PCT):* From Mount Shasta City, drive north on I-5 through the town of Weed. Exit at the Edgewood/Stewart Springs exit. Turn left and drive under the freeway, then turn right onto Old Highway 99. Continue north for a couple hundred yards and then turn left onto Stewart Springs Road. After 4 miles, FR 17 splits off to the right. Follow FR 17 to the Parks Creek trailhead. GPS: N41° 20' 35.13" / W122° 32' 15.14"

To the North Fork Trailhead: From Mount Shasta City, head west on West Lake Street, crossing over I-5. At the stop sign, turn left onto Old Stage Road. After 0.3 mile, veer right onto W A Barr Road. Continue south through the stop sign, and turn right onto North Shore Road. Paved at first, the road turns to gravel. Stay on the road for 4.5 miles, passing Lake Siskiyou and crossing over the wooden bridge that spans Deer Creek. After 4.5 miles, turn left onto the rough dirt road and continue for 0.3 mile to the large clearing near the trailhead. Park here and continue down the road for 100 yards to the trailhead. GPS: N41° 17' 11.71" / W122° 23' 7.30"

The Hike

With the exception of the Pacific Crest Trail, the Sisson–Callahan Trail (SCT) is the longest single trail in the Mount Shasta area. It measures a little over 8 miles from the trailhead near the confluence of the North Fork of the Sacramento River and the river's main fork to the junction with the PCT. Over the course of its journey, the trail follows a beautiful, wild river, passes through deep canyons and narrow gorges, crosses a large meadow complex, climbs through groves of rare and unusual trees, and travels through the spectacular Deadfall Basin.

Amazingly, with the exception of the section in the Deadfall Basin, this is one of the least used trails around Mount Shasta. The lack of hikers enjoying the SCT is not because of a lack of scenery. Instead, it probably has more to do with a paucity of

Sisson–Callahan Trail

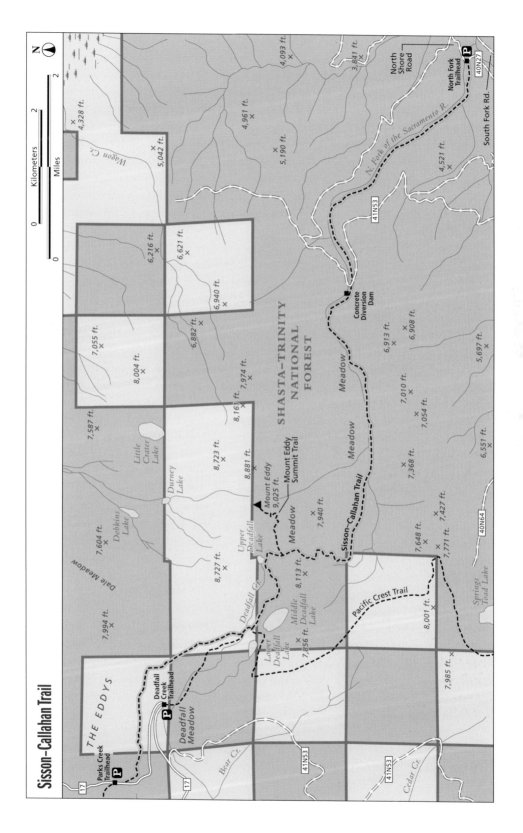

good information on the trail and the logistical challenges of hiking the entire trail. If you accept the challenge of the SCT, you will be treated to a wonderful journey with excellent scenery, deep solitude, and possibly the most diverse trail in the region.

The SCT is not only one of the least traveled trails in the Mount Shasta area but is one of the most historic. Loggers, miners, and cattlemen pushing up the North Fork of the Sacramento originally blazed its course in the nineteenth century. At the time, the town of Mount Shasta was known as Sisson. Eventually the route crossed over the crest of the Trinity Divide and descended the Upper Trinity River. It ultimately led to a route that reached the small town of Callahan, at the southern end of the Scott Valley. This linked Sisson with the primary stagecoach route that went from Weaverville to Yreka.

The trail originally climbed through the canyon of the North Fork and ascended the western headwall. From there it descended into the Bear Creek drainage. Sections of this route still exist. The most prominent is the path that traverses the rocky cliff at the west end of the canyon. It now connects to the PCT. A large part of the trail can still be followed down Bear Creek, but it eventually fades out. Early in the twentieth century, the forest service constructed a proper trail, linking sections that had already been constructed and establishing a new foot route out of the North Fork canyon and into Deadfall Basin. This was done to streamline the trail and connect it to the route from Parks Creek, which accessed the lookout tower on the summit of Mount Eddy. This is the route that exists today.

The logistics of the SCT are probably the single biggest deterrent to its use. The length and distance between trailheads poses a challenge. The best way to hike the SCT is to use a shuttle. To minimize the climbing, the Parks Creek trailhead is the best place to start. Park a car at the trailhead along the North Fork of the Sacramento, and then drive up to the PCT trailhead at Parks Creek. Hikers can either leave another car there when they depart or, better yet, arrange a ride up to the trailhead so that the car does not need to be retrieved. Setting up this way means that hikers must only climb 800 feet to the trail's high point on the shoulder of Mount Eddy, rather than climbing 4,500 feet. It also means that the bulk of the trail is a long, gentle descent.

This description of the SCT begins at the Parks Creek Trailhead on the PCT and ends at the North Fork trailhead, along the Sacramento River.

Begin the journey on the PCT. The trail departs Parks Creek Pass and maintains a level traverse across the northern flank of Mount Eddy. About 1.45 miles from the trailhead, the path crosses a large drainage that may have running water supplied from springs crossing the path. This begins a sporadic series of seeps and additional springs that cross the trail before it arrives in the Deadfall Basin. This area also has good views to the north and west, where the Scott Mountains loom close by and the distant Trinity Alps gnash at the sky.

When you arrive in Deadfall Basin, the PCT crosses one of the tributaries of Deadfall Creek and encounters a trail junction. To the right is the trail climbing out of Deadfall Meadow. Straight ahead is the PCT, heading north from the Eddy

Peering into the canyon of the North Fork of the Sacramento River.

Range. To the left is the beginning of the SCT and its climb through the heart of the Deadfall Lakes. This is the most popular and heavily used part of the SCT, with good reason. The scenery is spectacular.

Three beautiful lakes and a handful of unnamed tarns dot the basin, including Middle Deadfall Lake, which is nearly 25 acres, and Upper Deadfall Lake, which is the prettiest of the bunch, ringed with lush meadows and stunted trees. Behind the lake is the towering massif of Mount Eddy, rising 1,200 feet overhead. This is the steepest part of the entire trip. The trail eventually levels off, passing an unnamed tarn before reaching the upper lake.

After pausing to admire the wonderful view, continue on the trail, climbing once again but at a much more moderate grade. As the trail ascends the southern wall of the upper basin, be sure to look for yet another, obscure, unnamed pond. Soon the trail arrives at another trail junction. To the left is the trail that climbs to the summit of Mount Eddy and the one of the best views in Northern California. To proceed on the SCT, stay straight and begin an immediate descent from the junction.

Beyond the junction with the trail to the summit of Mount Eddy, the trail narrows considerably and shows few signs of use. As the trail begins to drop down into the North Fork of the Sacramento's canyon, the views to the south are excellent. The trail enters a magnificent old-growth forest of whitebark pine and rare foxtail pine. There are still views, especially of the rugged west end of the canyon into which the trail is descending, but they are now filtered through the trees. As the trail veers to the right, go cross-country to the left for a couple hundred yards to a lovely meadow. The summit of Mount Eddy looms high overhead. Back on the trail, descend to the west a little farther before making the first of eight switchbacks.

After the switchbacks, the SCT levels off and begins to head east into the canyon. Patches of grasses begin to appear, marking the beginning of an extensive patchwork of lush meadows. These meadows constitute the headwaters of the North Fork of the Sacramento River. They slowly seep water into the small stream that is the nascent North Fork. When the trail finally reaches the river, it is more like a creek, only a few feet across and easily crossed. Still, after the long descent, the water is a welcome sight. The trail crosses the river, and begins to parallel it on the south side. The SCT does not recross the river for the duration of the trip until the very end, where it is necessary to ford the river to get to the trailhead on the far side. There are a couple of very nice campsites near the upper crossing.

The complex of verdant meadows at the North Fork headwaters is one of the highlights of the trip. Populated by clusters of lodgepole pine, the meadow is broken up into patches of varying size, some of which are quite extensive. To the north, the red flanks of Mount Eddy rise high overhead. The river is almost always in sight from the trail and if it is not, it is audible.

About 0.6 mile from the river crossing, the trail begins to follow an old dirt road. At times the road and the trail are one, and other times the trail veers off the old road before reconnecting again. At the eastern end of the meadow complex, the old road becomes increasingly prominent. Soon, the trail passes a couple of large campsites. The larger of the two has a big fire ring situated in the middle of an old pullout. The pullout was once part of the road where it crossed the North Fork. When the crossing was washed out, what was left of the road made a natural spot to camp next to the water. The road and crossing incorrectly appear intact on the USGS topo maps.

This spot marks a major transition in the nature of the trail. For the last couple miles the path has maintained a fairly level grade as it followed the river through the meadow complex. Almost immediately after the pullout camp, the river begins a steep descent. The meadow comes to a sudden end and the water pours over a seemingly endless series of small cataracts formed by countless boulders obstructing the water.

This is one of the prettiest sections of the entire hike. Instead of just boulders and rocks channeling the water, the river enters a craggy gorge where the bedrock is exposed and the size of the boulders grows significantly. The river pours over several small waterfalls into beautiful, deep pools. Unfortunately, the trail stays high above the water, though the river is always visible. It is a beautiful scene and one of the noisiest parts of the river. If you want to stay close to the water, an old and extremely rocky road runs just a few feet above the racing river, though it takes a little route-finding to locate it. This lovely section of the river ends as the canyon makes a broad turn to the south. The trail stays high and bends away from the river, the first time separated since meeting up at the headwaters.

After a short distance away from the water, a few switchbacks through dense forest lead the path back alongside the river. A thick band of trees partially obscures the North Fork from view. Despite the obstructed view, watch for an old, partially overgrown trail between the SCT and the river. This path leads to a concrete diversion dam. It is neither easily seen from the river nor easily accessed, but hikers intent on climbing the 6-foot dam can do so.

Amazingly, this dam diverts water into a canal that transports it nearly 8 miles away to fill the Dwight Hammond Reservoir in the Hammond Ranch area, between Weed and Mount Shasta City. It is an impressive engineering accomplishment, considering the rough terrain and the distance between the dam and the reservoir. Interestingly, the canal takes water out of the Sacramento River watershed and delivers it into the Shasta River, which is part of the Klamath River watershed.

About 0.2 miles from the dam, the SCT emerges from the forest on the side of FR 41N53, the first (and only) bona fide, maintained road you'll encounter. The river passes under the road through a large culvert, but the road is designed to allow the river to go over it when water levels are high. This spot, 8.8 miles from the beginning of the hike, is a convenient place to take a break and dip your feet in the water.

When it is time to resume hiking, return to hike down the road, staying on the south side of the river. A couple of signs mark the trail's departure from the road. One new wrinkle you must deal with is the possible presence of mountain bikes. The road affords bikers access to the SCT, and they ride it all the way down to the trailhead and beyond. Despite this, it is one of the prettier sections of the SCT. The river rushes through the canyon and large boulders force it to find its way through the rocky maze. One of the highlights of this section of the trail is the large cascade pouring down the side of the canyon on the far side of the river. This creek begins in nearby Morgan Meadow.

The canyon widens a little as the river levels off. The trail follows suit, and its grade lessens. The area remains very scenic. Especially noteworthy are the small waterfalls formed when the river pours over small bedrock escarpments. None of them measure much more than 6 or 7 feet, but they still add a lot of interest to the trail, as do the lovely pools that form along this section of the North Fork. Some nice grassy areas also complement the river.

After a long steady descent to the east, the trail makes a sharp drop to the bottom of a road, and then veers to the south. The river also turns southward, but it does so out of sight of the trail.

Once on the old road, the SCT makes its only significant climb since its ascent out of the Deadfall Lakes Basin. Thankfully the climb is short, and the route soon deviates to the left, off of the road. Resuming singletrack, the path drops back down to the North Fork.

The return to the North Fork marks the beginning of the final leg of the SCT. At first the river is about 150 feet below the trail, but the two gradually move toward each other. Eventually, the trail settles in about 20 feet above the river. This part of the river generally lacks the interesting course and steeper drop found in earlier sections. One notable exception occurs about halfway between the old road and the trailhead. The canyon narrows and the trail passes through an unusual rock formation, where river rock aggregate is accreted together. When this strange rock is sighted, go off-trail a few feet to the edge of the cliff, high above the river. Down below, the accreted rock forms large boulders and chokes the river, creating several small waterfalls. Unfortunately, this interesting formation does not last, and the trail resumes along a more mundane stretch of river.

The remaining portion of the SCT follows the river for a little over a mile to the trailhead. The land surrounding the river becomes drier as it levels off. The trees become smaller, evidence of past logging activity. Eventually, the river makes a broad turn to the east again. This signals the journey is near its end. The path moves away from the river and enters a shallow gully. This does not last long and the SCT finally returns to the North Fork at a wide area on the far side of the river from the trailhead.

One last sign marks the end (or beginning, as it may be) of the trail. A use trail continues to the south, connecting mountain bikers back to the road near the Middle Fork, which they climbed to the SCT. Stay left and ford the river to get to the trailhead. When the water is high this can be a challenge. Thankfully, the river is very broad here and splits into numerous channels, allowing the volume of water to disperse a bit. On the far side of the ford, a few yards of singletrack connect to the dirt road leading to the parking area. This completes the SCT.

Miles and Directions

0.0 Begin the hike on the Pacific Crest Trail at the Parks Creek trailhead.

1.5 Pass a large spring above the trail.

2.8 Turn left at the junction with the Deadfall Meadow Trail to begin the Sisson–Callahan Trail.

3.8 Reach Upper Deadfall Lake and enjoy the prettiest spot in Deadfall Basin.

4.2 Climb to the top of the Deadfall Basin rim and stay straight at the junction with the trail leading to the summit of Mount Eddy.

5.3 Finish the last switchback on the descent to the bottom of the North Fork's canyon.

6.3 Cross over the North Fork of the Sacramento River.

7.9 Pass the washed-out road crossing of the North Fork.

8.8 Cross over FR 41N53.

9.4 Pass the cascade pouring into the North Fork from Morgan Meadow.

12.2 Ford the North Fork of the Sacramento and arrive at the North Fork trailhead.

30 Castle Lake Shore

The short hike along the shore of Castle Lake is a great introduction to the Trinity Divide. Full of awesome views of the massive cliffs above the lake, the trail is easy and level.

Total distance: 1.0 mile
Trail type: Out and back
Elevation gain: None
Difficulty: Easy
Trail surface: Packed earth, rocky
Hiking time: 30 minutes
Season: Year-round

Fees and permits: None
Canine compatibility: Dogs are permitted.
Land status: Shasta-Trinity National Forest
Trail contact: Mount Shasta Ranger District, 204 W. Alma St., Mount Shasta, CA 96067; (530) 926-4511; www.fs.usda.gov/stnf
Other: Water is available in Castle Lake.

Finding the trailhead: From Mount Shasta City, head west on West Lake Street, crossing over I-5. At the stop sign, turn left onto Old Stage Road. After 0.3 mile, veer right onto W A Barr Road. Continue south, crossing over the dam that impounds the Sacramento River and forms Lake Sis-kiyou. Just past the dam, make a left-hand turn onto Castle Lake Road, which climbs for 7 miles to the road's end at Castle Lake. GPS: N41° 13' 49.87" / W122° 22' 53.88"

The Hike

Castle Lake is one of the most spectacular landmarks around Mount Shasta. The largest lake in the Trinity Divide, it is the third largest in the entire Klamath Range. It occupies a deep basin surrounded by towering walls on the three sides. The southern wall is particularly memorable, rising 1,200 feet out of the water to the summit of Castle Peak. The beautiful alpine lake has always attracted visitors, and this still holds true. The presence of a paved road leading up from Lake Siskiyou enables everyone to visit the lake.

The trail along the lake's shore is a fantastic opportunity to enjoy the lake and observe many of its beautiful features from different angles. The road to the lake is plowed in the winter so it is possible to come here even when there is a lot of snow, and hike the trail on snowshoes. Whether you come up for mountain serenity or to enjoy the lake with your family, the lakeshore trail is a great option, and offers beautiful scenery and quick and easy access to the lake with minimal effort.

The Castle Lake Shore Trail begins at the north end of the large trailhead parking lot. Just past the trailhead sign is a ranger's cabin. It is seldom occupied. The path begins by passing through brush and rocks as it rounds a little finger of the lake. A small, grassy clearing lies just off the trail. When the water level is very high, this area is flooded and becomes part of the lake. As the water recedes, it forms a little pond and eventually a grassy clearing.

Castle Lake Shore; Little Castle Lake and Mount Bradley; Heart Lake

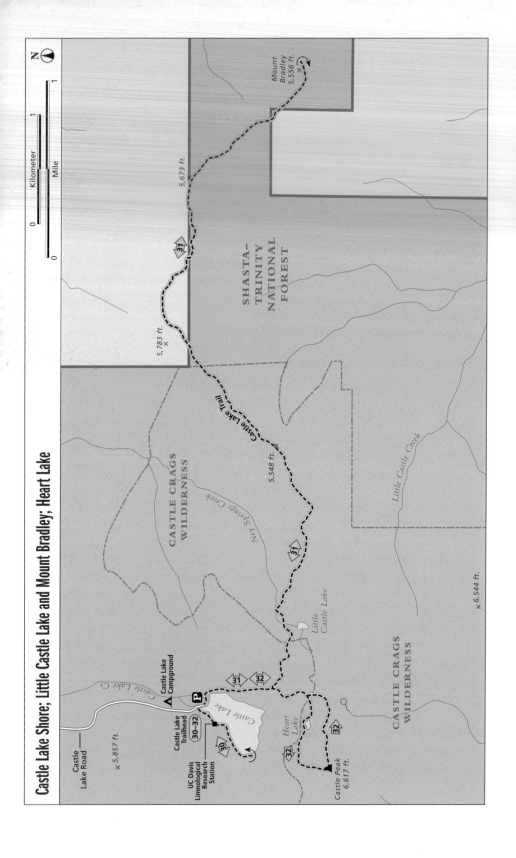

Castle Lake.

Past the little clearing the trail finally comes alongside the lake and runs parallel to the shore. Beautiful lodgepole pines line the trail. Away from the lake are some nice large boulders that present great scrambling opportunities for kids.

Soon the trail emerges from the trees and crosses a brushy area. Beyond this lies the UC Davis Limnological Station. A small pier lies below the station, where boats can be docked. The research station was established to study the lake's exceptional purity. (*It must be a miserable assignment.*)

Continuing past the research station, the nature of the trail changes considerably. The first half of the hike was a pleasant path through the woods at the edge of the lake. This part of the hike is slung on the edge of the steep wall that forms the western side of Castle Lake's large basin. The lake is about 10 feet below the trail. Despite brush encroaching on the path, it is still easily passable. The only obstacles are the sections of trail that have partially washed out. They are not difficult, but caution should still be employed.

Near the end of the trail there is a nice little beach. Scramble down the rocks to the pebbly beach and enjoy a fantastic spot to sit and enjoy the soaring cliffs that rise directly overhead. In the spring, giant cascades thunder down the cliffs and crash loudly into the lake. This makes a logical destination to end the hike. The trail continues a little farther, but ends on a rock outcropping near the base of the cliffs at the lake's south end. Below the outcropping, a large garden of carnivorous *Darlingtonia* plants clings to the rocks. Insects land in their large pitchers, are stuck to a sticky resin, and are then absorbed into the plant.

Past the outcropping, a narrow, precarious track weaves through the brush, leading to a talus slope that collapsed into the water. A very steep, rough route climbs from there up the cliffs to Heart Lake. Only experienced climbers should attempt this route.

Miles and Directions

0.0 From the trailhead, hike past a small ranger's cabin and follow the lake shore to the west.

0.3 The trail passes the UC Davis Limnological Research Station.

0.5 The path ends at a rocky drop off above the lake. Turn around here and retrace your steps to the trailhead.

1.0 Arrive back at the trailhead.

31 Little Castle Lake and Mount Bradley

This long hike begins at the edge of awesome Castle Lake and climbs to the edge of the lake's rocky headwall and then down to less-traveled Little Castle Lake. From there, it traverses a long, exposed ridge leading to Mount Bradley, with panoramic views all the way, highlighted by Mount Shasta, Mount Eddy, and the staggering Castle Crags.

See map on page 148
Total distance: 2.0 miles (Little Castle Lake), 11.0 miles (Mount Bradley)
Trail type: Out and back
Elevation gain: 1,200 feet
Difficulty: Moderate
Trail surface: Packed dirt, rocky, dirt road
Hiking time: 5.5 hours
Season: Summer, fall

Fees and permits: None
Canine compatibility: Dogs are permitted.
Land status: Shasta-Trinity National Forest
Trail contact: Mount Shasta Ranger District, 204 W. Alma St., Mount Shasta, CA 96067; (530) 926-4511; www.fs.usda.gov/stnf
Other: Water is available at Castle Lake and Little Castle Lake.

Finding the trailhead: From Mount Shasta City, head west on West Lake Street, crossing over I-5. At the stop sign, turn left onto Old Stage Road. After 0.3 mile, veer right onto W A Barr Road. Continue south, crossing over the dam that impounds the Sacramento River and forms Lake Siskiyou. Just past the dam, make a left-hand turn onto Castle Lake Road, which climbs for 7 miles to the road's end at Castle Lake. GPS: N41° 13' 49.87" / W122° 22' 53.88"

The Hike

The Castle Lake Trail is one of the longer hiking trails in the Mount Shasta area. About 11 miles round-trip, it offers up a spectacular feast of lakes and peaks, and a smorgasbord of some of the finest views in the region. Surprisingly, once you climb above Castle Lake, the trail is among the least traveled in the area. Aside from the hike up Mount Eddy, the Castle Lake Trail is one of the best introductions to the geography around Mount Shasta. It has great exposure to the lakes of Trinity Divide, Castle Lake being the finest specimen in the range and Little Castle Lake being a jewel in its own right. The hike out on the ridge to Mount Bradley allow hikers to examine most of the major features in the area, including the majority of the Trinity Divide and the Castle Crags, and the Cascade Crest running above the Shasta Valley on its way across the Oregon border. Of course, Mount Shasta consumes most of the attention, rising high above everything around it.

From the parking lot, follow the path east, crossing Castle Lake's outlet after only 30 yards or so. Past the outlet creek, which marks the beginning of Castle Lake Creek's journey down to Lake Siskiyou, the trail turns south and begins climbing up the

Mount Shasta and Little Castle Lake.

eastern wall above Castle Lake. As the route gains elevation, views of Castle Lake periodically open up through the trees. The 54-acre lake is one of the three largest in the Klamath Mountains, along with Caribou Lake in the Trinity Alps, which, at 72 acres, is the largest, and Ukonom Lake in the Marble Mountains. The summit of Castle Peak is visible above the sheer headwall rising directly out of the south end of the water. As you near the top of the climb, the trees give way and the trail becomes rockier. At 0.5 mile from the trailhead, the trail finally reaches a saddle 400 feet above Castle Lake.

From the saddle, the Castle Lake Trail turns east and passes a small tarn. The little pool often lasts all year, though it may dry up at the end of the season in drier years. Beyond the tarn, the trail begins to drop steeply. Spring's snowmelt has eroded the trail in some places. After descending for 0.3 mile, the route enters a lush meadow, with views of Mount Shasta peering from around a ridge. A short spur trail veers off to the right behind some trees. Beyond the glade lies Little Castle Lake. The appellation is derived not only from the lake's proximity to Castle Lake and the Castle Crags, but also from its tall headwall, a miniature edition of the massive cliff that towers above Castle Lake. Like the headwall of Castle Lake, this one also rises directly out of the water. Although it is not deep, the Little Castle Lake is attractive, and a great view of Mount Shasta is to be had for those who scramble up the wall behind it.

To continue to Mount Bradley, return to the main path, which descends another 300 feet before leveling off. From here, the trail begins a 0.5-mile stretch through a densely wooded area. This is the only part of the entire hike that is completely viewless. Nonetheless, the dense forest is permeated by a sense of great isolation that heightens the beauty of the area.

Soon the climbing begins in earnest, indicating that the crest of the ridge leading to Mount Bradley is nigh. When the trail arrives at the top of the ridge, the trees clear out and great views open up. The highlight is the looming presence of the spikey pinnacle of Battle Rock, the Castle Crags' highest point. This needle got its name as a monument to the Battle of the Castle Crags, which took place on the ridge between it and Castle Lake. The battle occurred in 1855 between pioneers and Native Americans from nearby tribes. Famed author Joaquin Miller was injured in the battle. This granite turret protrudes like a mighty thumb from the main crest of the Castle Crags. Sometimes known as Castle Spire, it is a destination for dedicated rock climbers.

Be sure to mark the point where the trail coming up from Little Castle Lake reaches the top of the ridge. The turnoff is a bit indistinct, and the trail on the ridge, which was once an old road, continues west beyond this point, obfuscating where the paths meet. Rocks are usually piled up to block the road and indicate where the trail turns north and begins to descend off the ridge on the return trip, but there are no guarantees that the rocks will always be there.

From this point, the Castle Lake Trail continues along the top of the ridge for another 3.5 miles. Although some sections pass through lightly wooded areas, it is generally open, with excellent, far-reaching, and often 360-degree views.

After hiking along the ridge for 1.3 miles, the trail skirts the edge of Peak 5,783, and turns due east. Another mile brings the route to the top of Point 5,673. Both of these summits are higher than Mount Bradley, and offer excellent views and destinations in their own right. In some ways they are better destinations—especially Point 5,673—because the trail beyond is wide, and follows a roadbed to Mount Bradley. If you choose to continue all the way to Mount Bradley, follow the roadbed downhill from Point 5,673 to where it merges onto the road climbing to the top of the peak from Dunsmuir. Follow the road to the summit, which has a lookout tower.

Mount Bradley's moniker might seem out of place for a small peak at the end of a ridge, particularly when compared to the other mounts in the area, Mount Shasta and Mount Eddy. However, from the peak's base 3,000 feet below in Dunsmuir along the Sacramento River, Mount Bradley seems like a mighty summit.

From Mount Bradley, retrace your steps to the Castle Lake.

Miles and Directions

0.0 Start at the Castle Lake trailhead. The path crosses the lake's outlet and starts to climb immediately.

0.5 Reach a junction at the top of the climb. Stay left, and go downhill.

1.0 Arrive at Little Castle Lake.

2.0 Climb to the top of the long ridge that leads to Mount Bradley. Be sure to mark this spot so you will not pass it on the return.

3.6 Traverse the slopes of Peak 5,783, just below the summit.

4.4 Climb to the top of Peak 5,673 for great views. This makes a good place to stop if you don't want to hike on dusty roads to the actual summit of Mount Bradley.

5.0 Join the road leading to the lookout tower on Mount Bradley.

5.5 Reach the lookout tower on the summit of Mount Bradley and enjoy the great view. Retrace your steps.

11.0 Arrive back at the trailhead.

32 Heart Lake

Tucked on a bench in the cliffs high above spectacular Castle Lake, little Heart Lake is one of the most stunning little bodies of water in Northern California. The tiny lake is graced with a spectacular view of Mount Shasta. It is one of the most iconic views in the area, yet it is also among the easiest to get to. Set beneath soaring cliffs and surrounded by small meadows, the lake's setting would be worth hiking to even if it did not have such a grand view. As if this were not enough, there is a rough path that leads to the top of Castle Peak, where there are sweeping views of the north country, highlighted by the awesome spires of the Castle Crags. This is one of the classic hikes in the Mount Shasta area.

See map on page 148
Total distance: 3.0 miles
Trail type: Out and back or lollipop
Elevation gain: 1,175 feet
Difficulty: Moderate to strenuous
Trail surface: Packed dirt, rocky
Hiking time: 1.5 hours
Season: Summer, fall

Fees and permits: None
Canine compatibility: Dogs are permitted.
Land status: Shasta-Trinity National Forest
Trail contact: Mount Shasta Ranger District, 204 W. Alma St., Mount Shasta, CA 96067; (530) 926-4511; www.fs.usda.gov/stnf
Other: Water is available at Castle Lake and Heart Lake.

Finding the trailhead: From Mount Shasta City, drive west on West Lake Street, crossing over I-5. At the stop sign, turn left onto Old Stage Road. After 0.3 mile, veer right onto W A Barr Road. Continue south, crossing over the dam that impounds the Sacramento River and forms Lake Siskiyou. Just past the dam, make a left turn onto Castle Lake Road, which climbs for 7 miles to the road's end at Castle Lake. GPS: N41° 13' 49.87" / W122° 22' 53.88"

The Hike

Although short, the hike to Heart Lake in the Trinity Divide is a titan in terms of scenery and vistas. Few trails offer as much alpine terrain and tremendous views for such little effort.

Beginning at the Castle Lake trailhead, a worthy destination in its own right, the trail climbs to a craggy bench high above large Castle Lake. There, nestled into the rocky cliffs, is small Heart Lake. Though diminutive in size, the lake offers one of the finest views of mighty Mount Shasta. The great volcano rises above the stony dike at the north end of the lake, looming majestically in the distance. It is a phenomenal sight set amid gorgeous surroundings, yet it is only half of the wonders the short trail offers.

A little loop that departs from Heart Lake Trail climbs to the top of Castle Peak. From the summit more fantastic views await, including the labyrinthine Castle Crags

Mount Shasta and the last shades of alpenglow reflect in Heart Lake.

and distant Lassen Peak. It is surprising that such mesmerizing views are obtained from such a short trail, but the Heart Lake Trail is barely 3 miles long. It is possibly the finest 3 miles in the Mount Shasta area.

This hike can also make a great snowshoe outing. The road to Castle Lake is plowed in winter. Other than the Everitt Memorial Highway on Mount Shasta, this is the only plowed road that climbs this high, making snow play and snowshoeing a fantastic option.

The Heart Lake Trail starts at the Castle Lake trailhead and follows the Castle Lake Trail for the first 0.6 mile. From the parking lot follow the path east, crossing the lake's outlet after only 30 yards or so. Once across Castle Lake Creek, the trail turns south and begins climbing up the eastern wall above Castle Lake. As the route gains elevation, views of Castle Lake periodically open up through the trees. The lake is one of the three largest in the Klamath Mountains, along with Caribou Lake in the Trinity Alps, which, at 72 acres, is the largest, and Ukonom Lake in the Marble Mountains. The summit of Castle Peak is visible above the sheer headwall at the southern end of the lake.

As you near the top of the climb, the trees thin out and the trail becomes rockier. After 0.5 mile of climbing, arrive at a rocky saddle 400 feet above the lake. Several paths split off to the right (west). These all converge quickly so that the main route will be obvious. If you stay on the Castle Lake Trail and reach a small pond, you have gone too far to the east. Continuing past the pond is described in the description for Little Castle Lake and Mount Bradley (Hike 31). Backtrack to one of the paths branching off to the west, and proceed to hike toward Heart Lake. Once on the main path, it heads west and climbs through a small, meadowlike area. The trail heads toward a notch between the cliffs of Castle Peak and a small rocky knoll. On the far side of this notch, the trail descends slightly to Heart Lake.

Heart Lake is small, not even a tenth of the size of Castle Lake. Nonetheless, it packs an extremely scenic punch, far outclassing many much larger lakes. The view from the south side of the lake is one of the finest of Mount Shasta, and one of the area's scenic apogees. Depending on the time of day, you can be graced with a gorgeous reflection of California's most spectacular mountain. During the summer, the lake warms up earlier than many of the other lakes due to its small size, making it a great place to take an afternoon swim. Castle Lake itself is not visible from this spot. To see the lake, climb the little rocky knoll just to the right of Heart Lake's outlet. From there, Castle Lake can be observed far below.

The ascent of Castle Peak forms a lollipop with the trail to Heart Lake. It can be climbed before or after heading to Heart Lake. This is an unofficial route, and the path is narrow but not difficult to follow. To start the loop, cross the outlet and follow the trail to the west for almost 0.3 mile from Heart Lake, beginning to climb as you pass a small tarn bordered by an attractive meadow. Soon the trail reaches a ridge, grows faint, and makes a sharp turn to the south.

This ridge is steep and the route is faint but not difficult to discern. It climbs steeply, gaining almost 400 feet in the 0.2 mile to the summit of Castle Peak. The peak, which is unofficially named, gets its moniker from its position between Castle Lake and the Castle Crags. The eastern flank of the mountain was the site of the Battle of the Castle Crags, between prospectors and Native Americans in 1855, the last confirmed battle in which the Indians fought solely with traditional weapons.

Once on the summit of Castle Peak, a tremendous, expansive scene opens up. Soaring above the foreground of Heart and Castle Lakes, Mount Shasta presides above the Strawberry Valley and all of its denizens, including Black Butte and Spring Hill. Mount Eddy rises on the west side of the valley, an impressive mountain in its own right. Between these two giants, the northernmost peaks of the California Cascades, including the Goosenest and Willow Creek Mountain, can be seen. Farther to the north, in Oregon, are Mount McLoughlin and Pilot Rock. The immense bulk of the Castle Crags rises south of Castle Peak, with the countless granite spires thrusting skyward. Far beyond this awesome rocky vision, Lassen Peak and the cadre of smaller peaks that make up the ruins of Mount Tehama—as well as Crater Peak and Burney Mountain—all line the horizon. It is a staggering panoply of alpine splendor.

When you are ready to depart this stunning panorama, follow the narrow but obvious path that leads east, down the opposite side of Castle Peak. The path stays right at the crest of the ridge, and the drop-off on the north side is very sheer. After 0.5 mile the cliffs soften and the slope is much more moderate. Simply head down this slope and across the level bench at the bottom until you intersect the Heart Lake Trail. Follow it to the intersection with the Castle Lake Trail, and then descend to the trailhead.

Miles and Directions

0.0 From the trailhead, cross over Castle Lake's outlet and begin climbing the trail above the lake.

0.5 Reach a junction at the top of the climb. Turn to the right and follow the winding trail around large rocks.

0.9 Descend to the edge of Heart Lake. To climb Castle Peak, continue west past the lake.

1.2 Climb to the top of the ridge west of Heart Lake. Turn left and follow the narrow path uphill.

1.5 Enjoy the awesome panorama from the summit of Castle Peak. To return to the Heart Lake Trail, follow the track down the ridge to the east as it hugs the edge.

2.1 Veer left off the ridge and descend cross-country down the easy slope.

2.3 Rejoin the Heart Lake Trail.

2.5 Reach the junction with the Castle Lake Trail. Stay left, and follow the trail back down toward the trailhead.

3.0 Arrive back at the trailhead.

33 Gray Rock Lakes

Set in a beautiful rocky bowl beneath the highest peaks of the Castle Crags Wilderness, the Gray Rock Lakes are a lightly visited slice of mountain paradise. The short trail leads to a trio of lakes set amid high, rocky cliffs. Hearty explorers can climb the surrounding peaks without too much difficulty to enjoy awesome views.

Total distance: 2.2 miles
Trail type: Out and back
Elevation gain: 600 feet
Difficulty: Easy to moderate
Trail surface: Packed dirt, rocky
Hiking time: 1.5 hours
Season: Summer, fall
Fees and permits: None

Canine compatibility: Dogs are permitted.
Land status: Shasta-Trinity National Forest
Trail contact: Mount Shasta Ranger District, 204 W. Alma St., Mount Shasta, CA 96067; (530) 926-4511; www.fs.usda.gov/stnf
Other: Water is available at the Gray Rock Lakes.

Finding the trailhead: From Mount Shasta City, head west on West Lake Street, crossing over I-5. At the stop sign, turn left onto Old Stage Road. After 0.3 mile, veer right onto W A Barr Road. Continue south, crossing over the dam that impounds the Sacramento River and forms Lake Siskiyou. From the dam, continue 9 miles to the west, passing the lake and continuing up the Sacramento River. After 9 miles turn left, crossing over the Sacramento River on a forest service bridge. Veer left after the bridge, then make a sharp right turn onto FR 39N45. The well-maintained dirt road may not be signed, but it is hard to miss. It parallels the river for 1.3 miles before intersecting FR 39N41. At the intersection, turn left onto FR 39N41. Again, this road may not be signed, but the level of wear on the road makes it obvious which way is correct. Continue up the road for 1.2 miles. At this point the road's condition degrades dramatically, and those with sedans or who are uncomfortable negotiating steep, severely eroded routes should park and hike the 0.3 mile to the Gray Rock Lakes trailhead. For those with a high-clearance vehicle, simply continue to the trailhead. GPS: N41° 13' 19.26 / W122° 26' 26.37"

The Hike

Looking up at the Trinity Divide from the town of Mount Shasta, visitors could be forgiven for thinking there were not many rugged and beautiful places in what seems to be a heavily wooded set of ridges. Fortunately, the Trinity Divide only presents its tamer profile to the town, hiding its many wonderful lake basins and craggy cliffs and peaks from casual view. The Gray Rock Lakes are a great example of this. The peaks, Gray Rock Dome and Soapstone Peak, look mildly craggy from town, but heading up the South Fork Canyon it becomes more apparent that these are large, rugged mountains.

Situated at the feet of these peaks are the beautiful Gray Rock Lakes, the only lake basin entirely within the Castle Crags Wilderness (the upper reaches of the Castle

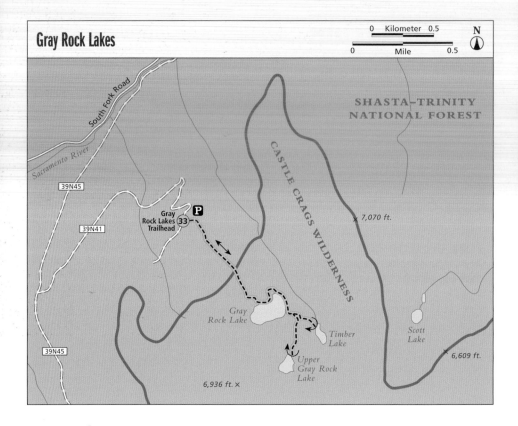

Gray Rock Lakes

0 Kilometer 0.5

0 Mile 0.5

N

South Fork Road

Sacramento River

SHASTA-TRINITY
NATIONAL FOREST

CASTLE CRAGS WILDERNESS

39N45

39N41

Gray
Rock Lakes (33)
Trailhead

P

× 7,070 ft.

Gray
Rock Lake

Timber
Lake

Scott
Lake

39N45

Upper
Gray Rock
Lake

× 6,609 ft.

6,936 ft. ×

Lake Basin, including small Heart Lake, are also within the wilderness boundary, but Castle Lake itself is outside the boundary). Gray Rock Lake, the largest of the three in the basin, along with Upper Gray Rock Lake and Timber Lake, are all deep alpine pools lined with impressive cliffs.

In many ways, the trail to the lakes is much easier than the drive to the trailhead. If driving a low-clearance vehicle or if you're unfamiliar with negotiating rough dirt roads, it will be necessary to park about a quarter-mile below the trailhead and hike up to the beginning of the trail.

Once on the main path, the Gray Rock Lakes Trail is fairly level at first. Slung on the slopes of a deep canyon, Gray Rock Dome looms ominously across the gorge. After only 0.1 of a mile, the trail begins to climb steeply. The steep pitch is mercifully short and levels off quickly. At this point, early in the summer, Gray Rock Creek can be heard crashing through the canyon far below. Later in the year its volume decreases significantly. As the trail advances, views of Soapstone Peak and the southern cliffs of the cirque come into view.

Soon the path begins descending to the lakes. Large Gray Rock Lake becomes visible as the trail nears the shore. The water sits in a rocky bowl with cliffs rising

Gray Rock Lake.

above the southern shore. Though a low ridge obscures the actual summit of Soap-stone Peak, most of the peak's rocky mass can be observed from the lake. Even better, the bulk of Gray Rock Dome forms a fine backdrop to the east.

A trail splits off to the right and skirts the lake's western shore. The Gray Rock Lakes Trail turns left at the junction with the lakeshore path, angling to the east, toward Gray Rock Lake's outlet. Several good campsites are here, although the best is on the east side of the outlet. A large fire pit marks the site. Though there are some rocky patches, it is possible to completely circle the lake.

Once on the east side of the lake, a small ridge begins to rise above the west end of the lake. The ridge is covered with huckleberry oak, and manzanita, which can obscure the trail once it departs the lakeshore and begins climbing. The path climbs above the lake for 200 yards to an unmarked junction amid the brush. Staying to the right leads to Upper Gray Rock Lake, the prettiest of the three bodies of water. Set amid high, vertical cliffs, it is a fantastic spot. The route up to the top of Soapstone Peak begins here. A little exploration at the north end of the lake reveals a pair of small ponds. Back at the junction amid the brush, bearing to the left leads downhill to a small meadow adjacent to pretty Timber Lake. A vertical cliff rises directly out of the water at the south end. This lake receives the fewest visitors of the three. The rugged route to the top of Gray Rock Dome begins here.

Miles and Directions

0.0 Start on the Gray Rock Lakes Trail. If you were unable to drive the last bit of the road, you must hike 0.15 miles up the road to reach the trailhead.

0.6 Descend to the edge of Gray Rock Lake.

0.8 Stay left at a fork next to the lake, and begin climbing up a brushy trail. A few yards beyond, stay right at a second fork to climb up to Upper Gray Lake. Timber Lake lies 0.3 mile down the trail that goes left from the fork.

1.1 Arrive at Upper Gray Rock Lake. Retrace your steps.

2.2 Arrive back at the trailhead.

34 Soapstone Trail

A route that receives almost no use, the Soapstone Trail accesses a small pond and climbs through beautiful forest to a high ridgecrest, where it joins the Pacific Crest Trail (PCT). Once on the PCT, hikers can make a short trip to one of the most incredible vistas in the Mount Shasta area.

Total distance: 4.6 miles (to both Soapstone Pond and the vista on the PCT)
Trail type: Out and back
Elevation gain: 980 feet
Difficulty: Moderate to strenuous
Trail surface: Packed dirt, rocky, dirt road
Hiking time: 3 hours
Season: Summer, fall

Fees and permits: None
Canine compatibility: Dogs are permitted.
Land status: Shasta-Trinity National Forest, Castle Crags Wilderness
Trail contact: Mount Shasta Ranger District, 204 W. Alma St., Mount Shasta, CA 96067; (530) 926-4511; www.fs.usda.gov/stnf
Other: No water is available.

Finding the trailhead: From Mount Shasta City, head west on West Lake Street, crossing over I-5. At the stop sign, turn left onto Old Stage Road. After 0.3 mile, veer right onto W A Barr Road. Continue south, crossing over the dam that impounds the Sacramento River and forms Lake Siskiyou. From the dam, continue 9 miles to the west, passing the lake and continuing up the Sacramento River. After 9 miles, turn left, crossing over the Sacramento River on a forest service bridge. Veer left after the bridge, then make a sharp right turn onto FR 39N45. The well-maintained dirt road may not be signed, but it is hard to miss. It parallels the river for 1.3 miles before intersecting FR 39N41. Stay straight on FR 39N45. Continue for 0.1 mile to another junction. High-clearance vehicles can stay left and proceed 1 mile up increasingly rough FR 39N45 to the trailhead. Those with low-clearance vehicles should park at the junction and hike up the road to the trailhead, then onward onto the Soapstone Trail. GPS: N41° 12' 14.69" / W122° 26' 50.86"

The Hike

Quite possibly the most forsaken and least-used trail in the Trinity Divide, the Soapstone Trail offers hikers the opportunity to disappear into mountains that rarely feel the tread of hiking shoes. While it does not boast grand lakes, massive cliffs, or vast meadows, the trail does offer many of the features hikers look for in trails, only on a somewhat moderated scale.

The trail accesses the small Soapstone Pond, passes through small grassy areas, and offers good views of beautiful cliffs, as well as vistas to the north that include pyramidal Porcupine Peak. All of this is arranged in an orderly fashion and makes for a pleasant hike. While it may lack scenery that rises to the level of the spectacular, it offers deep solitude and a chance to enjoy the mountains without the possibility of running into other hikers.

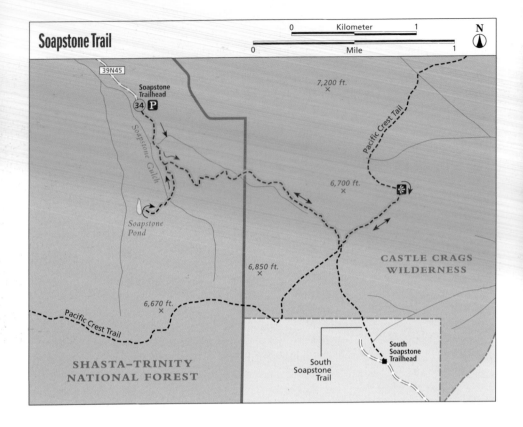

This is true of the Soapstone Trail, at least. The path is maintained as a rarely used route to access the Pacific Crest Trail during one of its longest roadless sections in all of Northern California. Understandably, isolation may be a bit harder to find once you reach the PCT. The payoff for the loss of solitude is the spectacle of one of the most magnificent views in the Mount Shasta area. The PCT's vista of Mount Shasta and the Castle Crags is monumental, and a worthy destination for hikers on the Soapstone Trail who yearn for more than a lonely walk through the mountains.

The Soapstone Trail begins at a wide parking lot at the end of a rough dirt road. The road is not passable for low-clearance vehicles. Hikers in these vehicles must park where the road splits and hike 1 mile up to the trailhead. At the trailhead, the pathway sets out to the south, crossing over large mounds intended to close the road off to vehicular traffic. The path is obviously an old road, though it quickly degrades into a more attractive singletrack.

About 0.2 mile from the trailhead the route crosses Soapstone Creek, which is likely to be dry later in the season. On the far side, the singletrack continues for a short distance before regaining the badly overgrown road. Roughly 100 yards from the creek, look for two large cairns on the left side of the trail marking the junction

The stunning view of the Castle Crags from the PCT.

of the Soapstone Trail and the spur trail that goes to Soapstone Pond. If you intend to visit the pond, head there first.

To reach Soapstone Pond, continue down the spur another 0.4 mile to the small body of water. On the way, pass a few marshy areas and cross another stream. About halfway between the junction and the Soapstone Pond, another pair of cairns lines the left side of the road. Disregard these. Though it looks like there may be a trail here, it disappears quickly and is not worth the effort. Right before the pond the old road ends, narrowing to singletrack as it climbs over a low rise. On the other side lies small Soapstone Pond. Ringed with trees, it only rises to the level of nice, especially late in the summer when the water level has receded.

Returning to the junction with the main stem of the Soapstone Trail, the path shrinks down to a faint singletrack. From this point onward the trail obviously receives very, very little use. Though the route is always obvious, at times it nearly fades away entirely.

The trail stays level for a little while, and then begins to climb a steep grade. After passing through a band of trees, it enters a large brush field. A few switchbacks ease the grade a little. Thankfully, this is one of the prettiest sections of the whole hike. Much of the Soapstone Basin is visible. The view includes a series of large cliffs immediately to the south, as well as the walls of the Devils Pocket a little farther to the west. A short distance beyond the brush, large grassy areas dotted with trees beckon explorers to delve deeper into the almost-never-traveled reaches of Soapstone Basin.

Rocky peaks on the rim of Soapstone Basin.

Eventually the views end, as the trail reenters the dense forest. As if in compensation for the lack of views, the trail levels off. It passes a small seep that still flows late in the year, and then arrives at the crossing of Soapstone Creek. Just beyond the creek a sign marks the passage across the boundary of the Castle Crags Wilderness.

The corner of the Castle Crags Wilderness through which the Soapstone Trail travels is among the most remote of the entire wilderness area. It consists of a small canyon tucked between the crest of the large central rib of the Trinity Divide and the summit of Soapstone Peak, the highest point in the Castle Crags Wilderness. As the path winds up a moderate grade, occasional views appear to the north, toward Porcupine Peak.

Soon the route settles in along the uppermost section of Soapstone Creek, and maintains a parallel course for approximately 0.3 mile. Finally, as the trail nears the headwall of the canyon, it steepens considerably. This section is thankfully short. After a dusty switchback near the top of the canyon, a large rock outcropping marks the end of the climb. The view to the north includes the vast, oppressively brushy summit of Soapstone Peak. The crest of the ridge offers no views to the south due to the presence of a dense forest of mountain hemlock. The trail descends another 0.2 mile to an obvious junction with the PCT.

Though the Soapstone Trail officially continues south of the junction for another 0.5 mile to the South Soapstone trailhead, it is much better to turn left onto the PCT.

The trail initially goes through a forest, but soon clears out a bit, and the Castle Crags emerge to the southeast. Though the view is awe-inspiring, maintain course a little farther: The view ahead is incomparable.

Eventually the forest recedes altogether, as the trail arrives at a shoulder on the edge of a vast basin and the grand vista unfolds. Immediately ahead is the giant headwaters basin of the North Fork of Castle Creek. The tall, brush-covered point straight ahead is the backside of Castle Peak. Above the peak is the mighty cone of Mount Shasta, crowning the horizon. Below and to the right is the awesome bulk of the Castle Crags. The endless granite spires form a giant, rocky knot.

The clear line of the PCT can be observed zigzagging along the flank of this incredible formation. An obvious side trail leads to a level clearing on the shoulder, where PCT thru-hikers have established an obvious camp with room for four or five tents. Down below, to the north, is a small, seasonal pond lying a couple hundred feet below the trail. When it has water, it is a welcome diversion along this long, waterless section of the trail. You must proceed a little farther along the PCT to reach a suitable place to travel cross-country down to the little lake. For those who opt to camp at this incredible vista, the sense of vastness and epic proportion will not be soon forgotten. Sunset is tremendous.

Miles and Directions

0.0 Start by climbing over some large mounds that block the road at the trailhead.

0.3 At the junction, turn left to continue on the Soapstone Trail. Staying right, the trail reaches little Soapstone Pond in 0.4 mile. The pond is pretty, but not impressive.

0.9 Enter the Castle Crags Wilderness.

1.4 After a short, steep climb, reach the top of a long ridge that runs from the crest of the Trinity Divide to the Castle Crags. Hike down the other side of the ridge.

1.5 Arrive at a junction with the Pacific Crest Trail. Turn left and continue hiking on the PCT.

1.9 Where the trail turns left and begins a traverse of a massive basin, a clearing on the right of the trail has an epic vista of Mount Shasta and the Castle Crags. It is stupendous. This is the turnaround; retrace your steps.

3.8 Arrive back at the trailhead. With the out-and-back leg to Soapstone Pond, the round-trip total is 4.6 miles.

35 Cliff Lakes

The Cliff Lakes are the source of the South Fork of the Sacramento River, the largest of the river's three headwaters forks. Given that the Sacramento is the Golden State's longest and largest river, this has special significance. However, without an official trail leading to the lakes, they tend to go under the radar. This is unfortunate because getting to them is easy, and they are among the most spectacular lakes in Northern California.

Total distance: 3.0 miles to Cliff Lake; 4 miles to Terrace Lake
Trail type: Out and back
Elevation gain: 250 feet to Cliff Lake; 720 feet to Terrace Lake
Difficulty: Easy to moderate
Trail surface: dirt road, rocky, packed dirt
Hiking time: 2.5 hours
Season: Summer, fall

Fees and permits: None
Canine compatibility: Dogs are permitted.
Land status: Shasta-Trinity National Forest
Trail contact: Mount Shasta Ranger District, 204 W. Alma St., Mount Shasta, CA 96067; (530) 926-4511; www.fs.usda.gov/stnf
Other: Water is available at numerous lakes. The west side of Cliff Lake is private property. Do not enter this area.

Finding the trailhead: From Mount Shasta City, head west on West Lake Street, crossing over I-5. At the stop sign, turn left onto Old Stage Road. After 0.3 mile, veer right onto W A Barr Road. Continue south, crossing over the dam that impounds the Sacramento River and forms Lake Siskiyou. From the dam, continue 11.9 miles to the west, passing the lake and continuing up the Sacramento River. At 11.9 miles look for unsigned FR 39N05Y veering off to the left. There is usually a painted blaze on a tree, but there is no other identification of the turnoff. The dirt road does have a bit of climb to it and is surrounded by brush. It is only 30-40 feet up the road to the parking area. GPS: N41° 13' 1.82" / W122° 29' 22.34"

The Hike

Because the Mount Shasta region has an abundance of great hikes and exceptional scenery, it should come as no surprise that a real gem of a hike slips through the cracks every now and then, and escapes notoriety. What is surprising is that such a gem could be as spectacular as Cliff Lake, a deep lake that is one of the most beautiful bodies of water in the Trinity Divide.

As the name implies, there is a magnificent cliff rising out of the lake, soaring 1,500 feet above the alpine waters. As if this were not enough, there are four more lakes in the giant basin. Two of the lakes, Cedar and Lower Cliff Lakes, are passed by the trail en route to Cliff Lake. The other two, Terrace and Upper Cliff Lakes, are nestled in high cirques tucked into the rocky cliffs. Adding interest to all of these fantastic features is the proliferation of Port Orford cedars, an extremely rare species of tree found in high

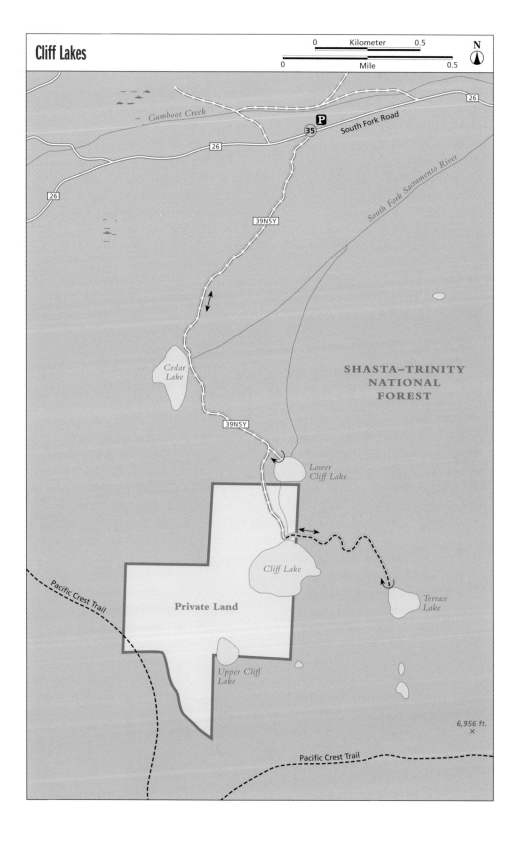

concentration around Cliff Lake. The abundance of the Port Orford cedar around the Cliff Lake area has led to the basin being unofficially referred to as Cedar Basin.

However, having expounded the superlatives, two caveats need to be pointed out. The first is that the hike is mostly on a dirt road rather than on a normal hiking trail. The road is very rugged, with one 70-yard stretch composed entirely of large boulders. It would take great patience to negotiate a vehicle up this road. It is rarely driven on, but there are rare occasions when it is necessary to watch out for slow driving vehicles. The other caveat to be aware of is the presence of a large block of private land at the lake. The entire west half of Cliff Lake, and lands surrounding it, are privately owned. There are a couple of cabins and a few out buildings on the land, as well as an odd dock constructed of large, floating logs. Please be respectful of the property owners and do not trespass. A good rule of thumb is to stay on the east side of the outlet creek, where the national forest owns the land.

The parking area right off of South Fork Road is large enough to accommodate several cars, in the unlikely event that there are more than one or two present. Park in the large clearing and begin hiking down the road. It is very level as it passes through a mixed forest of cedar, ponderosa pine, and various firs. Be on the lookout for Port Orford cedars, which begin to appear along the road. These are technically cypress trees despite their name, and the foliage does resemble that of a cedar. Some of the most distinguishing characteristics are the blue tint of the sprays, and the blue-and-red cones that form on the sprays' tips.

Continuing down the road, the grade is very gentle. A few creeks cross the way, but none are large and they will most likely be dry by mid- to late summer.

About 0.8 mile from the trailhead, the forest around the road opens up as Cedar Lake comes into view. This is the shallowest of all the lakes in Cedar Basin. Some good campsites are scattered around the lake for those inclined to camp, though better sites lie ahead. The road skirts the northern end of the lake before you come to an impressively built rocky causeway. The outlet of Cedar Lake has created a very marshy area, and to cross it the road has been built up by piling large boulders. Driving over this section would not be fun, but walking over it is easy.

Beyond the causeway, the trail veers away from Cedar Lake and makes the only noticeable climb of the entire hike. It is very short and only gains about 100 feet. Just past the grade Lower Cliff Lake comes into view. It is smaller and deeper than Cedar Lake, and is backed by an attractive peak on its east side. A short spur off of the main road drops down to the lakeshore, where some great campsites are found. From the shore of Lower Cliff Lake, you get your first view of the giant cirque surrounding the Cliff Lakes.

Returning to the main road, proceed for 0.3 mile to the north shore of Cliff Lake. The sound of the lake's outlet creek should be audible before arriving. Stay left when you pass a gated dirt road splitting off the main route. This leads to a cabin on private property on the lake's west side. Please respect the owner's privacy and stay on the road or the area on the east side of the lake's outlet. From here, it is just a short walk to the end of the road. It comes to an abrupt end at the edge of the water.

Cliff Lake.

Cliff Lake is a sublime slice of alpine splendor. The lake is large and deep and surrounded by cliffs on three sides. The enormous wall at the south end of the lake emerges directly from the lake's blue waters and climbs 1,500 feet to the summit of Peak 7,149. Numerous snow-fed cascades crash down the face of the cliff, and two large streams, falling precipitously out of Upper Cliff and Terrace Lakes, also contribute to the symphony of cataracts.

Be sure to remember that to the right of the road that leads to Cliff Lake is the private inholding, where there are a couple of cabins and some outbuildings. Do not venture to this side of the lake. Instead, cross the lake's outlet creek. There is a well-established use trail a few dozen feet north of the outlet. It is also possible to cross over the logs clogging the outlet.

On the far side of the outlet creek is a nice little campsite that has a very old forest service fire pit. The rocks have been piled up and mortared together with a small iron chimney, and a large piece of iron plate has been placed on top of the fire to form a griddle. From the campsite, look east (left) as you face the lake. There, the large trunk of a dead tree stands not far away. Close inspection will reveal a faint use trail just to the left of the trunk. This is the beginning of the route that leads up to Terrace Lake.

The path is narrow, and passes through a large expanse of pinemat manzanita, huckleberry oak, and chinquapin. After climbing for about 0.5 miles the trail deposits you at the edge of Terrace Lake.

The basin holding the lake is not nearly as rocky as the one holding Cliff Lake, but it is still very pretty. The crest of the ridge that branches off the main spine of the Trinity Divide and runs to the Castle Crags is visible behind the blue waters. The Pacific Crest Trail courses along the far side of this crest. There is a nifty view looking down on this basin just a few feet off of the trail. There are no established campsites here, but it is a nice place to camp nonetheless. The basin holding Terrace Lake contains the highest-elevation Port Orford cedars that have been found. A few hidden ponds in the back of the basin, and a cross-country route onto the cliffs above Cliff Lake, beckon those hungry for exploration.

Miles and Directions

0.0 Start at the large clearing that functions as a trailhead. Begin by walking south along the dirt road.

0.7 The road comes alongside Cedar Lake, where there are some campsites. An impressive rock causeway skirts the east side of the lake.

1.2 A spur trail descends to the left and leads to Lower Cliff Lake, which is 0.1 mile away.

1.5 The road ends at the north end of Cliff Lake. Do not go to the right, where the lakeshore and lake are on private property. Cross over the outlet creek and explore the east side of the lake. Locate the remnants of the old campground with a stone stove. This is the landmark needed to find the trail up to Terrace Lake. From the stove, look east toward a large, broken, tree trunk. Near the base of the trunk there is a path through the brush. This is the trail to Terrace Lake.

2.0 The narrow path ends at Terrace Lake. Retrace your steps.

4.0 Arrive back at the trailhead.

36 Gumboot Lake

The hike from Gumboot Lake follows a simple trail that visits Upper Gumboot Lake and a couple of tiny meadows. Combined with a short trip on the Pacific Crest Trail, the trail leads to a fantastic vista of the Trinity Alps, the Eddy Range, the South Fork of the Sacramento River, and mighty Mount Shasta.

Total distance: 2.8 miles
Trail type: Out and back
Elevation gain: 550 feet
Difficulty: Easy
Trail surface: Packed dirt, dirt road, rocky, paved road
Hiking time: 1.5 hours
Season: Summer, fall

Fees and permits: None
Canine compatibility: Dogs are permitted.
Land status: Shasta-Trinity National Forest
Trail contact: Mount Shasta Ranger District, 204 W. Alma St., Mount Shasta, CA 96067; (530) 926-4511; www.fs.usda.gov/stnf
Other: Water is available from the Gumboot Lakes.

Finding the trailhead: From Mount Shasta City, head west on West Lake Street, crossing over I-5. At the stop sign, turn left onto Old Stage Road. After 0.3 mile, veer right onto W A Barr Road. Continue south, crossing over the dam that impounds the Sacramento River and forms Lake Siskiyou. From the dam, continue 12.5 miles to the west on FR 26, passing the lake and continuing up the Sacramento River. At 12.5 miles, veer left at the fork onto paved FR 40N37. Proceed to the trailhead at Gumboot Lake a short distance ahead. GPS: N41° 12' 44.78" / W122° 30' 38.41"

The Hike

Situated at the far end of the South Fork of the Sacramento River's canyon, the Gumboot Trail is a modest hike that connects Gumboot Lake with the Pacific Crest Trail. The lake is a pleasant spot in a shallow, rocky bowl, with meadows scattered throughout the forest. It is a serene location where relaxing seems like it ought to be at the top of the list of things to do. Yet, in the midst of the idyll, there is a nice little hike that boasts some superlative scenery.

The trail begins at the outlet of Gumboot Lake, climbs near Upper Gumboot Lake, and then passes a pair of small meadows on the way to its junction with the Pacific Crest Trail (PCT). Despite the presence of a campground at the beginning of the trip and the paved road where it meets the PCT, the Gumboot Trail has a sense of great isolation. This is most pronounced when you look out over the windswept basin at the head of the South Fork's canyon. It is an invigorating place and worth the effort, even if you are planning on a relaxing afternoon at the lake.

The hike begins at the parking area at the east end of Gumboot Lake, next to the small dam at the lake's outlet. Although the lake is natural, the dam raises the water level and increases Gumboot's size. The route initially follows the road down to a ford

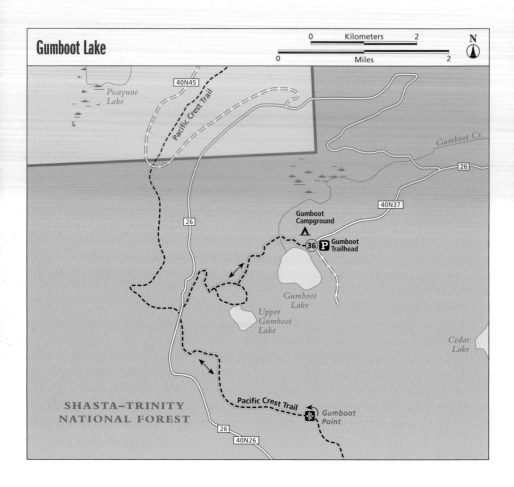

across Gumboot Creek and past a couple of the campsites. The only amenity supplied at the campground is a vault toilet, which is off to the right. A few dozen yards past the creek crossing, a yellow sign sets the boundary of the area where fires are permitted. It also marks the beginning of the trail.

Once on the trail, which was once an old, narrow road, you begin to climb steadily. While it is never too steep, the grade is just enough to make hikers take note that they are gaining a fair amount of elevation. It maintains a westerly course for approximately 0.3 mile from the beginning of the singletrack before it arrives at a junction marked by a series of cairns. The obvious main trail stays to the right. If you go left, the trail descends through some brush and arrives at the edge of Upper Gumboot Lake.

The small lake is not as attractive as its bigger sibling, but it is still a pleasant place to enjoy some solitude. A faint trail follows the north shore and then climbs up a slope as it angles to the north, reconnecting with the main trail. Whether you choose to bypass the lake or make the short Upper Gumboot detour, the main trail continues to climb a little farther, with occasional views of the basin to the north.

Gumboot Point vista of Mount Shasta.

Soon the trail passes two small meadows and turns to the right. Climbing a little farther, the path encounters one tight switchback. After a final ascent, the trail ends at the edge of the paved road accessing the PCT trailhead at Gumboot Saddle. This is the official end of the Gumboot Trail.

To continue on to Gumboot Point and the excellent vista, proceed a few yards along the road to the beginning of the PCT. Initially passing through dense stands of trees, the trail soon leaves the forest canopy and crosses a brushy area. The path generally stays just below the crest of Trinity Divide. After reentering the forest, the trail passes a few primitive campsites. Soon the route crosses an area of exposed, gray rock. Leave the trail and scramble up the rock to the obvious high point. From here an incredible vista unfolds. Immediately below is Gumboot Lake. The Eddy Range, a subrange of the Trinity Divide, extends to the north, capped by Mount Eddy. The canyon of the South Fork of the Sacramento drops away to the east, its southern side lined by the high peaks of the Trinity Divide's great rib, which leads to the mighty Castle Crags.

The entire scene is crowned by magnificent Mount Shasta, holding sway over the entire region. It is a stunning sight, particularly in the afternoon as the sun prepares to set. If you are hiking to the Seven Lakes Basin, this vista is only the beginning of a spectacular journey, but it makes a great climax to a hike from Gumboot Lake.

Miles and Directions

0.0 Start at the small parking area at the edge of Gumboot Lake. Follow the road past the little dam and through the campground. At the end of the campground, begin hiking on the trail beside a yellow sign.

0.4 The spur leading down to Upper Gumboot Lake descends to the right.

0.7 The trail ends at the paved road near the Gumboot Saddle trailhead. Turn left and walk along the road for a dozen yards, then begin hiking on the Pacific Crest Trail.

1.4 Scramble uphill a short distance above the PCT to end the hike on Gumboot Point. This is the turnaround; retrace your steps. The PCT continues south to the Seven Lakes Basin.

2.8 Arrive back at the trailhead.

37 Porcupine and Toad Lakes

Located in awesome, rocky cirques, Porcupine and Toad Lakes are isolated, magnificent, alpine lakes. The long hike to the two lakes follows the Pacific Crest Trail north from Gumboot Saddle, passing long ridges, small meadows, and epic vistas. Either lake makes a great destination for a backpacking trip with lots of potential for exploration.

Total distance: 11.5 miles to Porcupine Lake; 13.4 miles to Toad Lake
Trail type: Out and back
Elevation gain: 1,300 feet
Difficulty: Difficult due to length
Trail surface: Packed dirt, rocky, dirt road
Hiking time: 6-8 hours
Season: Summer, fall

Fees and permits: None
Canine compatibility: Dogs are permitted.
Land status: Shasta-Trinity National Forest
Trail contact: Mount Shasta Ranger District, 204 W. Alma St., Mount Shasta, CA 96067; (530) 926-4511; www.fs.usda.gov/stnf
Other: Water is available from Porcupine and Toad Lakes.

Finding the trailhead: From Mount Shasta City, head west on West Lake Street, crossing over I-5. At the stop sign, turn left onto Old Stage Road. After 0.3 mile, veer right onto W A Barr Road. Continue south, crossing over the dam that impounds the Sacramento River and forms Lake Siskiyou. At the intersection with Castle Lake Road, stay straight. The road becomes FR 26. Follow this road for nearly 12 miles. A signed fork indicates Gumboot Lake is 0.5 mile to the left. Continue to the right, climbing up into the cirque that contains the Gumboot Lakes. The Pacific Crest Trail's Gumboot Trailhead is located at the summit, with a good parking lot. GPS: N41° 12' 31.40" / W122° 31' 9.97"

The Hike

The Eddy Range is a subsection of the Trinity Divide. It extends from Parks Creek Pass on the north side of Mount Eddy to Gumboot Saddle above the headwaters of the South Fork of the Sacramento River. This is the highest part of the Trinity Divide. In addition to Mount Eddy, several unnamed peaks here exceed 8,000 feet, the only part of the divide to climb that high. Although nine lakes are found in the Eddys, six of them are on Mount Eddy. The other three, Porcupine, Toad, and Chipmunk Lakes, are all found at the headwaters of the Middle Fork of the Sacramento River.

Porcupine and Toad Lakes are large, deep, first-rate lakes set in high bowls near the crest of the Trinity Divide. Despite being only 0.5 mile apart, they are remarkably different. Porcupine Lake has a rocky shoreline and is surrounded by towering granitic cliffs. In contrast, Toad Lake is more than twice the size of Porcupine, sits in a broad, forested, peridotite basin, and is surrounded by small meadows. As unlike as they may be, together they make a fantastic hike along the Pacific Crest Trail (PCT).

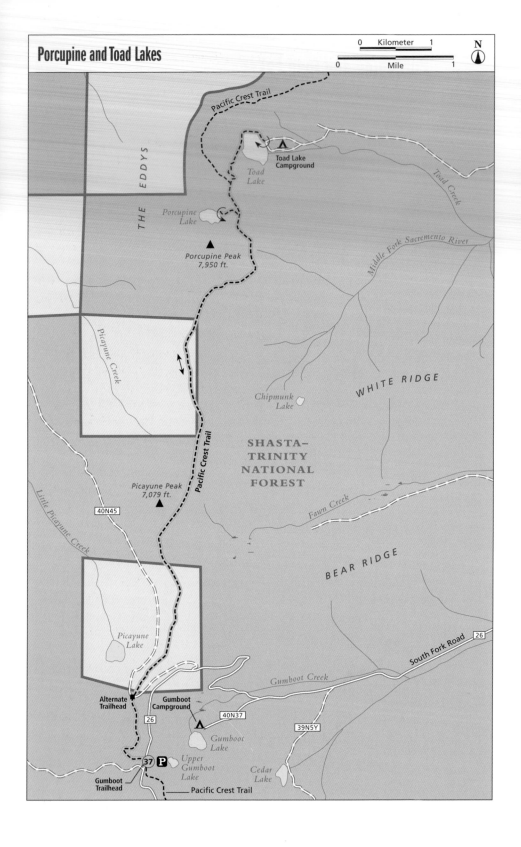

Porcupine and Toad Lakes

The route to the lakes begins on the PCT at Gumboot Saddle. The trail sets out to the north, climbing a couple of switchbacks before settling into a northerly trajectory along the eastern shoulder of Mumbo Peak. This section of the PCT crosses open country with views to the east toward Mount Shasta. To the south, glittering Gumboot Lake sits amid forest and meadows 400 feet below the trail.

After 0.6 mile the trail descends to a saddle and crosses wide FR 40N45. A small campsite marks the crossing, and the PCT is visible across the road. This crossing is an alternate trailhead that cuts off 0.6 mile one-way and 300 feet of elevation gain. To get to this trailhead, stay right at the fork near Gumboot Lake and continue driving up two long switchbacks. About 1.4 miles from the fork, turn right onto FR 40N45. The road is well maintained, made of gravel, and in good condition. Although this shaves a fair amount of distance off the trip, the views from the beginning of the trail are worth the extra distance.

From the road crossing, the PCT continues north, now traversing the west side of the Eddy Range. After passing beneath the western terminus of Bear Ridge, the path crosses a long saddle above Fawn Creek Canyon. Mount Shasta looms majestically above the canyon. Fawn Creek begins in a large meadow just below the saddle and feeds into the South Fork of the Sacramento. It is the only tributary of the Sacramento River that begins on the crest of the Eddy Range alongside the three main forks of the river. To the west is Picayune Lake, 600 feet below the PCT. Picayune Peak is the highest point immediately to the north. Traverse the east flank of the peak and pass through a second saddle that lies between Picayune Peak and White Ridge. If you want to climb Picayune Peak, go up the slopes above the second saddle for a nifty view.

North of the saddle between Picayune Peak and White Ridge, traverse the latter's western slope. Here you get the first good look at the dark mass of Porcupine Peak. From the main crest of the Eddy Range, White Ridge extends eastward, descending gradually to the confluence of the Middle and South Forks of the Sacramento River. It is similar in many respects to Bear Ridge, although it is a little higher. The trail crosses over the western face of the ridge, with good views westward. A small but fairly reliable spring is found about 20 feet below the trail in this section. For PCT travelers, it is the first water in many miles. Watch for lush grass and damp ground around the trail.

Proceeding north from White Ridge, the PCT crosses the long western rim of the canyon of the Middle Fork of the Sacramento River. Hidden from view, small Chipmunk Lake is the lone lake in this part of the canyon. A large meadow blankets an area just below the trail, providing excellent views of Mount Shasta to the east. In season, the meadow fills with an excellent display of wildflowers. Small springs provide the necessary water for the meadow, but are not productive enough to resupply hikers. Beyond the meadow, the PCT begins a wide arc to the east, passing beneath Porcupine Peak. Another small meadow filled with carnivorous pitcher plants is found just south of the trail along this stretch.

Porcupine Peak rises above Porcupine Lake.

Soon the PCT turns north again, rounding a shoulder at the base of Porcupine Peak. Views of Mount Shasta and the Castle Crags Wilderness are excellent. Up until this point, the PCT has managed to persevere at a remarkably level grade. At this point it begins to climb at a more taxing incline. Thankfully it is only a brief break from the pleasantly level trail.

As the path turns north, watch for a small cairn marking the junction with the spur trail leading up to Porcupine Lake. Follow the trail up to the east shore of the lake. Surrounded on three sides by high, rocky peaks, Porcupine Lake is a gorgeous gem set amid harsh, beautiful stone. The best perspective is from the north shore. Circle around the lake to the north and scramble up the brushy talus slope to get an incredible view of the great triangular tower of Porcupine Peak rising above the sapphire waters. If you keep circling the lake to the west you will find a hidden, densely forested basin. Though steep, there is a simple cross-country route through the basin to the top of Porcupine Peak. There are a few good campsites at the east end of the lake.

If you wish to continue to Toad Lake, return to the PCT and hike north for 0.3 mile to a junction with a great overlook above Toad Lake. The deep blue waters are set amid orange and pink walls cloaked with green forests. Peering over a ridge behind the lake is magnificent Mount Shasta, 18.5 miles to the east but looking like it is close enough to touch. Stay right at the junction, and descend 0.6 mile to the shore of Toad Lake. Follow the trail around the north shore of the lake to the east side. Here, a short trail leads to the Toad Lake Campground in 0.4 mile. Reach the campground via a long dirt road that climbs up the Middle Fork of the Sacramento River's canyon. Small, remote, and little used, the camp seems a bit out of place in the wild canyon.

Miles and Directions

0.0 Start at the Gumboot Saddle trailhead. The Pacific Crest Trail begins at the east end of the parking area.

0.7 Cross FR 40N45. You can start the hike here, shaving almost 1.5 miles off the round-trip mileage of the hike.

1.8 The PCT travels along the saddle above Fawn Creek Canyon.

2.8 To climb Picayune Peak, veer left off the trail and scramble up the bare slope to the summit.

4.1 Pass a small meadow with a beautiful view of Mount Shasta.

5.0 Round Porcupine Peak's broad shoulder. This marks the final leg of the PCT before the spur that leads to Porcupine Lake.

5.5 Turn left onto the spur trail to Porcupine Lake. The lake is 0.3 mile down the trail. This can be a turnaround; the round-trip distance is about 11.5 miles. To reach Toad Lake, continue hiking on the PCT.

5.8 At a junction, the spur trail leading to Toad Lake turns right and begins to climb down toward the lake.

6.2 The trail reaches the bottom of the canyon and skirts the edge of a meadow. The lake lies just ahead.

6.7 After passing through trees, the trail breaks out into the open and follows the edge of the lake around to its east side, where it ends at the junction with the short trail coming from the Toad Lake campground. The campground is 0.5 mile down the trail. Retrace your steps.

13.4 Arrive back at the trailhead.

38 Seven Lakes Basin

The journey to the Seven Lakes Basin is one of the classic hikes in the Mount Shasta area. Traveling south on the Pacific Crest Trail, there unfolds plentiful and spectacular views of the Trinity Alps to the west and Mount Shasta to the east. Leave the PCT above the beautiful Seven Lakes Basin and follow the easy trail to Lake Helen for a shorter destination. A road continues into the basin and accesses Upper and Lower Seven Lakes, which are beautiful, cliff-lined, alpine treasures. Hikers looking to explore seldom-traveled country can try to reach awesome Echo Lake, lying at the foot of the 1,000-foot vertical north face of Boulder Peak.

Total distance: 5.4 miles to Lake Helen; 7.6 miles to Upper Seven Lake
Trail type: Out and back
Elevation gain: 300 feet to Lake Helen; 850 feet, including the return climb, to and from Upper Seven Lake
Difficulty: Moderate to difficult
Trail surface: Packed dirt, rocky, dirt road
Season: Summer, fall

Fees and permits: None
Canine compatibility: Dogs are permitted.
Land status: Shasta-Trinity National Forest
Trail contact: Mount Shasta Ranger District, 204 W. Alma St., Mount Shasta, CA 96067; (530) 926-4511; www.fs.usda.gov/stnf
Other: Water is available from the lakes along the trail.

Finding the trailhead: From Mount Shasta City, head west on West Lake Street, crossing over I-5. At the stop sign, turn left onto Old Stage Road. After 0.3 mile, veer right onto W A Barr Road. Continue south, crossing over the dam that impounds the Sacramento River and forms Lake Siskiyou. At the intersection with Castle Lake Road, stay straight. The road becomes FR 26. Follow this road for nearly 12 miles. A signed fork indicates Gumboot Lake is 0.5 mile to the left. Continue to the right on FR 26, climbing up into the cirque that contains the Gumboot Lakes. The Pacific Crest Trail's Gumboot Trailhead is located at the summit, with a good parking lot. GPS: N41° 12' 31.40" / W122° 31' 9.97"

The Hike

Providing maximum scenery for minimal effort, the trip along the Pacific Crest Trail to the Seven Lakes Basin is one of the finest hikes around Mount Shasta. Far-reaching views are constant throughout the entire trip and while Mount Shasta is scenery nonpareil, vistas of the mountain are complemented by Mount Eddy, the Trinity Alps, the Russian Wilderness, the Castle Crags, Grey Rocks, and the many lakes found in the Trinity Divide. Boulder Peak, the rugged sentinel towering above the Seven Lakes Basin, is not the least of these spectacles.

The trail itself is an exciting part of the hike. It follows the crest of the Trinity Divide, traveling over naked rock, along cliffs, and traversing large talus fields. After

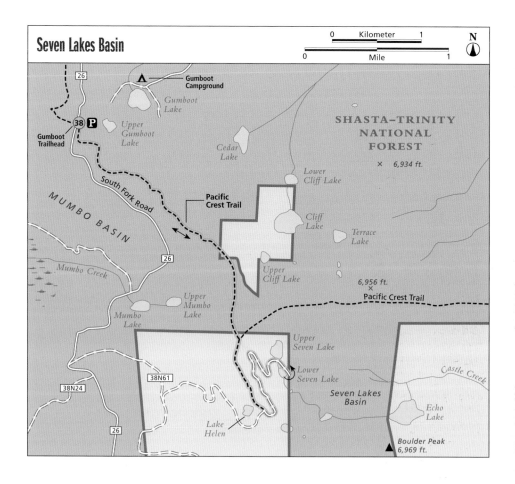

Seven Lakes Basin

departing the PCT, hikers can follow a path to Lake Helen, the highest of the seven lakes. This makes a nice panorama-filled outing that is abundant with memorable sights. You also have the option of descending to the Seven Lakes Basin, where Upper and Lower Seven Lakes await. The upper lake in particular is a first-rate body of water, with cliffs towering above its west side. In terms of the quantity and quality of scenery, the hike to the Seven Lakes Basin is in the upper echelon of trails in the Trinity Divide.

The trail begins at the PCT trailhead on Gumboot Saddle. Follow the trail south as it weaves around the beginning of the Trinity Divide's main ridge. The trail climbs through forest before rounding a brushy shoulder and dropping to a wooded saddle that contains a primitive campsite. The trail then climbs out of the saddle and across another brushy slope, where the trail tops out on the rocky outcropping of Gumboot Point. The views of Mount Eddy, Gumboot Lake, the South Fork of the Sacramento, and Mount Shasta are staggering.

From here, the PCT maintains a fairly level grade as it travels south across the crest of the Trinity Divide. The trail winds through some large, rocky outcroppings, shifting

Looking down on the Seven Lakes Basin.

first to the east side of the ridge, then back to the west side. The crest begins to gain elevation, but the trail stays level. Consequently the trail falls well below the top of the ridge. If you want an unbelievably tremendous overlook, follow the ridge to the top of Peak 7,149. Seldom seen, it is one of the grandest sights around Mount Shasta. The climb is rugged, cross-country, and worth it.

Staying on the PCT, look down from the trail to observe the Mumbo Lakes in a basin directly below. The upper lake is shallow, but the lower lake is deeper. Views of the Trinity Alps continue to improve. Some peaks in the Trinities, especially Billys Peak and the craggy spire of Billys Peak Lookout, are less than 14 miles distant and seem particularly close. The Russian Wilderness, far to the north, is also visible beyond the northernmost mountains of the Trinity Alps. The crest's slope gets steeper as the trail heads south, leaving the route slung somewhat precariously high above the Mumbo Basin. Finally, the trail rounds a bend and arrives at a large saddle with a trail junction.

At the saddle, the magnificent view of the Seven Lakes Basin unfolds. Here Boulder Peak comes into view for the first time. Its sharp summit and the sheer, rugged cliff rising out of the deep blue waters of Echo Lake are fine to behold. The wide valley drops away from the saddle rapidly to a flat, forested area. Tall cliffs ring the basin and are most dramatic on the west and south sides. Boulder Peak on the southern end of the basin is an imposing sentinel guarding the eastern end of the cliffs. The lakes are all situated at the bottom of the cliffs that ring the south and west ends of the basin.

The Castle Crags peek over a ridge beyond Boulder Peak and Echo Lake.

Upper and Lower Seven Lakes and a small, nameless pond, the tiniest of the seven lakes, lie immediately below the saddle. Along the southern cliffs lies a meadow-ringed, nameless lake, and awesome Echo Lake is at the foot of Boulder Peak. Lake Helen and another unnamed lake are on a bench near the top of the cliffs on the west side of the basin. Looming ominously above the scene are the dark, brooding crags of the Grey Rocks, a mysterious cluster of peaks that see few hikers. No trail penetrates these peaks, and they are essentially a forsaken, albeit spectacular, corner of the Mount Shasta area.

From the saddle, the PCT swings east, running along the flank of the ridge that separates the Seven Lakes Basin from the headwaters of the Sacramento River. The ridge eventually leads to the Castle Crags. If you follow the PCT to the east for 0.8 mile, the trail comes to within 50 feet of a low notch on the ridge. Scramble up the notch for a terrific view of Mount Eddy and Mount Shasta, as well as Terrace Lake and a few unnamed ponds.

Back at the junction when the PCT first arrives at the saddle above the Seven Lakes Basin, turn right and proceed along a prominently visible path. It quickly joins a rugged four-wheel-drive road. Follow the road as it passes through some trees and then crosses an open area. Just as it reenters a large group of trees, veer right off the road and go cross-country for a few yards to the edge of Lake Helen, about 0.5 mile from the junction at the saddle.

Lake Helen is the highest of the seven lakes. Not as spectacular as Echo Lake or as scenic as Upper Seven Lake, it is still a very pretty spot. A large pinnacle rises above the north side of the lake, which is a shoulder of Tri-Counties Peak, where Siskiyou, Shasta, and Trinity Counties converge. From the west shore of the lake, it is possible to see Mount Shasta poking out above the edge of the cliffs.

To reach the lakes at the bottom of the basin, return to the rough road and follow it down a series of switchbacks. After 1 mile it arrives at the shore of Upper Seven Lake. Aside from Echo Lake, this is the prettiest of the lakes in the basin. Cliffs tower above the west side of the lake, and the high ridge along the crest of the Trinity Divide is almost 1,000 feet overhead. This is a wonderful spot. Lower Seven Lake is just to the south but not as pretty as the upper lake.

Unfortunately, the basin's most amazing lake, Echo Lake, is on private property. However, the west corner of the lake is publicly accessible and is an incredible place to view the lake and the towering north face of Boulder Peak. To get there, look for a narrow path heading east from between Upper and Lower Seven Lakes. Follow this rough, brush-choked path for 1 mile. It ends at the western corner of Echo Lake, where a meadow leads along the base of the cliffs to the water. If you are fortunate to find your way here, relax and enjoy the accomplishment. Return as you came.

Miles and Directions

0.0 Start by hiking south on the Pacific Crest Trail.

0.7 Scramble above the trail for the grand vista from Gumboot Point.

2.3 The PCT rounds a shoulder and arrives at a junction with a great view of the Seven Lakes Basin. To reach the lakes, go right at the junction, leaving the PCT. The trail merges onto a rough dirt road.

2.7 Leave the trail and go cross-country to the right to reach Lake Helen. To get to Upper Seven Lake at the bottom of the Seven Lakes Basin, continue hiking on the trail.

2.8 The road makes a wide switchback and begins to descend into the basin.

3.8 At the end of a series of switchbacks, the old road arrives at the edge of Upper Seven Lake, a beautiful, alpine lake. Lower Seven Lake is not quite a nice as its upper twin, but is still worth visiting. Stay straight at the end of the road to reach it. Retrace your steps.

7.6 Arrive back at the trailhead.

39 Tamarack and Twin Lakes

The easy hike to remote Tamarack and Twin Lakes is the sole hiking trail in the southern third of the Trinity Divide. Obscure and seldom used, the hike leads to some of the most attractive lakes in the Mount Shasta area, complemented by high, craggy cliffs and beautiful meadows.

Total distance: 5.0 miles
Trail type: Out and back
Elevation gain: 670 feet
Difficulty: Moderate
Trail surface: Dirt road, packed dirt, rocky
Hiking time: 2.5 hours
Season: Summer, fall

Fees and permits: None
Canine compatibility: Dogs are permitted.
Land status: Shasta-Trinity National Forest
Trail contact: Mount Shasta Ranger District, 204 W. Alma St., Mount Shasta, CA 96067; (530) 926-4511; www.fs.usda.gov/stnf
Other: Water is available from the lakes.

Finding the trailhead: From Mount Shasta City, travel south on I-5 and take the Castella exit. Turn right onto Castle Creek Road. After climbing 3,500 feet in 11.5 miles, you reach Whalan Summit. Pass the road on the right leading to the Pine-gri-la resort. Continue another mile, then turn left onto FR 38N17. Follow the road for about 3 miles, crossing Twin Lakes Creek once and stopping at the second crossing. Park on the far side of the creek, and walk back to the rough road that climbs steeply uphill. This is the beginning of the hike. GPS: 41° 7' 13.91" / W122° 28' 9.31"

The Hike

It is a surprising irony that the southern third of the Trinity Divide's high country has some of the range's most dazzling scenery and yet sees dramatically less visitation than the northern two-thirds. The reasons are clear: checkerboard land ownership, an extreme paucity of developed recreation infrastructure, and the general obscurity of the fantastic sights that await hikers in this region.

While these challenges reduce the number of people who hike here, those who do are treated to some of the most breathtaking scenery in all Northern California. The mighty Grey Rocks, one of the least known yet most rugged mountain strongholds in the North State, crown the southern divide and are complemented by numerous lakes and meadows. The best and easiest way to sample the exceptional landscape of the southern Trinity Divide is to hike the Tamarack Lake Trail. This incredibly under-used route visits not just Tamarack Lake, but also the excellent Twin Lakes. The upper of the pair is a first-rate alpine lake on its own, and would be worth a long hike on its merits alone. However, as excellent as Upper Twin Lake is, it is Tamarack Lake that is the unrivaled limnic monarch in this region. A large, deep lake ringed with lush meadows and backed by a massive bank of enormous cliffs, Tamarack Lake is one of

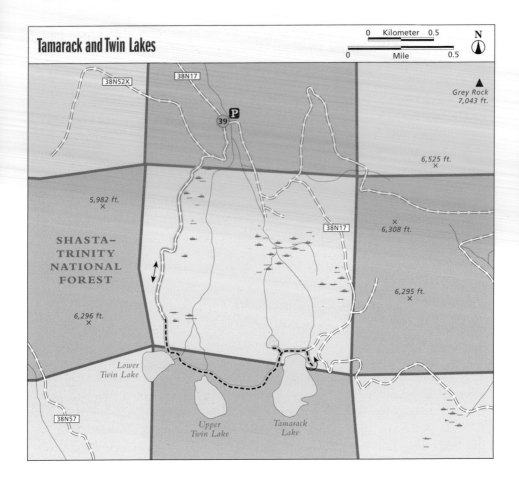

0   Kilometer   0.5

0   Mile   0.5

N

38N52X

38N17

Grey Rock
7,043 ft.

P
39

6,525 ft.
×

5,982 ft.
×

38N17

×
6,308 ft.

SHASTA-
TRINITY
NATIONAL
FOREST

6,295 ft.
×

6,296 ft.
×

Lower
Twin Lake

38N57

Upper
Twin Lake

Tamarack
Lake

the prettiest in the Klamath Mountains and one of the top-tier lakes in the greater Mount Shasta area.

Though the Tamarack Lake Trail technically begins at Tamarack Meadow just south of Lower Twin Lake, most hikers will want to park on the side of Road 38N17, next to where Twin Lakes Creek passes under the road. There is a small pullout on the road, on the east side of the crossing. The road connecting to the Tamarack Lake Trail initially parallels the creek, though the water is out of sight—in a gully and obscured by trees.

After a short, steep dogleg to the west, the road sets its course to the south and makes a long, gradual climb along a series of small meadows that spread out on the east side of the road. Many sections of the road are in good shape and passable by low-clearance vehicles. However, just enough rough spots exist to make driving a regular car up this road unrealistic.

After nearly a mile, the road makes another steep dogleg to the west. It then arrives on the edge of a large and beautiful Tamarack Meadow. To the south, the tall cliffs that mark the lakes' backdrop loom beyond the dense forest of lodgepole pine that rings the meadow. To the northeast, the dark towers of the Grey Rocks have an ominous, if beautiful, presence.

Once at the meadow, the road comes to a theoretical end and the Tamarack Lake Trail actually begins. In reality it is hard to distinguish between the two because the path is nearly as wide as the road as it skirts the western edge of the large, grassy clearing. The wide path proceeds to the south a short distance, and then makes a short, steep climb. If anyone had any thoughts this was still a road, the rocky climb should put this assumption to rest. It would take a very stout jeep to make it up this section of the hike.

Soon the path arrives at the edge of Lower Twin Lake. Though fairly shallow, the lake is large and clear. A wooded ridge rises to the west. The tall cliffs above Tamarack and Upper Twin Lake are visible over the trees to the south. In most places this lake would be a first-rate destination, but do not tarry too long here. Better sights await only a stone's throw away.

Back on the trail, the route turns to the east, away from Lower Twin Lake. As it proceeds the trail begins to narrow, looking less like a road. It quickly arrives at the north end of Upper Twin Lake, near the lake's outlet. As noted, this lake is a top-tier alpine lake. Roughly the same size as its lower twin, it is much deeper, has fewer trees choking its shores, and more rocks populate the area. Most importantly, bright white cliffs soar nearly 1,000 feet above the water. It is a dramatic sight that is worth the effort of the hike even if you were to progress no farther. For hikers with little time or small children, this could be a satisfying end to the hike.

From the outlet of Upper Twin Lake, the path finally narrows to singletrack. It crosses the outlet and begins to loop around to the south, on the east side of the lake. After following the shore for a little while, you arrive at a junction. Stay to the left and climb away from the lake. The track to the right continues along the shore of Upper Twin Lake.

As the Tamarack Lake Trail climbs, it leaves the trees behind and enters a large brush field. The path winds over the low divide that separates Upper Twin Lake from Tamarack Lake. Though some sections tend to be a bit overgrown, cairns help to navigate. Unfortunately, near the top of the divide the trail may disappear altogether. Maintain a course to the east. If you veer too far to the north, backtrack until you find a path that continues to the east, toward Tamarack Lake. This is the most frustrating part of the trail and may cause some to get lost. If you go too far to the north, it is possible to pick a way through the brush, maintaining an easterly direction, and then intersect the trail. However you proceed, the views of the Gray Rocks are excellent!

Once off the ridge, the trail continues to the south, moving gradually closer to Tamarack Lake. About 0.2 mile past the point where the path levels off on the far side of the divide, it arrives at another junction. Here the trail is obvious, and is even marked by two tree-mounted signs that indicate destinations. At the junction, a short trail splits off to the left and travels about 100 yards to the shore of a small, shallow, and

Tamarack Lake.

unnamed lake. Despite not being nearly as large as any of the other lakes in the area, it is still quite pretty and worth a visit. Particularly appealing is the sense of elevation you get looking across the lake and seeing nothing but sky beyond a thin band of trees. Beyond the trees a steep slope falls away to the north.

Returning to the main trail, the route now stays very close to the north shore of Tamarack Lake. The views south across the water are superb. The tall cliffs, looming 800 feet overhead, are as impressive as they are sheer. The path finally reaches a meadow-fringed outlet of Tamarack Lake. It is a stupendously beautiful spot.

Be aware of the presence of a rough road coming down to the lake. This road is sometimes used by extremely motivated four-wheel-drive enthusiasts who make the journey to the lake to camp at the few campsites with large stone fire pits found here. A few other great sites are a few hundred yards south, right on the shore. The campsites are well shaded by trees and complemented by open grassy areas and great views of the lake. For most hikers, this is the best place to turn around.

Miles and Directions

0.0 Start by crossing Tamarack Creek on the main road, then turn left and begin hiking up the rough dirt road.

0.3 Pass some pleasant meadows alongside the trail.

1.1 The road ends at Tamarack Meadow, where there are great views of the Grey Rocks' dark towers and the gleaming, white cliffs above Tamarack Lake. The Tamarack Lake Trail begins at the far end of the meadow.

1.5 Pass the edge of Lower Twin Lake.

1.6 The trail skirts the north end of spectacular Upper Twin Lake. This is one of the finest lakes in the Trinity Divide, yet it is overshadowed by neighboring Tamarack Lake.

1.8 The path splits. To the right, it continues along the edge of Upper Twin Lake. To reach Tamarack Lake, turn left and climb through brush over a low divide. At the top of the divide, the trail can be difficult to follow. If you lose it, go due east until you reach the lake. Follow the shore to the north and you will eventually run into the trail again.

2.2 A spur trail goes left and leads to a pretty, unnamed lake.

2.5 The trail ends at the northeast end of Tamarack Lake, where there are nice campsites and a stunning view of the giant cliffs looming above the lake. Retrace your steps.

5.0 Arrive back at the trailhead.

Part VI. Castle Crags Trails

Apart from Mount Shasta, the Castle Crags are the area's most spectacular and recognizable landmark. A part of the rock cocktail that is Trinity Divide range, the Crags are a chaotic jumble of massive granite walls, spires, domes, and canyons. Towering over 3,000 feet above the Sacramento River, they are a powerfully imposing reminder that there is more to the Mount Shasta area than just a vast sea of trees crowned by a glorious volcano. The Crags also demand homage, and travelers respond gladly, rendering honor to these incredible mountains.

Yet the Castle Crags tempt hikers cruelly. As awe-inspiring as they are, they are equally impenetrable, because little trail access into the heart of their granite majesty exists. For the most part, you must be satisfied with gazing up at the cold, sheer granite from far below. Of course, this should not be a deterrent from hiking the trails in the Castle Crags. Many national parks don't have scenery this breathtaking.

The trails that do travel the lower reaches of the Castle Crags are divided between the Shasta–Trinity National Forest and Castle Crags State Park. An entrance fee is required to get into the park and no overnight camping is allowed at the trailheads. Dogs are not permitted inside the state park.

The national forest has fewer restrictions on activities, which is fortunate because it administers most of the best scenery in the Crags. Indeed, most of the Castle Crags outside the state park fall into the Castle Crags Wilderness, which enshrines and protects their wild state. Of course, this is a great example of the law only recognizing what nature itself has already accomplished: The Castle Crags are simply too impenetrable for any kind of development to take hold.

Most hikes in the Castle Crags travel through the dense forests on the lower flanks of the formation. Frequent clearings yield grand vistas of the mountains. Because the trails are on the lower slopes of the Crags, the winters are not as severe as they are on the higher mountains. This makes the Castle Crags a fantastic place to hike while the other mountains are still buried in snow.

Hiking is particularly good here in the spring, when the snows are melting. Surprisingly, water plays a prominent role along most of the trails in the Castle Crags. Numerous creek crossings and springs enliven the trails, and add a refreshing contrast to the rock towers that inevitably dominate your attention. The vertical terrain means that there are waterfalls when the water is flowing. Be sure not to overlook the east side of Castle Crags State Park, where the Sacramento River flows through. There are campgrounds and picnic areas right by the water, as well as the only opportunity in the Mount Shasta area to hike along the banks of the river. This area is frequently overlooked and lightly used.

40 Root Creek

Root Creek Falls is one of the great waterfalls of the Mount Shasta area. The cataract pours over several tall tiers cut through a narrow granite chute. Towering high overhead is the mighty spire of Castle Dome, elevating the scene to the sublime. While the falls are the highlight, most of the hike is a pleasant trip through the woods.

Total distance: 5.0 miles
Trail type: Out and back
Elevation gain: 700 feet
Difficulty: Easy
Trail surface: Packed dirt, rocky
Hiking time: 2.5 hours
Season: Year-round, but the falls flow best in the spring

Fees and permits: None
Canine compatibility: Dogs are not allowed.
Land status: Castle Crags State Park, Shasta-Trinity National Forest, Castle Crags Wilderness
Trail contact: Castle Crags State Park, 20022 Castle Creek Rd., Castella, CA 96017; (530) 235-2684; www.parks.ca.gov/?page_id=454
Other: Water is available in Root Creek.

Finding the trailhead: From I-5, take the Soda Creek exit. Go to the west side of the freeway and park at the Pacific Crest Trail (PCT) trailhead. The trailhead is only yards from the southbound freeway exit. GPS: N41° 9' 44.90" / W122° 17' 53.56"

The Hike

The Root Creek Trail has a bit of a split personality. Most of the hike is a pleasant walk through the woods. It is quiet, mild-mannered, and lacking anything particularly noteworthy. The latter part of the hike follows boisterous Root Creek to a vista with a wonderful view of Root Creek Falls and Castle Dome. The multitiered falls pour gracefully through a granite gorge. High above, Castle Dome's gray spike floats overhead, its sheer east face an imposing presence above the falls. It is a scene you would expect to see in Yosemite, or other grand places in the Sierra Nevada. For all of the magnificence of the sight, it is not well known, but deserves an iconic status. At the very least, it is an exceptional payoff for a fairly easy-going trail. The falls are best seen during the spring runoff. This is convenient because the trail is at a lower elevation and can be done when trails in the high country are still covered in snow.

There are two options to reach Root Creek. One is to begin the hike at the PCT trailhead by I-5. The second option is to begin at the Castle Dome trailhead inside Castle Crags State Park, a route that is almost 1 mile shorter and has 400 fewer feet of elevation gain. Since it is in the state park, this trailhead requires an entry fee. If you decide to make the trip from the Castle Dome Trailhead, hike 0.4 mile on the Castle Dome Trail and turn left onto the PCT. About 0.1 mile later, where the PCT splits off to the right, stay left on the Root Creek Trail.

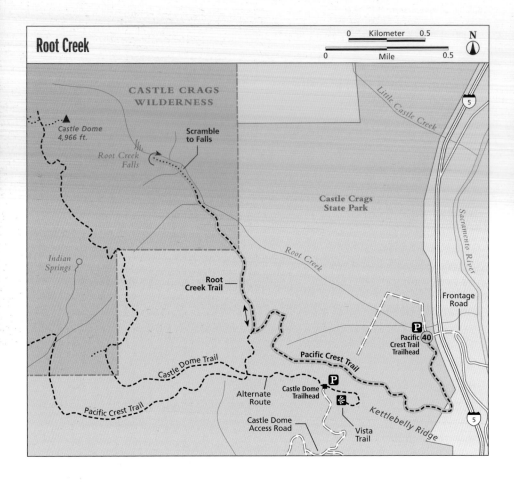

0   Kilometer   0.5

0   Mile   0.5

N

CASTLE CRAGS
WILDERNESS

Little Castle Creek

Castle Dome
4,966 ft.

Scramble
to Falls

Root Creek
Falls

Castle Crags
State Park

Indian
Springs

Root Creek

Root
Creek Trail

Frontage
Road

Sacramento River

Pacific 40
Crest Trail
Trailhead

Castle Dome Trail

Pacific Crest Trail

Castle Dome
Trailhead

P

P

Alternate
Route

Kettlebelly Ridge

Pacific Crest Trail

Castle Dome
Access Road

Vista
Trail

5

This trail description begins at the Pacific Crest Trail trailhead at the Soda Creek exit on I-5. Walk past the gate and turn left onto an old road. The trail soon enters the forest and narrows down to a normal single track. The trail initially travels south for 0.4 miles, before turning west. At the turn, note a track continuing south into the trees. Follow this for a few yards past the trees to a nice view of Mount Shasta. This is the only opportunity to see the mountain on the hike to Root Creek Falls.

Back on the main trail head west, climbing through the woods that blanket the feet of the Castle Crags. The trail maintains a steady westward orientation, climbing moderately through the forest for about 1.2 miles. While climbing, stay right at a junction with the Kettlebelly Ridge Trail. This path connects to the Castle Crags State Park's campground. Eventually the PCT makes a broad switchback just before a junction with the Root Creek Trail. Turn right onto the Root Creek Trail and continue to the north.

Once on the Root Creek Trail, the path maintains a level grade as it meanders through dense forest cover. Recent work has made this trail ADA (Americans with

Castle Dome looms above Root Creek Falls.

Disabilities Act)-compliant. It is a wide path and retains its moderate grade. Notice the narrow gullies beside sections of the trail. This was an old mining ditch that channeled water diverted from Root Creek.

After about 0.4 mile, the sound of Root Creek becomes audible. The slope to the right of the trail becomes steeper, falling away into Root Creek's increasingly narrow canyon. Another 0.3 mile finally brings the trail to the banks of Root Creek. The creek crashes over granite rocks as it heads toward its confluence with the Sacramento River. Large rusty pipes protrude from the creek and its banks. These were installed to divert water to the ditches for mining operations. The Root Creek Trail officially ends at the creek.

To see Root Creek Falls, stay on the south side of the creek. Climb above the high embankment, above the point where the trail meets the creek. From this point on, the route is a track made by people visiting Root Creek Falls. It can be difficult to find and requires some route-finding skills. The path is very faint but it parallels the creek. If you lose the trail, just maintain a cross-country course above Root Creek. As you approach the falls, the trail should become more obvious as the canyon narrows. Eventually the use trail reaches a point where the falls and Castle Dome are visible. It is a bit precarious and there is not much room, but the view is worth the effort. Indeed, it is one of the most fantastic sights in the Mount Shasta area, seemingly transporting those lucky enough to behold it to the granite majesty of Yosemite and the Sierra Nevada.

Miles and Directions

0.0 The trailhead is right off of the Soda Creek exit on I-5. Pass the gate and turn left, beginning the climb up the Pacific Crest Trail.

0.5 Stay right at a junction with the Kettlebelly Ridge Trail.

1.5 Turn right at the junction onto the Root Creek Trail.

1.9 Cross the boundary into the Castle Crags Wilderness.

2.2 The trail ends at Root Creek. Above the creek, look for a narrow, unofficial path heading upstream to the west. This is the path to the Root Creek Falls vista.

2.5 Reach a precarious overlook on the side of steep slope for a sublime view of Root Creek Falls and Castle Dome. Retrace your steps.

5.0 Arrive back at the trailhead.

41 Castle Dome

The hike up to Castle Dome is the only trail to climb into the granite wonderland of the Castle Crags. While the other trails in the Crags afford hikers great views of the splendid spires, they fail to give hands-on experience with these magnificent peaks. Much of the hike up the Castle Dome Trail follows suit, but the final third of the trip is out in the open, with incredible views of Mount Shasta and the great walls and towers of the Castle Crags. It ends at the base of Castle Dome, where there is ample room to explore a broad bench with numerous vistas and rocks to scramble on.

Total distance: 5.0 miles to Castle Dome; 6.0 miles including Vista Point Trail and Indian Springs Spur
Trail type: Out and back
Elevation gain: 2,135 feet
Difficulty: Strenuous
Trail surface: Packed dirt, rocky, rock scrambling
Hiking time: 4 hours
Season: Spring, summer, fall

Fees and permits: There is an entrance fee for the state park.
Canine compatibility: Dogs are not allowed.
Land status: Castle Crags State Park, Shasta-Trinity National Forest, Castle Crags Wilderness
Trail contact: Castle Crags State Park, 20022 Castle Creek Rd., Castella, CA 96017; (530) 235-2684; www.parks.ca.gov/?page_id=454
Other: Water is usually available at Indian Springs. The park is open from 6 a.m. to 8 p.m. There is no overnight parking at the trailhead.

Finding the trailhead: From the Castella exit on I-5 six miles south of Dunsmuir, proceed a few hundred yards west on Castle Creek Road to the entrance to the Castle Crags State Park. Turn right into the park entrance and pay the fee at the guard station. Turn right immediately beyond the guard station and continue through the campground. Just beyond the campground is a turnaround; use it if your vehicle does not have a tight steering radius. From the turnaround, it is a little over 1.0 mile up a winding, one-lane road to the trailhead. GPS: N41° 9' 34.11" / W122° 18' 21.14"

The Hike

The Castle Crags are a frustratingly awesome formation to explore. They are so rugged that no trails penetrate the spire-covered heart of the massive granite pluton. Although a few trails wind around the lower reaches of the Castle Crags, most notably the Pacific Crest Trail, all of these generally avoid the features that make the Crags the amazing spectacle they are.

The lone exception to this rule is the Castle Dome Trail (alternately referred to as the Castle Crags Trail or Crags Trail). This steep route climbs the forested slopes before finally topping out on a brushy saddle slung between Castle Dome and the high towers of the Crags' eastern face. Although most of the trail is steep and lacks

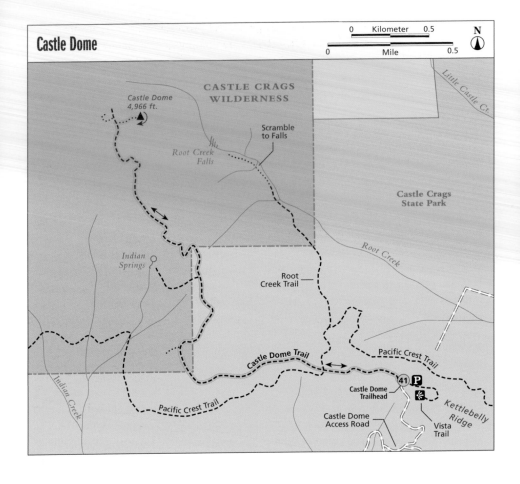

0   Kilometer   0.5

0   Mile   0.5

N

CASTLE CRAGS
WILDERNESS

Little Castle Cr.

Castle Dome
4,966 ft.

Scramble
to Falls

Root Creek
Falls

Castle Crags
State Park

Indian
Springs

Root Creek

Root
Creek Trail

Castle Dome Trail

Pacific Crest Trail

41 P

Castle Dome
Trailhead

Kettlebelly
Ridge

Indian Creek

Pacific Crest Trail

Castle Dome
Access Road

Vista
Trail

any interesting scenery, the final third of the trail is an exceptional ascent through gray pinnacles, and presents amazing views of the Grey Rocks, Castle Dome, and Mount Shasta.

When the trail finally fades out at a saddle by Castle Dome, it is not exactly in the bosom of the mighty crags, but it is as close as hikers are going to get by means of a maintained trail. Still, it is an amazing destination with great views in all directions. The great turrets of the Castle Crags soar 1,000 feet overhead, foreboding in their inaccessible grandeur. Over all of this presides lonely Mount Shasta, seen from one of its classic perspectives.

The Castle Dome Trail begins at the end of a one-lane road. The parking area has room for about twenty cars, some picnic tables, and a restroom. Before heading out on the main trail, it is a worthwhile warm-up to walk the easy 0.3 mile path to a vista point. Though this adds 0.5 mile to the overall effort, the trail is ADA-compatible and very easy. At the vista point, you'll have a great opportunity to observe the Grey Rocks, the Castle Crags, and Mount Shasta. An interpretive display informs that these three formations resulted from different geological processes, and each are formed from different types of rock. The Grey Rocks are composed of metamorphic greenstone, the Castle Crags from hardened and glaciated granite, and Mount Shasta from volcanic andesite and dacite. In addition to having a great view of the surrounding region, the vista point also affords the opportunity to survey the route up to Castle Dome. Don't worry: It is as steep as it looks.

When done enjoying the view from the vista, return to the parking lot and proceed down the paved road for about 100 yards to the beginning of the Castle Dome Trail. The trail maintains a very level, wide grade for the first 0.4 mile. This section of trail is shared with the Root Creek Trail, which is also ADA-compatible. After 0.3 mile, the Castle Dome splits off to the left of the main trail.

The easy grade of the first part of the hike is immediately forgotten, and the route now climbs in earnest. It switchbacks a few times and then straightens out. It passes through a clearing where power lines crackle overhead. The Castle Dome Trail crosses over the Pacific Crest Trail in the clearing. Climbing past the clearing, the path begins to traverse the forested slopes above the PCT, climbing toward a junction with the Bob's Hat Trail. Here the trail begins a sustained northward march through thick forest. After 0.2 mile of climbing, the trail reaches a switchback and begins heading east. Right at the switchback, a small clearing is visible about 30 yards away. From the clearing, which is used as a small, waterless campsite, you get your first chance to gaze up at the mighty Castle Crags. The countless granite spires are astounding.

Back on the trail, it turns north again a short distance from the lone switchback. It continues to climb, though not as severely as before. Tufts of grass, sporadic at first, thicken and carpet the forest floor as the trail levels off. The path traverses the south side of an open slope and has good views of the Grey Rocks and a small part of the Castle Crags. The visible portion is the south side of Six Toe Rock, one of the most popular rock climbing destinations in the Crags.

Too soon, the level section of trail comes to an end at a junction with a spur leading to Indian Spring. Though it is 0.2 mile each way on the spur trail, it is a worth the extra effort. Here are more good views of Six Toe Rock, the Grey Rocks, and Castle Creek. If you are short on water, the side trip is mandatory because Indian Spring is the only source of water on the entire trail. The small spring gushing out of the rocks has created a verdant grotto. It is a refreshingly cool place to take a rest before beginning the final, steep push up to Castle Dome.

Returning to the junction with the Castle Dome Trail, the path begins to climb once again. A sign marks the trail's departure from Castle Crags State Park and entry into the Castle Crags Wilderness, which is administered by the Shasta–Trinity National Forest. Near the wilderness sign, the trail affords its most iconic view: Castle Dome towers overhead on the left, while far to the north looms lofty Mount Shasta, the mightiest peak in Northern California.

The route soon turns away from the vista and climbs through forest canopy before finally passing through a series of granite pinnacles. Weaving around the small towers

The Castle Dome Trail has great views of the granite dome and towering Mount Shasta.

and along narrow benches beneath high granite walls, the trail has finally entered the granite portion of the Crags.

The grade gets steeper and switchbacks a few more times, gaining elevation quickly. Now Castle Dome is in constant sight, as is Mount Shasta. After passing a small, watery seep, the trail finally comes to an open point with great views. The path levels off and plunges into thick manzanita as it nears the bench at the base of Castle Dome. It winds through the brush before finally ending at a notch high above Root Creek Canyon.

Fine views of the Sacramento River Canyon, as well as the Castle Creek drainage, capped on its west end by the Gray Rocks, are to be seen here. Castle Dome rises above the saddle on the east side, and a cluster of smaller domes lines the north edge of the bench. On the other side of these domes is an 800-foot drop down into Root Creek Canyon. On the south side of the saddle is the low summit of Six Toe Rock, which is far more impressive when looking at it from below. (From the saddle, it fails to impress.) Soaring above all are the high towers of the Castle Crags, a seemingly endless maze of granite spires and pinnacles. No trails penetrate this part of the Crags, and it remains one of the most remote and inaccessible wildernesses in Northern California.

From the notch overlooking upper Root Creek Canyon, which marks the terminus of the maintained trail, a rough use trail plows through the brush across the saddle to the base of the cliffs. The dome that forms the left side of the notch at trail's end is called the Observation Deck. From the end of the trail, skirt the base of the dome to the south side. There is some brush, but hugging the rock makes the short jaunt pretty easy. There is also a use trail from farther down the Castle Dome Trail that accesses the backside of the Deck. It is an easy scramble to the top. From the top of the Observation Deck you can enjoy great views in all directions, taking in the Crags, Castle Dome, and Mount Shasta. Savor the views of this majestic land.

Miles and Directions

0.0 The hike begins at the end of the narrow, twisting road above the park's campground. It is worth the time to hike the short vista trail before setting out for Castle Dome. The overlook has a great view of the Castle Crags, Gray Rocks, and Mount Shasta.

0.2 Turn left at a fork, leaving a wide, level path and beginning to climbing steeply. At the intersection with the Pacific Crest Trail, stay straight and continue climbing.

0.7 Stay right at the junction with the Bob's Hat Trail.

1.5 Arrive at the junction with the short side trail that accesses Indian Spring. It is 0.2 mile to the left to the spring, the only water on the hike. There are great views of the Castle Creek drainage, including the awesome Gray Rocks. Stay straight to get to Castle Dome.

1.6 Enter the Castle Crags Wilderness.

2.1 The trail passes a great vista with a view of Mount Shasta and Castle Dome. Past the overlook, the trail begins to level as you hike onto the bench at the foot of Castle Dome.

2.5 The trail fades away near the large rock known as the Observation Deck. Retrace your steps.

5.0 Arrive back at the trailhead.

42 Flume Trail

Without demanding too much effort, the Flume Trail offers hikers a good introduction to the Castle Crags. Beautiful creeks, human history, lovely forests, and sweeping vistas all combine to make a satisfying outing that can be undertaken throughout most of the year.

Total distance: 5.8 miles
Trail type: Double lollipop
Elevation gain: 850 feet
Difficulty: Moderate
Trail surface: Packed dirt, rocky
Hiking time: 3 hours
Season: Year-round
Fees and permits: There is an entrance fee for the state park.

Canine compatibility: Dogs are not allowed.
Land status: Castle Crags State Park, Shasta-Trinity National Forest, Castle Crags Wilderness
Trail contact: Castle Crags State Park, 20022 Castle Creek Rd., Castella, CA 96017; (530) 235-2684; www.parks.ca.gov/?page_id=454
Other: Water is available from Indian Springs Creek. The park is open from 6 a.m. to 8 p.m. There is no overnight parking at the trailhead.

Finding the trailhead: From the Castella exit on I-5 six miles south of Dunsmuir, proceed a few hundred yards west on Castle Creek Road to the entrance to Castle Crags State Park. Turn right into the park entrance and pay the entrance fee at the guard station. Turn left immediately after the guard station and park in the large parking lot. GPS: N41° 8' 52.69" / W122° 19' 18.13"

The Hike

The Flume Trail in Castle Crags State Park is a nice way to experience a number of the park's great features without putting out too much effort. The first half of the trail is an easy, level path through beautiful forests, over a boisterous creek, and along a historic flume, from which the trail gets its name. The flume was built to supply water to the nearby town of Castella. Much of the flume is gone, but small sections of ditch and rotting timbers still remain and line the trail in places. The latter half of the hike is more demanding, as the trail climbs up onto the lower flanks of the Castle Crags to connect with the Pacific Crest Trail. The two trails combine to form a nice little loop that has great views of granite walls of the Castle Crags and sweeping vistas overlooking Castle Creek, where the dark peaks of the Grey Rocks gaze down ominously on their domain. While it lacks the close exposure to the granite of the Crags themselves, the diversity of the Flume Trail makes it a good option for a well-rounded experience in one of the Mount Shasta area's premier landmarks.

To reach the Flume Trail, it is first necessary to hike on the Indian Creek Nature Trail. Find the beginning of the trail at the north end of the parking lot. The trail immediately drops down into the woods and arrives at a junction after only 0.1 mile.

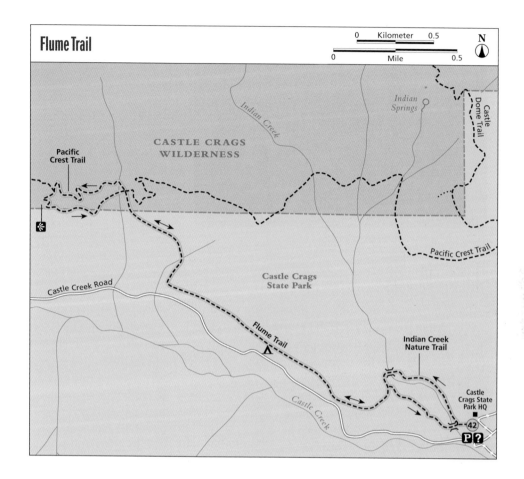

CASTLE CRAGS
WILDERNESS

Pacific
Crest Trail

Indian
Springs

Castle
Dome
Trail

Castle Creek Road

Castle Crags
State Park

Flume Trail

Indian Creek
Nature Trail

Castle
Crags State
Park HQ

Castle Creek

Pacific Crest Trail

The Indian Creek Trail is a 1-mile loop. The Flume Trail begins at the far end of the loop, which makes returning on the second half of the loop a good option.

Stay to the right and continue hiking through the woods. As you approach the end of the loop, cross Indian Creek over a beautiful, rustic bridge. The creek originates from productive Indian Springs, 1,400 feet higher up the flanks of the Crags. Even when other creeks have dried up, the spring keeps Indian Creek flowing strong throughout the year. The spring can be visited on the Castle Dome Trail (Hike 41). Just past the bridge, the trail arrives at a fork, 0.6 mile from the trailhead. Turn right and begin hiking on the Flume Trail.

Once on the Flume Trail, the path descends gradually through thick forest and crosses over a small, seasonal stream on a rickety bridge. This is followed quickly by a short, rocky causeway. Begin looking for wooden planks on the left side of the trail. These are remnants of the old flume. The middle section of the hike follows the original path of the flume. The water flowed through chutes constructed from the wood planks or through ditches. The remains of the water-transporting system are evident for nearly a mile.

Indian Creek races beneath the second bridge.

After following the flume for 0.7 mile, the trail passes a small environmental campground. Outhouses, tables, and other amenities are visible from the trail, and a short spur drops down to the campground. If you are satisfied with the easy stroll to this point, the campground makes a good place to turn around and head back to the trailhead. If you want to climb high enough to enjoy views of the Crags and Castle Creek canyon, continue hiking to the west on the trail.

About 0.3 mile past the campground, the path makes a sharp turn to the north and begins to climb steeply. It soon turns back to the west and passes through a large, lovely oak forest. At the far end of the oak woods, the trail arrives at the junction that begins the loop into the Crags, 2.4 miles from the beginning of the hike. Turn right to start the loop.

Near the junction is small Dump Creek. Pass the creek though a pair of switchbacks that soon lead you away from the water. Join the Pacific Crest Trail (PCT) at the top of the switchbacks, and turn left. The PCT quickly crosses over the creek and begins to climb out of the small drainage. Nearly 0.3 mile from the creek, the PCT climbs up out of a small gully and makes a tight, hairpin turn. Look to the north for a fantastic view of the imposing granite cliffs of the Castle Crags. These peaks seem like misplaced towers of the Sierra Nevada. Another 0.2 mile brings you to another junction. Turn left to return to the Flume Trail. The path climbs to the top of a knoll, where a short, easy scramble over small rocks leads to an awesome overlook above Castle Creek. The creek can be seen and heard crashing through the canyon 700 feet below. To the east, wooded Girard Ridge rises above the canyon of the Sacramento River. To the west, the

The first bridge over Indian Creek.

mysterious Grey Rocks stand guard over the region.

From the overlook the trail begins to descend, making several switchbacks down a remote, rarely traveled hillside. The trail crosses Dump Creek and arrives at the junction at the beginning of the loop 0.6 mile after leaving the overlook.

From the junction, hike back along the Flume Trail for 1.8 mile to the junction with the Indian Creek

Remnants of the old flume.

Nature Trail. This time, turn right and hike the second half of the little loop. The path travels through the woods, but offers a brief open spot that has a nice view of the Castle Crags. It then descends to Indian Creek and crosses an unusual but very scenic bridge. This spot on Indian Creek is one of the prettiest on the entire hike and makes a good place to sit and put your feet in the water. Beyond the creek it is only 0.1 mile back to the trailhead.

Miles and Directions

0.0 To reach the Flume Trail, begin the hike on the Indian Creek Nature Trail.

0.6 After crossing over Indian Creek, turn right onto the Flume Trail.

1.4 Pass the small environmental campground.

2.4 Begin the loop at the end of the hike. Turn right and climb up two switchbacks, then turn left onto the Pacific Crest Trail.

2.8 There is a fantastic view of the Castle Crags where the trail makes a hairpin turn.

2.9 Turn left back onto the Flume Trail.

3.0 Scramble off the trail a few yards for an incredible overlook above Castle Creek.

3.6 Stay right to complete the loop and continue hiking back toward the trailhead on the Flume Trail.

5.4 Stay right at the junction to hike the second half of the Indian Creek Nature Trail.

5.8 Arrive back at the trailhead.

43 Burstarse Falls

The Castle Crags are one of the most spectacular features in Northern California, but few trails penetrate into the jumbled, awesome heart of the formation. This hike along the Pacific Crest Trail may not explore the interior of the Crags, but it does offer a glimpse of what the journey might look like. The highlight is beautiful Burstarse Falls, hidden at the end of a narrow, beautiful, and waterfall–filled canyon.

Total distance: 5.0 miles
Trail type: Out and back
Elevation gain: 1,060 feet
Difficulty: Moderate
Trail surface: Packed dirt, rocky, rock scrambling
Hiking time: 3 hours
Season: Spring, summer, fall

Fees and permits: None
Canine compatibility: Dogs are permitted.
Land Status: Shasta-Trinity National Forest
Trail contact: Mount Shasta Ranger District, 204 W. Alma St., Mount Shasta, CA 96067; (530) 926-4511; www.fs.usda.gov/stnf
Other: Water is usually available at Popcorn Spring and in Burstarse Creek.

Finding the trailhead: From I-5, take the Castella exit. Head west on Castle Creek Road for 3.3 miles. Turn right into the clearing that serves as a parking area. A Pacific Crest Trail (PCT) sign marks the parking area. GPS: N41° 9' 42.95" / W122° 22' 10.64"

The Hike

The Pacific Crest Trail courses 37 miles through the Trinity Divide, one of the Klamath Mountain's scenic ranges. The first part of the Trinity Divide that PCT hikers encounter is the fantastic Castle Crags, the massive jumble of granite spires and domes. Beginning at the Sacramento River, the PCT climbs along the southern flank of the Crags. While the section of the PCT through the Trinity Divide passes beautiful lakes, meadows, and rugged peaks, it is only on the lower flanks of the Crags that the PCT encounters one of the divide's waterfalls.

Burstarse Falls is an attractive 50-foot plunge followed by a series of smaller cataracts that include a second waterfall about 25 feet in height. This series of waterfalls is easily accessed via a pleasant hike on the PCT. Once at the mouth of Burstarse Creek's canyon, you must climb through the narrow, beautiful gorge to get to the base of the falls. One of the route's great features is that the trail is a great early-season hike. The falls are located on the Crags' south-facing side, which means the snow tends to melt off quickly, and the trail is open for much of the year. The hike to the falls is an excellent opportunity to enjoy a wild and scenic place while most of the mountains are still covered in snow.

The route to Burstarse Falls begins at the Dog Trailhead, just off of Castle Creek Road. The trailhead is marked with a small sign for the PCT. The east half of the

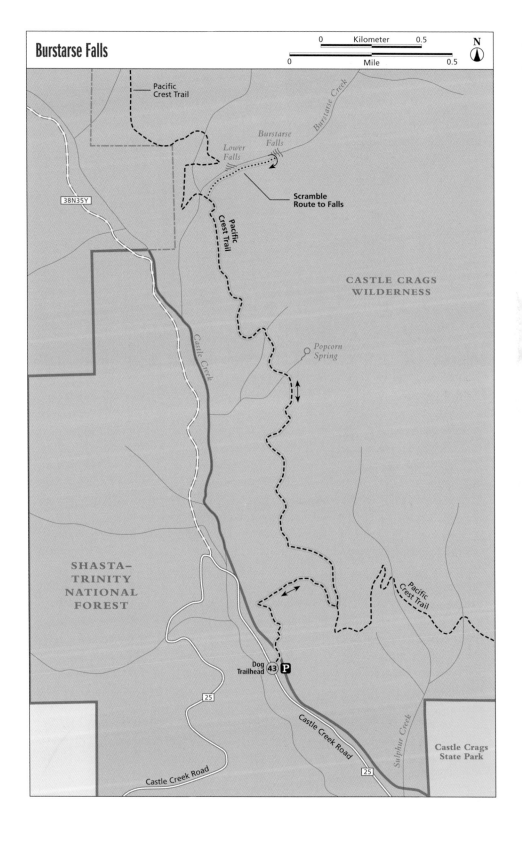

Burstarse Falls

Kilometer
0 0.5

Mile
0 0.5

N

Pacific
Crest Trail

Burstarse Creek

Burstarse
Falls

Lower
Falls

Scramble
Route to Falls

38N35Y

Pacific
Crest Trail

CASTLE CRAGS
WILDERNESS

Castle Creek

Popcorn
Spring

Pacific
Crest Trail

SHASTA–
TRINITY
NATIONAL
FOREST

Dog
Trailhead 43 P

25

Castle Creek Road

Sulphur Creek

Castle Crags
State Park

Castle Creek Road

Castle Creek Road

25

Burstarse Falls.

parking area is often used as a firing range, so be sure to park on the west side if possible. The Dog Trail connects with the PCT after 0.5 mile of fairly steep climbing. The trail is so named because people hiking the Pacific Crest Trail in the company of dogs use it. To the east of the Dog Trail junction, the PCT passes through Castle Crags State Park, which does not allow dogs. The Dog Trail thus provides a bypass through the park. Unfortunately it also bypasses a lot of great scenery.

Although the Dog Trail climbs at a moderately steep grade (nearly 600 feet in 0.5 mile), this is the steepest part of the trip to Burstarse Falls. Though significantly eroded, in some places it is possible to see that the trail was once an old road. Look for the collapsed timbers of an old mine just before the trail meets the PCT. When the trail intersects the PCT, turn left and begin hiking west on the Pacific Crest Trail.

Continuing west on the PCT, the trail maintains an easy grade for about 1.7 miles. Though the trail is climbing, it does so very gently, making the elevation gain almost imperceptible. Views of the granite spires and domes of the Castle Crags, as well as distant glimpses of the Gray Rocks, grace the trail when it occasionally passes through clear areas. The Gray Rocks are an awesome cluster of dark towers at the southern end of the Castle Creek watershed. These mysterious peaks are composed of greenstone, an unusual stone in the largely granitic and ultramafic Trinity Divide.

The trail passes over a few seasonal creeks, which will likely be dry after the early summer. The only reliable water is at Popcorn Spring, about 0.9 mile beyond where the Dog Trail meets the PCT. After repeatedly scalloping through a seemingly endless series of small drainages, the trail finally arrives at Burstarse Creek. The trail swings around a low shoulder and then descends into the creek's gulch.

Although a wooden sign hanging on a tree identifies the creek, two landmarks also indicate arrival at Burstarse Creek. The first indicator is the confluence of another, smaller stream where the trail crosses the water. Later in the season this stream may be dry, but the channel is still obvious. The second indicator is an interesting chute just below the trail, where the creek races over the smooth granite.

Immediately upstream from where the PCT meets Burstarse Creek is a 10-foot tiered cascade, which only presages bigger things to come. From the PCT, a faint use trail branches off to the right and parallels the east side of the creek. Above the first cascade, the creek courses through a series of granite channels and troughs. This area is very reminiscent of creeks in the Sierra Nevada.

Beyond the channels is the first big waterfall. About 25 feet high, it is sometimes referred to as Lower Burstarse Falls. Many stop here, thinking that this is, in fact, Burstarse Falls. The trail grows harder to follow at this point because it passes under some low-hanging trees and through brush.

Staying on the east side of the creek, climb above the lower falls and continue up the increasingly narrow canyon. Watch for some rare yew trees above the lower falls. These trees have firlike needles, and the bark tends to flake off like that of a madrone tree.

The east side of the canyon becomes too steep to pass above the lower falls, so cross over the creek and continue up the west side of the canyon. Soon it will be possible to cross back over to the east side. At this point, Burstarse Falls finally comes into view. The falls rocket off the cliff and free fall about 50 feet onto a pile of rocks below. A series of cascades below the falls adds to the beauty of the scene. There is a nice area to sit down and relax while enjoying the spectacle of the falls.

Miles and Directions

0.0 Start on the Dog Trail. Begin hiking uphill from the large parking area.

0.5 Turn left onto the Pacific Crest Trail. Follow the PCT for 1.7 miles.

2.3 The trail descends to Burstarse Creek. Follow the east side of the creek upstream to reach the lower falls. A narrow footpath winds up the steep-walled gorge.

2.5 The footpath ends near the base of awesome Burstarse Falls. Retrace your steps.

5.0 Arrive back at the trailhead.

44 Lower Castle Crags Traverse

Leaving the Sacramento River, the Pacific Crest Trail (PCT) makes a long ascent to the crest of the Trinity Divide, the mountain range immediately to the west of Mount Shasta. The first part of the ascent follows the lower flanks of the mighty towers of the Castle Crags. This shuttle hike climbs up to the PCT and then follows it down to the Soda Springs trailhead near I-5 and the Sacramento River. Along the way, it crosses many remote creeks and has fantastic views of the Crags' awesome towers.

Total distance: 6.8 miles
Trail type: Shuttle
Elevation gain: 1,575 feet
Difficulty: Moderate
Trail surface: Packed dirt, rocky
Hiking time: 4 hours
Season: Spring, summer, fall
Fees and permits: None
Canine compatibility: Dogs are not allowed.

Land status: Shasta-Trinity National Forest, Castle Crags Wilderness, Castle Crags State Park
Trail contact: Mount Shasta Ranger District, 204 W. Alma St., Mount Shasta, CA 96067; (530) 926-4511; www.fs.usda.gov/stnf
Other: Water is usually available at several creek crossings.

Finding the trailhead: To reach the Dog Trailhead from I-5 south of Dunsmuir, take the Castella exit. Head west on Castle Creek Road for 3.3 miles. Turn right into the clearing that serves as a parking area. A PCT sign marks the parking area. GPS: N41° 9' 42.95" / W122° 22' 10.64"

To reach the Soda Creek trailhead from I-5 south of Dunsmuir, take the Soda Creek exit. Go to the west side of the freeway and park at the Pacific Crest Trailhead. The trailhead is only yards from the southbound freeway exit. GPS: N41° 9'44.90" / W122° 17' 53.56"

The Hike

Next to Mount Shasta, the Castle Crags are the most recognizable landmark in the region. The longest stretch of trail in the Crags is the Pacific Crest Trail, which winds across the formation's southern flank. A few trails connect to the PCT, creating some options for exploration. The best way to connect to the PCT is to climb the Dog Trail, and then hike east to the PCT trailhead at Soda Creek. Along the way are opportunities to observe the towering granite walls and turrets.

Views of the Crags are not the only highlight on this trip. The hike includes excellent vistas of the Castle Creek drainage and the mysterious Grey Rocks. This part of the PCT also boasts six major creek crossings. In the spring, when the water flows strong, these are attractive, refreshing sights. Spring is also the best time to hike this section of trail because temperatures are cooler, and the higher trails are typically still smothered in snow. It should be noted that the best way to hike this trail is to utilize a shuttle. Park one vehicle at the PCT trailhead at the Soda Creek exit on I-5, then drive to the trailhead for the Dog Trail and begin the trip.

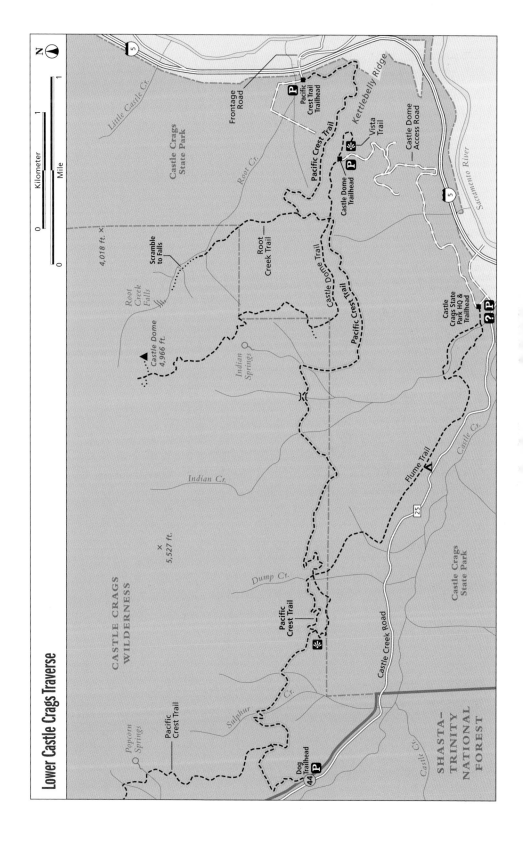

Lower Castle Crags Traverse

N

0 Kilometer 1

0 Mile 1

Little Castle Cr.

Castle Crags State Park

Frontage Road

5

P Pacific Crest Trail Trailhead

Pacific Crest Trail

Kettlebelly Ridge

Root Cr.

Castle Dome Trailhead P

Vista Trail

Castle Dome Access Road

5

Sacramento River

4,018 ft. ×

Scramble to Falls

Root Creek Trail

Castle Dome Trail

Root Creek Falls

Pacific Crest Trail

Castle Dome 4,966 ft. ▲

Indian Springs

Castle Crags State Park HQ & Trailhead

? P

Indian Cr.

× 5,527 ft.

CASTLE CRAGS WILDERNESS

Flume Trail

25

Dump Cr.

Castle Cr.

Pacific Crest Trail

Castle Creek Road

Castle Crags State Park

Sulphur Cr.

Popicorn Springs

Pacific Crest Trail

SHASTA–TRINITY NATIONAL FOREST

Castle Cr.

Dog Trailhead P

44

The Dog Trailhead is located at an old quarry. The east half of the parking clearing is often used as a firing range, so be sure to park on the west side if possible. The Dog Trail connects to the PCT in 0.5 mile; it is so named because people hiking the Pacific Crest Trail in the company of dogs use it. To the east of the Dog Trail, the PCT passes through Castle Crags State Park, which does not allow dogs. The Dog Trail thus provides a bypass through the park. Unfortunately it also bypasses a lot of great scenery.

Although the Dog Trail climbs at a moderately steep grade—nearly 600 feet in 0.5 mile—this is the steepest part of the entire journey. Initially open and climbing an old road, the trail eventually swings to the east as it passes beneath the forest canopy. Watch for a pile of rough-hewn timbers just above the trail, the remains of an old mine. The original road that the Dog Trail now follows was constructed to access this mine.

Where the trail intersects the PCT, head right (east). Immediately after the junction the trail rounds a corner and reveals a spectacular view of Battle Mountain, one of the largest towers in the Castle Crags. The trail then reenters the forest canopy and makes a descent to Sulphur Creek.

Though the creek is quite scenic, it lacks much of the sulfuric odor for which it is named. However, the smell is quite evident from Castle Creek Road, farther downstream. As the trail makes a gradual ascent it crosses the east fork of Sulphur Creek. This is also a very scenic stream. Near the top of the long grade the PCT arrives at a junction with the Flume Trail. This trail (Hike 42) begins at Castle Crags State Park. Continue hiking a little farther down the PCT to where the trail begins to descend into another drainage, blessing hikers with yet another incredible view of sheer face of Battle Mountain. The path soon arrives at small Dump Creek. Despite its small size, the creek has numerous scenic cascades and clear pools.

Just beyond Dump Creek, the PCT crosses the Flume Trail a second time. There is a nice little loop at the end of the Flume Trail, and the second junction with the trail marks the route that leads back down to the main trail. Stay left at the junction and continue east on the PCT. The trail soon emerges from the forest cover, revealing great views to the west. Castle Creek, the largest early tributary of the Sacramento River, flows through a wide valley nearly 400 feet below the trail. Towering high above the landscape are the dark towers of the Grey Rocks. These seldom-climbed peaks harbor spectacular, isolated canyons and tiny but gorgeous lakes. Few venture into that mountain stronghold.

Proceeding east on the PCT, the trail rounds a small shoulder and crosses the boundary into Castle Crags State Park for the first time. Here, round the corner and make a steep climb, leaving the forest canopy once again. The views are even better as the trail crosses open granite for the first time, and skirts the top of an impressive cliff. Far below the Castle Creek valley unfolds, this time topped not only by the Grey Rocks but also Soapstone Peak, the high point of the Castle Crags Wilderness (though not the Crags themselves) and the Crags' own Battle Mountain. It is a

The granite glory of the Castle Crags.

Six Toe Rock, another popular rock climbing destination. This marks the final creek crossing of the hike.

Proceeding past the crossing, the PCT arrives at the first of many junctions that dot the last leg of the trip. The first intersection is with the Bob's Farm Trail, which descends to state park headquarters. Stay on the PCT, following the well-marked signs. The trail reaches at a second junction, this time with the Castle Dome Trail beneath a large power line. Again, follow the signs to stay on the PCT. A third intersection joins the PCT to the Root Creek Trail. Stay right at the junction, on the PCT. The PCT begins the last leg down to the interstate. It crosses beneath the power line again, and then passes a final trail junction, this time with the Kettlebelly Ridge Trail, which leads to the state park's campground.

As the sound of the freeway becomes audible, the trail makes one last, sharp switchback to the left. At this point look for a use trail cutting through the brush to the right. This path enters an old clear-cut where hikers get the only view of Mount Shasta from this low section of the PCT. Back on the main trail, the journey ends after walking a short distance on a decaying asphalt road, and then passing through a hiker's gate at the Soda Creek trailhead.

Miles and Directions

0.0   Start on the Dog Trail, climbing from a large parking area up to the Pacific Crest Trail.

0.5   Turn right onto the Pacific Crest Trail. As you round a corner on the PCT, an awesome view of the Castle Crags opens.

1.1   The PCT crosses Sulphur Creek, followed by the east fork of Sulphur Creek 0.3 mile later.

1.8   Stay left at the junction with the Flume Trail.

2.1   Stay left at the second junction with the Flume Trail, and then cross over small Dump Creek.

2.8   The trail traverses an open granite ledge with great views of the Castle Creek drainage and the Grey Rocks.

3.3   The PCT crosses the west fork of Indian Creek.

3.8   The PCT crosses a creek for the final time at the east fork of Indian Creek.

4.4   Continue straight through the junction with the Bob's Hat Trail.

4.9   The PCT intersects the Castle Dome Trail in a clearing beneath a power line. Stay straight as the trail descends. A little farther, the PCT is joined by the Root Creek Trail.

5.2   At a fork where the PCT and Root Creek Trails separate, turn right and continue on the PCT.

6.3   Continue to the left at the junction with the Kettlebelly Ridge Trail.

6.8   The PCT arrives at the Soda Creek trailhead near I-5.

45 Sacramento River

The Sacramento River, California's longest and largest, begins in the Trinity Divide just west of Mount Shasta. Below Lake Siskiyou and the Box Canyon of the Sacramento, there are very few places to hike along the river. The longest section of trail on the upper Sacramento River is the Sacramento River Trail in Castle Crags State Park. This easy hike offers great views of the wild, raucous river, beautiful flora, and some interesting geology.

Total distance: 2.6 miles
Trail type: Out and back
Elevation gain: 30 feet
Difficulty: Easy
Trail surface: Packed dirt
Hiking time: 1.5 hours
Season: Year-round
Fees and permits: None

Canine compatibility: Dogs are not allowed.
Land status: Castle Crags State Park
Trail contact: Castle Crags State Park, 20022 Castle Creek Rd., Castella, CA 96017; (530) 235-2684; www.parks.ca.gov/?page_id=454
Other: Water is plentiful in the Sacramento River.

Finding the trailhead: From I-5 south of Dunsmuir, take the Castella exit. Head east toward the river. Turn left onto Frontage Road. Proceed 0.6 mile to a wide pullout beside the road. Find a small sign marking the beginning of the trail. It is also possible to park at Castle Crags State Park and follow a path that passes through a tunnel beneath the freeway. GPS: N41° 9' 3.65" / W122° 18' 21.33"

The Hike

The upper Sacramento River begins high in the Trinity Divide, west of magnificent Mount Shasta. The river is impounded to form Lake Siskiyou shortly after the three headwaters forks—the South, Middle, and North Forks—converge. More than 30 miles downstream from the lake, the river's energy is again stilled at massive Shasta Lake. Between these two reservoirs, the Sacramento is a boisterous, wild waterway. It flows through rocky gorges and over rapids. While the river is understandably popular with rafters and kayakers, it is less of a draw with hikers, primarily because of the lack of developed trails.

The best opportunity to experience the interlake section of the river is along Castle Crags State Park's Sacramento River Trail. This trail has somehow managed to stay off the radar, and is used primarily by local residents. Despite its near anonymity, the trail is a very scenic hike. It is never out of sight or sound of the Sacramento. Numerous opportunities exist to climb down to the river and observe its glorious whitewater, interesting bedrock, and a few small, rocky beaches.

The Sacramento River Trail begins inconspicuously at a large pullout on the side of Frontage Road at the north end of Castella. Just up the road a tunnel passes under I-5 connecting the trailhead to the Castle Crags State Park. The River Trail itself

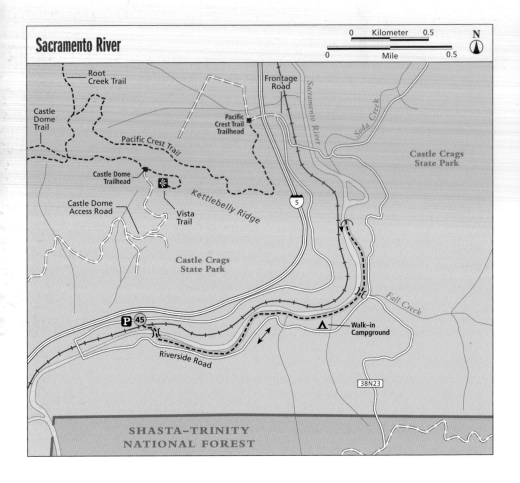

immediately dives into the forest, passing through oak, ponderosa pine, and cedar. It drops down some short rock-stepped switchbacks and passes through a small, narrow tunnel beneath the railroad tracks. Beyond the train tracks, the trail reenters the woods briefly before encountering the Sacramento River.

To allow access to the far side of the river, a swinging suspension bridge has been constructed. It is a unique and exciting way to cross the large river. From the bridge are good views up- and downstream. On the far side is an attractive picnic area with tables overlooking the water. The picnic area is accessible via a road that parallels the trail for the duration of the hike. Fortunately, the road is situated well away from the trail and is lightly traveled, meaning that it barely intrudes on the natural setting.

Pick up the trail just left of the bridge. Heading upstream to the east, the path is nearly level, with only gradual ups and downs. The Sacramento is about 40 feet below the trail at this point, and fairly wide. Thick wooden planks periodically cross small, spring-fed streams. Through the trees are glimpses of the Castle Crags high above the river. The Grey Rocks also make brief appearances.

The Sacramento River Trail crosses over Fall Creek.

The river maintains a wide course along this section of the trail, which is heavily forested. Among the numerous species of trees are yew and Port Orford cedars, two rare types. Yews have needles similar to fir trees and red, peeling bark similar to that found on a madrone. Port Orford cedars, which are actually cypress trees, are endemic to the Klamath Mountains in northern California and southern Oregon.

About 0.7 mile from the bridge, the trail crosses a small footbridge over a large, unnamed creek. A noticeable side trail heads away from the river to the road. Stay left on the main trail.

Shortly after crossing the creek, the Sacramento River Trail descends to river level. Here the Sacramento narrows considerably as it roars through a gorge cut into the exposed bedrock. This marks a distinct change in the river's personality. Up to this point it has been wide and swift-moving, with few significant rapids. Now, amid exposed bedrock, the Sacramento consists of a long series of whitewater cataracts and rapids. Many nice pools in bedrock coves make great swimming holes. Ironically, as the trail proceeds along the narrowing river, the valley widens. Here are some very pleasant walk-in campsites operated by Castle Crags State Park. The sites have bear boxes, picnic tables, and fire pits, as well as vault toilets. The campsites are adjacent to the river and very lightly used.

Beyond the campsites the river valley narrows again, though the trail stays at or near the river's level. Here are more rapids and exposed bedrock. Soon the path reaches another bridge over a tributary of Sacramento River. This is Fall Creek, which begins high up on Girard Ridge to the east. The Pacific Crest Trail crosses the headwaters of the creek. The confluence of the Sacramento River with Fall Creek is possibly the prettiest spot on the entire hike. A massive, fallen ponderosa lines the side of the creek, diverting the waters toward a final series of cataracts as it falls into the river. The bridge is supported by a huge fallen tree and a stone pier. On the far side of the creek, a small grassy area is beside the trail. Below is a large, bedrock beach. It is an attractive area with scenic places to sit and enjoy the creek and the river.

Past Fall Creek, the trail presses on for another 0.3 mile. The Sacramento widens a bit and goes over a few wide, low rapids. Near the end of the trail, large chunks of columnar basalt poke out of the sediment beside the trail. Finally, the trail enters another wide area along the river and turns, for the first time, directly toward the river. The path fades out at a fallen tree, beyond which is a rocky area next to the river itself.

Continuing onto the rocky area reveals a large, stone retaining wall across the river, evidence of a bridge that once crossed the Sacramento here. This marks the end of the trail, but one more point of interest that beckons. Backtracking on the trail a few yards reveals increasingly faint use trails that climb up to a bench perched beneath a long wall of columnar basalt. The basalt blocks are about 20 feet high. A couple of fallen trees have made travel a bit more difficult along the wall, but the flowers, lichen, seeps, and vines all add interest to the basalt. Once the area has been explored, return to the trailhead on the Sacramento River Trail.

Miles and Directions

0.0 Start at the pullout parking area. From the trailhead, the path descends stone-steped switchbacks and passes through a tunnel beneath the railroad tracks.

0.1 Cross over the Sacramento River on a large suspension bridge. Turn left at the far end of the bridge and continue hiking on the River Trail.

0.9 Pass the primitive campsites to the right of the trail. With bathrooms, tables, fire pits, bear boxes, and great access to the river, this is a wonderful place to camp.

1.1 The River Trail crosses over Fall Creek on an unusual but very pretty bridge. Across the creek, the rocky area by the river is one of the prettiest spots on the trail.

1.3 The trail ends next to the river with a view of a huge retaining wall, evidence that a bridge once crossed the water here. Retrace your steps.

2.6 Arrive back at the trailhead.

Part VII. McCloud River Trails

The McCloud River is one of Northern California's most scenic and famous waterways. The river's renown is built on its fantastic waterfalls and excellent fishing. Both deserve their reputations, but there is more river to be investigated. While it may follow a single course, the McCloud is really two very different rivers. It might not be apparent to the casual observer, but the McCloud River, more than any landmark around Mount Shasta, unites the two great mountain regions of the Cascade Range and the Klamath Mountains.

The upper McCloud flows across the gentle McCloud Flats. Its journey is highlighted by extensive volcanic features, including ancient lava flows and thick layers of basalt. The great drama of this part of the river comes when the water meets the dense basalt and, failing to wear it away, pours over it instead.

Below the falls the river is impounded at the Lake McCloud reservoir. Downstream from the dam, the lower McCloud enters a deep, wild canyon. The powerful river races through the canyon, hurtling over rocky rapids until it disappears into lonely recesses where only rough private roads reach. The contrast between the two areas is striking. The McCloud River has made an unheralded crossing from the volcanic Cascade Range into the dizzyingly complex Klamath Mountains zone. The fire-forged basalt has given way to marine sediment.

The trails that explore the McCloud River are divided between the two zones. The hikes on the upper McCloud highlight the swift but gentle river and the awesome evidence of past volcanic activity that shaped it. Hiking on the lower McCloud is to experience deep seclusion, as you hike through lost canyons that are seemingly cut off from the outside world. Whichever trail you hike, the beauty of crystalline water will be your constant companion.

46 McCloud Falls

The McCloud River's trio of waterfalls are among the most spectacular landmarks in the Mount Shasta area. They are certainly the finest collection of waterfalls around the mountain. The section of the McCloud River Trail that connects the Lower, Middle, and Upper Falls is one the most popular in the region, with good reason. Traveling through a beautiful canyon rife with volcanic features, the easy, level trail links the three waterfalls with minimal elevation gain. With opportunities to get exhilaratingly close to the large cataracts, this trail has major payoff for very little effort.

Total distance: 4.0 miles (farther if desired)
Trail type: Out and back
Elevation gain: 300 feet
Difficulty: Easy to moderate
Trail surface: Paved, packed dirt
Hiking time: 2 hours
Season: Spring, summer, fall

Fees and permits: None
Canine compatibility: Dogs are permitted.
Land status: Shasta-Trinity National Forest
Trail contact: McCloud Ranger Station, 2019 Forest Rd., McCloud, CA 96057; (530) 964-2184; www.fs.usda.gov/stnf
Other: Water is available in the McCloud River.

Finding the trailhead: From the main intersection in the town of McCloud, drive east on CA 89 for 5.5 miles. Turn right on the signed road for the McCloud River Loop. Continue for 0.7 mile. Stay right at the first intersection (turning left leads to Middle and Upper Falls). Pass the Fowlers Camp campground and turn left into the signed parking lot for the Lower Falls picnic area. GPS: N41° 14' 24.92" / W122° 1' 30.29"

The Hike

Without doubt, the three waterfalls on the McCloud River are among the premier attractions around Mount Shasta. Few trails deliver such awesome scenery for such minimal effort. The trail is almost entirely level. Only one climb, eased by some gently graded switchbacks and a set of stairs, must be surmounted to complete the short hike. Yet, for this little contribution in sweat, hikers are treated to nearly constant views of the gorgeous McCloud River as it flows through a striking volcanic canyon or thunderous over sheer cliffs and explodes into clouds of spray.

Each waterfall has a distinct character, which only heightens the excitement of discovering the cataracts as you round the corner and they come into view. Of course, such awesome beauty requiring so little effort has not gone unnoticed, and the trail is among the most popular around Mount Shasta. Do not let the traffic on the trail dissuade you from enjoying the spectacle of awesome spectacle. The scene is too awesome to be avoided.

The trip to the McCloud Falls is actually a segment of the larger McCloud River Trail (Hike 47), which extends beyond the beginning and end of the waterfall hike.

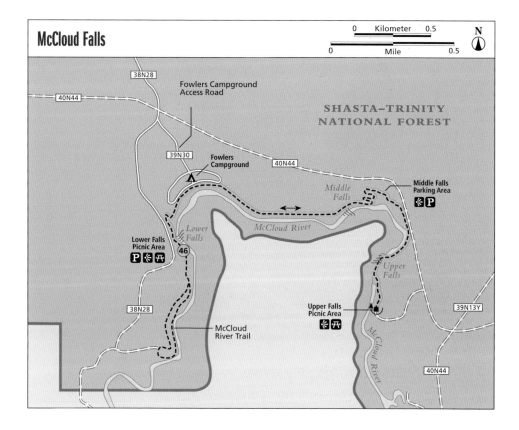

McCloud Falls

0   Kilometer   0.5

0   Mile   0.5

N

38N28

40N44

Fowlers Campground
Access Road

**SHASTA–TRINITY
NATIONAL FOREST**

39N30

Fowlers
Campground

40N44

*Middle
Falls*

Middle Falls
Parking Area

McCloud River

*Lower
Falls*

Lower Falls
Picnic Area

46

*Upper
Falls*

38N28

Upper Falls
Picnic Area

39N13Y

McCloud
River Trail

McCloud River

40N44

Numerous trailheads service the trail over its entire 15 miles. The hike to the falls can
be extended in either direction by continuing on the McCloud River Trail.

The most commonly used trailhead for the hike to the falls is the picnic area
at Lower Falls. The River Trail continues 0.6 mile south of the picnic area to the
Pine Tree Hollow boat launch area, the western terminus of the River Trail and a
very scenic little hike on its own. The river travels through a rocky gorge lined with
columnar basalt.

To start the hike at the typical trailhead, park in the large parking area for the
Lower Falls picnic area. Walk through the tables toward the overlook above the Lower
Falls of the McCloud River. The fall is formed where the river pours 15 feet over a
large basalt block into a deep pool. Native Americans noted that this was the place
where spawning fish stopped traveling upstream. Prior to the falls, fish spawning up
the river would have encountered a few rapids but had a fairly straightforward passage. It is unlikely that a fish could leap up the falls.

The trail departs the overlook to the left and climbs down an attractively built set
of stone stairs; a little farther away is a ramp. The section of the trail between Lower
Falls and Fowlers Camp is ADA-compatible. Consequently it is paved and very level.
Above Lower Falls, the basalt continues along the banks of the river, creating a broad,

Middle McCloud Falls.

sunny bench to relax on while the river roars by. After lingering a bit, the trail veers briefly away from the river, climbs some very slight switchbacks and then nears the river again. The path is now on the outskirts of the Fowlers Camp campground. Below the level area where the camp sits, the river roars through a rocky gorge. Still paved, the trail follows a railing along the rim of the canyon.

After skirting the campground, the trail becomes a dirt path. It remains wide and is level. The river runs 20–50 feet to the right, now at the same level as the trail. This is because the river enters a deeper canyon once it passes the campground. However, rather than being on the canyon rim, the trail is now at its bottom. Paralleling the river under a shady forest canopy, the path encounters large boulders and rocky areas. Be sure to look for Pacific yew trees, which thrive in wetter spots in the area. The tree is identified by its firlike needles and red, peeling bark, similar to a madrone tree.

The river is almost always in view and can always be heard. This is the longest unbroken stretch of the McCloud River Trail. It is about 0.7 mile from Fowlers Camp to Middle McCloud Falls. This incredible waterfall is the unrivaled highlight of the hike. Far more impressive than either of its siblings, it is about 50 feet high and 130 feet across. The river reaches the precipice of the falls and pours over in a broad, rectangular sheet. It is audible long before it is visible, but when you approach its base the roar of Middle Falls is deafening.

The trail comes within 30 feet of the edge of the falls' pool, where the water surging over the precipice is an awesome view. From this point, the path switches back and begins to climb out of the river canyon. The grade is moderate while the trail climbs a short series of switchbacks before finally coming to a well-built wooden staircase. Go up the stairs to finish the climb out of the canyon. The staircase is necessary because the rim of the canyon is capped with a layer of hard volcanic rock unsuitable for trail construction. The lone ascent of the entire hike now done, hike along the canyon rim to a great vista above the falls. A railing along this section of trail is both for safety and to allow you to get right up to the edge for the best possible view of the falls.

From the Middle Falls overlook, the trail continues upstream, following the rim of the canyon. The path is slung precariously above the river but the railing makes the going safe while permitting the great views. In the distance to the west, the high peaks of the Castle Crags Wilderness, specifically Gray Rock Dome and Soapstone Peak, line the horizon. Mount Shasta is visible but partially obscured by trees. A short distance from the end of the railing, the trail drops a little below the rim of the canyon but remains high above the river, which tumbles through a series of enormous boulders far below. The hard basalt cap that the stairs bypassed now forms a wall on the left side of the trail. Eventually the basalt comes to an end, and Upper McCloud Falls appears in the distance through the trees.

The beginning of a second railing marks the arrival at Upper Falls. Follow this to an overlook high above the waterfall. Though not as spectacular as Middle Falls, Upper Falls is still impressive. It is the geology of the waterfall rather than its scale that makes it such an awesome sight. At the falls, the McCloud River has encountered a 70-foot wall of erosion-resistant basalt. The water has worn a long gorge through the basalt. It rockets through the narrow chute, tumbling over little cataracts into bathtub-size pools excavated out of the hard rock. It culminates in a 35-foot plunge through a large notch cut into the basalt cliff. It is an interesting sight and gives the Upper Falls a very distinct personality.

Beyond the Upper Falls overlook, the trail parallels the river through a picnic area. Most people end the hike here and turn around to head back to the trailhead at Lower Falls.

While the spectacle of the three McCloud waterfalls is left behind, those who want to hike longer and enjoy the river more can continue on the trail. Beyond the Upper Falls area, the trail stays close to the river as it winds through rocky outcroppings and dense forest. At times the trail is constructed of piles of rugged lava rock. A few more decaying picnic trails are scattered randomly along the trail, but most are falling apart. Keen observers will also notice a few concrete pylons, remnants of a pipe network that once carried water from the river to the town of McCloud. About 0.5 mile past the Upper Falls picnic area, the trail comes to the Lakin Dam, a small diversion dam that once fed water into the pipes. Another picnic area lies past the dam. This is the beginning of the bayoulike Bigelow Meadow area, and a good place to stop and turn around. Pressing on for another mile brings hikers to the Bigelow Bridge, which has some nice swimming holes. Few people hike the trail after the Upper Falls and you are likely to have this area to yourself.

Miles and Directions

0.0 Start at the Lower Falls Picnic Area. From the falls overlook, go down the stairs to the rocky bench and pick up the trail.

0.2 The trail skirts the edge of the Fowlers Camp campground.

0.5 Leave Fowlers Camp and hike alongside the McCloud River.

1.2 The trail reaches the base of awesome Middle Falls.

1.5 Look down on Middle Falls from the overlook.

1.8 Enjoy the view of powerful Upper Falls.

2.0 Relax at the Upper Falls picnic area before turning around heading back to the trailhead.

4.0 Arrive back at the trailhead.

47 McCloud River Trail

Although the section of the McCloud River Trail that links the three McCloud River waterfalls is very popular, the other 13 miles are among the most obscure trails around Mount Shasta. As it winds along the McCloud River, the trail journeys through tall forests, lush riparian zones, and along rocky gorges and beautiful meadows. Long stretches of the hike seem to be forgotten and given up to those who seek solitude. While the trail can be hiked in one long outing, especially as a shuttle, it can also be broken up into shorter hikes.

Total distance: 15.5 miles
Trail type: Out and back or shuttle
Elevation gain: Minimal
Difficulty: Easy to moderate
Trail surface: Packed dirt, rocky, paved
Hiking time: Up to 9 hours
Season: Spring, summer, fall

Fees and permits: None
Canine compatibility: Dogs are permitted.
Land status: Shasta-Trinity National Forest
Trail contact: McCloud Ranger Station, 2019 Forest Rd., McCloud, CA 96057; (530) 964-2184; www.fs.usda.gov/stnf
Other: Water is available in the McCloud River.

Finding the trailhead: The McCloud River Trail begins at the Algoma campground and ends at the Pine Tree Hollow boat launch. There is road access at a few places along the trail, and these make good trailheads for shorter hikes.

Algoma Campground: From the main intersection in the town of McCloud, drive east on CA 89 for 13.4 miles. Turn right on paved FR 39N06. Continue for 0.8 mile to a bridge over the McCloud River. Park off the road, just before the bridge, on the north side of the river. Cross the road to find the beginning of the McCloud River Trail. GPS: N41° 15' 23.88" / W121° 52' 59.02"

Nitwit Camp: From the main intersection in the town of McCloud, drive east on CA 89 for 11.4 miles. Turn right onto an unpaved dirt road. There is no signage, but the turnoff comes at a low point in CA 89. There is a large parking area near the campsites. The trail runs parallel to the river.

Cattle Camp Swimming Hole: From the main intersection in the town of McCloud, drive east on CA 89 for 10.1 miles. Turn right on the paved McCloud River Loop Road, which is the east entrance to the loop. Be sure to drive past the closer west entrance. Proceed south for 0.9 mile on the loop road and turn right at the signed turn for the Cattle Camp swimming hole. GPS: N41° 15' 2.08" / W121° 56' 39.98"

Camp 4 Group Camp: From the main intersection in the town of McCloud, drive east on CA 89 for 5.5 miles. Turn right on the signed road for the McCloud River Loop. Continue for 0.7 mile. Turn left at the stop sign and drive 2.5 miles to the intersection with the dirt road leading to Camp 4, passing the stops for Middle and Upper Falls and the unsigned road leading to the Lakin Dam en route. Turn right on the dirt road accessing Camp 4 and proceed a short distance to the camp and parking area. GPS: N41° 14' 5.32" / W121° 59' 16.25"

Lower Falls Picnic Area: From the main intersection in the town of McCloud, drive east on CA 89 for 5.5 miles. Turn right on the signed road for the McCloud River Loop. Continue for 0.7 mile. Stay right at the first intersection (turning left leads to Middle and Upper Falls). Pass the Fowlers Camp campground and turn left into the signed parking lot for the Lower Falls picnic area. GPS: N41° 14' 24.92" / W122° 1' 30.29"

McCloud River Trail

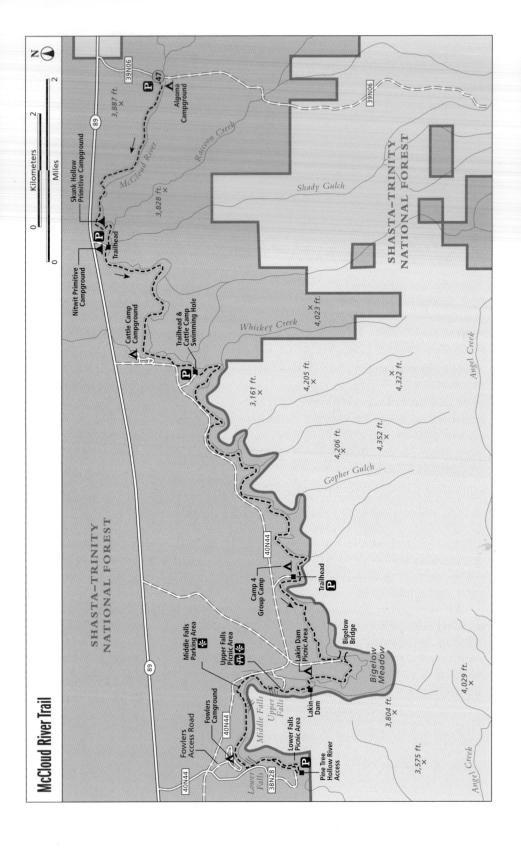

The Hike

The McCloud River is one of the great waterways of Northern California. Known for its fantastic fishing and three great waterfalls, it is a river steeped in primeval beauty. With the exception of the impoundment that forms Lake McCloud, it is a wild, free-flowing river until finally being captured by Shasta Lake. The McCloud River rises in the lowlands around the division between the Lassen and Shasta Cascade regions, to the east of Mount Shasta. It flows west, passing through the McCloud Flats before finally pouring into the McCloud River Canyon, which contains the river until it concludes its journey to Shasta Lake.

Over the course of the river's 77 miles, most hikers intent on exploring do so by hiking through the McCloud River Preserve (Hike 50) and to the McCloud River Falls (Hike 46). However, this is by no means the extent of the trails that explore the river. The McCloud River Trail follows the awesome river for 15 miles. Most hikers are unaware that the path that links the falls is in fact a short section of the longer McCloud River Trail. Other than the segment passing the falls, the rest of the trail receives little use and even less attention. Hikers justifiably gravitate to the spectacular waterfalls, to the exclusion of the rest of the trail. This leaves more than 12.5 miles of riparian pathway almost unused. It is a perfect opportunity to enjoy a beautiful river with some quality isolation.

While the trail is generally quite scenic, McCloud River Trail can be a bit of a mixed bag at times. The river passes through less interesting terrain that is not as exciting as sections along narrow gorges or through large meadows. Furthermore, the engineers that laid out the route often shifted the path away from the river. The intent was to stay above the river's high water mark and prevent the trail from being washed away when the river swelled with rainwater or heavy spring thaws. While in most cases this simply means being slung on steep slopes directly above the McCloud, in some instances the trail swings well away from the water. Consequently, the trail, as nice as it is, does not offer consistent access to the river, and the commensurate beauty and interest. Despite this, the majority of the McCloud River Trail is very pretty, offering intimate exposure to the river and plenty of interesting geology.

One of the great features of the McCloud River Trail is that it has road access at several different points, which makes it easy to hike single sections of the trail as individual hikes. It can best be broken up into five segments ranging in length from 2.5 to 4 miles. If these are done as out-and-back hikes, each is the perfect distance for an easy hike. Another great way to hike the trail is to utilize car shuttles. The most ambitious shuttle would be to hike the entire trail from end to end. Considering the level, easy grade, this is certainly a realistic option for a day hike. Shorter sections can also be connected with shuttles.

Lastly, the trail is described east to west. This follows the flow of the river and explores the least used sections first. It also leaves the waterfalls for last, allowing them to conclude the journey in climactic fashion. However, the sections are just as easily hiked in the opposite direction. You can choose for yourself which direction you want to hike.

Algoma to Nitwit—2.5 miles one way

The McCloud River Trail begins at the Algoma campground, which is located in a bend in the river just past a bridge over the river. Being the farthest part of the trail from McCloud, it is rarely used. Algoma simply does not come to mind when thinking of places to go hike.

It may not get attention but the hike from Algoma to the Nitwit camp is one of the prettiest parts of the entire river trail. For the first 1.2 miles it passes through a shallow canyon where the river maintains a consistently swift-moving course. Even though the canyon is only about 100 feet deep, the outside world does not intrude and hikers are left alone to enjoy the river. Once you emerge from the canyon, the water slows for a while as it meanders through a small floodplain before picking up speed again. Past the floodplain, the river flows through beautiful riparian forest until it reaches the primitive campsites at Skunk Hollow and Nitwit. There are some nice places to swim in the river here.

Nitwit to Cattle Camp Swimming Hole—3 miles one way

The section of the McCloud River Trail that runs from Nitwit to the Cattle Camp swimming hole is without doubt the least interesting portion of the trail. This is not to say that it is terrible. On the contrary, some sections are among the most scenic sections of the McCloud River. Unfortunately, these highlights tend to be fewer and farther between than on other parts of the hike. This is a result of the way the trail was routed. It stays above the high-water mark, so that when the McCloud is swollen with spring runoff or heavy rains, the trail is not at risk of being inundated and destroyed. However, there is a major drawback to this. When the river flows through flat, broad areas, the high-water mark is pushed well away from the water. For hikers this is a frustration, because the river is the prime draw for the trail and these sections hold little interest other than the forest.

This is the case on the segment from Nitwit to the Cattle Camp swimming hole. The trail follows the river for the first 1.7 miles past Nitwit to a nice swimming hole. However, from there the trail veers well away from the McCloud as it skirts a wood plain. This is followed by a mile of hiking through the woods, with no water in sight. However, this section concludes on one of the prettiest parts of the entire river trail. Just before the McCloud flows into the large, deep Cattle Camp swimming hole, it rips through a small gorge composed of volcanic basalt blocks. Short cliffs rise above the swimming hole, adding some dramatic relief to the deep blue pool.

Cattle Camp Swimming Hole to Camp 4—4 miles one way

The segment of the McCloud River Trail between the Cattle Camp swimming hole and the Camp 4 group camp is one of the trail's least traveled sections. The river,

The McCloud River surges through a small basalt gorge.

having been filled by some larger creeks, is larger than along previous sections. For most of the nearly 4 miles between the swimming hole and the group camp, the river passes through another shallow canyon, which means the trail is almost always within sight of the river. Indeed, most of this section sees the trail slung on the canyon slope just above the water.

The frustrating trail engineering that diminished the quality of the previous section is almost entirely absent here. Passage through the shallow canyon also means that the river is rarely placid. Instead, it travels swiftly through the canyon. The ubiquitous sound of rushing water is a welcome addition to any trail and on this section of the McCloud River Trail is present in spades. Adding to this section's qualities is the lack of use. Solitude is practically guaranteed. The shallow canyon runs almost the entire distance between the swimming hole and Camp 4. At the camp the canyon levels out and there is a nice meadow alongside the river.

Camp 4 to Upper Falls—3 miles one way

The portion of the McCloud River Trail between Camp 4 and Upper Falls is the last of the little-used sections before traffic explodes along the falls. The segment leading up to Upper Falls is best hiked from east to west. This hike has the most varied terrain of any part of the river trail. It includes some usual riverside scenery, as well as some forested hiking when the trail veers frustratingly far from the water to avoid the high-water mark.

Thankfully, the trail passes some interesting new features, such as the large bayou-like area where the river's current is stilled and it meanders through several channels as it cuts through dense brush. The Lakin Dam, a small diversion dam that once supplied water for the mill in McCloud, will fascinate history buffs. Although it is not a natural waterfall, the river pouring over the dam is still a pleasant sight. Below the dam, the river is swift as it flows through increasingly common volcanic features, including a significant amount of basalt and some ancient lava flows. The ever-more-rugged geology hints at what lies a short distance ahead, when the river pours over the three famed McCloud River Falls.

Upper Falls to Pine Tree Hollow Boat Launch—2.5 miles one way

The section of the McCloud River Trail that passes the three waterfalls is described in the opposite direction in Hike 46. Below Upper Falls the river's canyon is deeper than it has been at any point along the hike. The trail travels just below the basalt-capped rim before arriving at overlook above the awesome Middle Falls, the best of the three waterfalls.

After descending a series of switchbacks to drop back down to the river's level, the trail stays alongside the large river until it arrives at the Fowlers Camp campground. The river runs through a little gorge again, and the trail drops down a shorter set of switchbacks. The path parallels the river as the water runs over large rocky slabs until it flows over Lower Falls. Downstream from the last waterfall, the trail continues to follow the river for another 0.6 mile to the Pine Tree Hollow boat launch. This is one of the prettiest parts of the entire trail. The water passes through a rocky gorge and then flows through another shallow canyon. The trail stays well above the water, but then drops down to the riverbank at Pine Tree Hollow and follows the McCloud back upstream to a set of switchbacks. Climb up to rejoin the trail just downstream from Lower Falls.

Miles and Directions

0.0 Start at the bridge that crosses the river at Algoma Camp. There is a little parking area on the east side of the road below the bridge. Cross the road and hike through the beautiful little canyon.

1.2 The trail emerges from the canyon and travels the outskirts of a plain.

2.2 After coming alongside the river again, the trail cuts through the primitive Skunk Hollow campground.

2.6 Arrive at the primitive Nitwit campground.

3.8 Pass a nice swimming hole. The route follows the river a little farther and then veers away as it skirts a large riparian plain.

4.7 Hike past the edge of Cattle Camp campground.

5.4 The trail reaches Cattle Camp swimming hole. This is one of the prettiest spots on the entire hike.

Deep forests surround the McCloud River.

6.2   The trail enters another shallow canyon. This one will extend almost the entire distance to Camp 4.

9.5   Arrive at Camp 4. There is a small meadow next to the river on the north side of the camp.

10.0   The path veers away from the river again at the Bundoora Spring. It skirts the edge of another riparian plain for 0.9 mile.

10.9   When the trail reaches a dirt road, turn left and walk about 50 yards to the Bigelow Bridge. There are good swimming holes below the bridge. Return to the trail and continue hiking.

11.6   The trail reaches the Lakin Dam picnic area. The dam lies just a little farther down the trail.

12.3   Reach the Upper Falls picnic area, followed by the interesting Upper Falls.

12.7   Look down on Middle Falls from the overlook.

12.9   Climb down to the bottom of a series of switchbacks to return to the river's level. There is a fantastic view of the Middle Falls from here.

13.6   Hike along the edge of the Fowlers campground.

14.9   The trail ends reaches Pine Tree Hollow boat launch and loops back along the river.

15.5   Trail merges back onto the main trail and quickly arrives at Lower Falls

48 Squaw Valley Creek

The trail along large Squaw Valley Creek is an easy and scenic hike with good access to a beautiful creek in a lovely, wild canyon. In addition to some narrow gorges and large rocks, the hike passes a couple of small waterfalls. There is also a great loop option that combines the main trail, the Pacific Crest Trail, and a dirt road.

Total distance: 5.8 miles out-and-back to second waterfall; 8.0 miles for the loop connecting the Pacific Crest Trail (PCT) and Bear Trap Creek Road.
Trail type: Out and back or loop
Elevation gain: 300 feet on the out-and-back option; 1,000 feet on the loop option
Difficulty: Easy to moderate
Trail surface: Packed dirt, dirt road, rocky
Hiking time: 3.5-5 hours

Season: Spring, summer, fall
Fees and permits: None
Canine compatibility: Dogs are permitted.
Land status: Shasta-Trinity National Forest
Trail contact: McCloud Ranger Station, 2019 Forest Rd., McCloud, CA 96057; (530) 964-2184; www.fs.usda.gov/stnf
Other: Water is available in the McCloud River and at the Ah-Di-Na campground.

Finding the trailhead: From the main intersection of CA 89 and Squaw Valley Road in McCloud, drive south on Squaw Valley Road for 6 miles. Turn right onto a dirt road signed for Squaw Valley Creek. Proceed for 3 miles on this well-graded road to the large, signed parking area for the Cabin Creek Trailhead. GPS: N41° 8' 36.60" / W122° 10' 13.82"

The Hike

Squaw Valley Creek begins its journey high on Mount Shasta, bursting from the mountain in a series of large springs at South Gate Meadows. It tumbles down the flanks of the massive volcano before finally settling down and winding its way through Squaw Valley. At the south end of the valley the creek bends to the west and begins to flow through a deep, heavily forested canyon. After passage through the canyon, it finally contributes its waters to the McCloud River, deep in the remote mountains north of Shasta Lake. The springs at the headwaters and the extensive meadows in Squaw Valley mean that the creek has good flow all year. Even in the driest parts of the summer, when other creeks have dried up or shrunk to insignificance, this is a good option for a hike.

The Squaw Valley Creek Trail is the only hike in the McCloud area (with the exception of the Pacific Crest Trail) that does not parallel the McCloud River. Despite not being on the famed river, the trip along Squaw Valley Creek shares many of the McCloud's best qualities. Swift-moving water, banks choked with flowery Indian rhubarb, rock-strewn water with nice rapids, and falling water are all great features along Squaw Valley Creek. Perhaps most notable are the pair of small waterfalls.

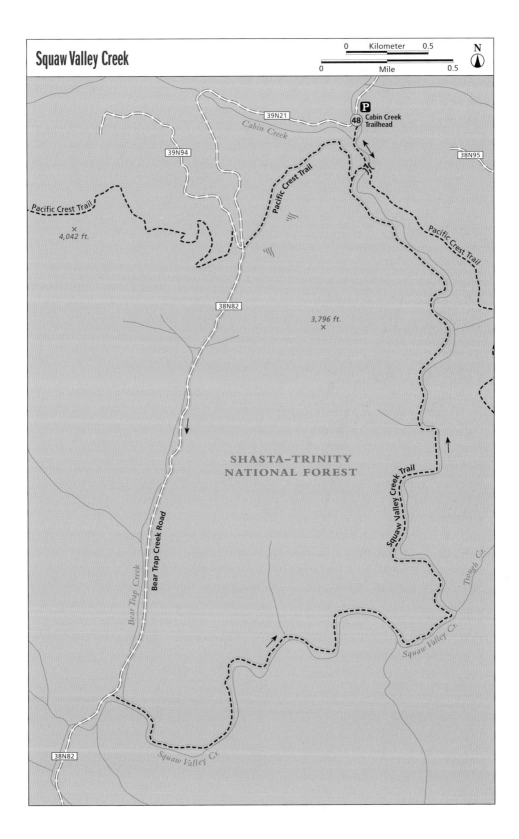

Squaw Valley Creek

0 Kilometer 0.5

0 Mile 0.5

N

39N21

Cabin Creek

P
48 Cabin Creek
Trailhead

39N94

38N95

Pacific Crest Trail

Pacific Crest Trail

Pacific Crest Trail

×
4,042 ft.

38N82

3,796 ft.
×

SHASTA–TRINITY
NATIONAL FOREST

Squaw Valley Creek Trail

Bear Trap Creek

Bear Trap Creek Road

Trough Cr.

Squaw Valley Cr.

38N82

Squaw Valley Cr.

Though they are not nearly as large as the waterfalls on the McCloud River, Squaw Valley Creek has a couple of pretty little cataracts.

Not all of its charms imitate the creek's larger neighbor. Squaw Valley Creek crashes through a short but very scenic, rocky gorge. Moreover, unlike any of the other trails in the McCloud area, this one has the option of being done as a loop. The Squaw Valley Creek Trail proper follows the creek for 5 miles to its confluence with Bear Trap Creek. Because a dirt road runs the length of Bear Trap Creek, there are two possible ways to complete the hike along Squaw Valley Creek. First is to do a simple out-and-back. Although you can hike the entire distance to Bear Trap Creek, the second waterfall makes a good place to turn around. This option is about 2.9 miles one way.

The other option is to create a loop by connecting the beginning of the route on Squaw Valley Creek with Bear Trap Road by hiking on the Pacific Crest Trail. By hiking down Bear Trap Road, you can connect with the Squaw Valley Creek Trail, and then hike its entire length back to the trailhead. This option is 8 miles long. This description of the hike starts with a brief overview of the first short option, followed by a full treatment of the loop option. It should also be noted that whichever option you choose, some signs refer to the Squaw Valley Creek Trail as the Cabin Creek Trail.

5.8-mile out-and-back option

For hikers not looking for a lengthy endeavor, the best way to see the highlights of the Squaw Valley Creek Trail is to hike only the first 3 miles. This permits hikers to enjoy the first scenic 0.5 mile, where the creek flows through a rocky gorge; it then tumbles through a canyon for the next 1.5 miles. About 2 miles from the trailhead a waterfall becomes audible. Obvious spurs lead down to the small, 10-foot waterfall. A nice little pool for swimming waits at the base of the falls—one of the highlights of the entire hike.

Beyond the waterfall, the path continues for another mile, staying close to the creek nearly the entire time. Eventually it comes within earshot of another small waterfall. Again, obvious tracks lead down to a vantage point, where you can see the falls. Smaller than the first, the falls is only 4- or 5-feet tall. However, the canyon has narrowed significantly and gotten quite rocky around the falls, so that the waterfall pours through a fairly tight space. This heightens the drama of the small waterfall significantly. This is a good spot for a picnic. Turn around here and begin the trip back to the trailhead.

8-mile loop option

If you are looking for a longer and more varied trip, the loop option is a great choice. By combining the Pacific Crest Trail, the road along Bear Trap Creek, and the Squaw Valley Creek Trail, this very scenic loop offers a fair amount of variety without having to retrace your steps.

The PCT bridge over Squaw Valley Creek.

To begin, hike south from the trailhead, crossing a bridge over diminutive Cabin Creek. From here the path and Squaw Valley Creek maintain the same course for 0.1 mile until it reaches the junction with the Pacific Crest Trail. Here, the creek drops through a narrow, rocky gorge. The PCT crosses over the chasm on a well-constructed wooden bridge. It is one of the more memorable sights of the trail. Although it is worth walking onto the bridge and looking down into the creek, do not cross it. Following the PCT in this direction leads to Ah-Di-Na Camp on the McCloud River.

Stay straight on the trail and pass the bridge. Another 0.1 mile leads to a second junction. This time, the PCT breaks away to the right and the Squaw Valley Creek Trail continues to follow the creek to the left. To take the loop option, turn to the right and follow the PCT as it climbs out of Squaw Valley Creek's canyon. Soon the trail swings to the left and climbs through the upper reaches of Cabin Creek's watershed. Eventually the trail widens and follows an old roadbed.

About 0.8 mile from the junction with the Squaw Valley Creek Trail, a sign on a tree indicates the PCT's arrival at the Octopus, a nexus of trails and dirt roads. This is the highest point of the hike. Turn to the left and head down the main road. A short distance from the Octopus a gate blocks vehicles from driving into Bear Trap Creek's canyon. Go around the gate and hike down the road as it stays alongside the creek.

For the first mile, the road maintains a fairly steep grade and will make hikers glad they tackled this part of the loop first. Notice how there is little to no water in the creek bed at the head of the canyon. As it drops deeper into its canyon, seeps and springs feed an increasingly larger creek. About halfway down the road, the canyon narrows and the creek comes right up against the roadbed at a very tight choke point. Shortly after this, a significant tributary joins Bear Trap Creek and increases its size substantially. Finally, about 2 miles from the Octopus, the road crosses over Bear Trap Creek. A couple hundred yards farther up the road, a sign indicating the Cabin Creek Trail is on the left, where the trail joins the road.

Squaw Valley Creek is immediately audible from the trail, and soon you will see it as well. The path travels through oak woodlands dotted with a few conifers. The wooded canyon walls are often visible high above the creek. The route winds its way through the small drainages that feed into the creek, staying in forest cover for the most part. Although it is pretty, there is a lot of poison oak in this area. The stuff is pretty thick along the trail in places, and requires a lot of vigilance to avoid.

Eventually, 2 miles from the junction with Bear Trap Creek Road, the roar of a small waterfall becomes audible. An obvious path leads off to the right and provides access to a vista overlooking the small cataract. It is not high, but the entire creek is funneled through a notch between a large boulder and a bedrock dike, dropping its cascade of water about 5 feet or so.

To continue the hike, keep following the creek. At one point, it seems a trail splits off to the left. The main route, straight ahead, is blocked by wood debris. Stay to the left as the trail climbs over a small knoll. This recently constructed section of trail is bypassing a portion of the Squaw Valley Creek Trail that collapsed into the creek. The collapse is visible when the detour and the original route meet.

About 1 mile from the small waterfall, the larger cataract becomes audible. Again, an obvious path drops down to the south and leads to an overlook of the waterfall. It is 8- to 10-feet high. It is an attractive sight and adds a lot of interest to the creek scenery. A small pool at the base of the falls is a good spot for a quick dip in hot weather.

Beyond the waterfall, the path stays close to Squaw Valley Creek for the last 2 miles back to the trailhead. Periodic spurs lead down to the creek. Typically, the channel is lined with dense bunches of Indian rhubarb, which sprouts attractive pink flowers in the spring. Note that there has been a transition in the type of forest the trail passes through. When the trail began at Bear Trap Creek, it passed through a dominantly oak forest. By the time the route reaches the second waterfall, the forest has become populated by conifers, mostly the usual ponderosa pine, Douglas fir, and cedar. Now, however, the trail passes through some of the finest stands of Pacific yew found in the Mount Shasta area. This tree looks like an odd combination of madrone and coast redwood. The trees can also be seen along the trails that follow the Sacramento and McCloud Rivers, though neither have yews as impressive as those found along Squaw Valley Creek.

As the trail nears the trailhead, it veers away from the creek for the first time. As it approaches the creek again, it passes one of the most scenic sections of Squaw Valley Creek. The creek shoots through a series of narrow, rocky gorges. At the beginning of the gorge section, a prominent use trail leads to some view points above the chasm. From here, it is a short distance to the junction with the Pacific Crest Trail. As you pass the bridge at the beginning of the trail, it becomes apparent that the rocky gorge crossed by the bridge is part of the same sequence of rugged little canyons you have been hiking along. Beyond the bridge, it is only a short distance back to the trailhead, completing the 8.0-mile loop.

Miles and Directions

5.8-mile out-and-back option

0.0 Start by hiking south from the Cabin Creek trailhead, crossing small Cabin Creek and coming alongside Squaw Valley Creek.

0.2 At the junction with the Pacific Crest Trail, stay right and pass the bridge. The PCT soon splits off to the right. Stay to the left.

2.0 The larger of two little waterfalls is just below the trail to the left.

2.9 The second, smaller of the two cataracts is just off the trail, surrounded by a small, rocky gorge. This makes a good place to turn around and head back to the trailhead.

5.8 Arrive back at the trailhead.

8-mile loop option

0.0 Start by hiking south from the Cabin Creek trailhead, crossing small Cabin Creek and coming alongside Squaw Valley Creek.

0.2 At the junction with the Pacific Crest Trail, stay right and go past the bridge. The PCT then splits off to the right. Turn right onto the PCT and begin climbing.

1.0 The PCT comes to the Octopus, a nexus of roads and trails. Turn left onto Bear Trap Creek Road, pass the gate, and begin hiking down into Bear Trap Creek canyon.

3.0 Just before Bear Trap Creek joins Squaw Valley Creek, turn left onto the Squaw Valley Creek Trail, which is signed as the Cabin Creek Trail.

5.0 The smaller of the two waterfalls is just below the trail to the right.

6.0 The larger waterfall is off the trail to the right.

7.8 Stay right at the junction with the PCT. Stay left when you pass the bridge.

8.0 Arrive back at the trailhead.

49 Ash Camp to Ah-Di-Na

The hike from Ash Camp to Ah-Di-Na Campground is a pleasantly level section of the Pacific Crest Trail that parallels the McCloud River through a remote and rugged canyon. The river boasts really impressive cataracts as it flows through the canyon, although they are difficult to access. The Ah-Di-Na Campground features the historic ruins of a large, early twentieth-century fishing camp, and great river access.

Total distance: 7.8 miles
Trail type: Out and back
Elevation gain: 400 feet
Difficulty: Moderate
Trail surface: Packed dirt, dirt road
Hiking time: 4 hours
Season: Spring, summer, fall
Fees and permits: None

Canine compatibility: Dogs are permitted.
Land status: Shasta-Trinity National Forest
Trail contact: McCloud Ranger Station, 2019 Forest Rd., McCloud, CA 96057; (530) 964-2184; www.fs.usda.gov/stnf
Other: Water is available in the McCloud River and at the Ah-Di-Na Campground.

Finding the trailhead: From the main intersection in McCloud, drive south for 9.2 miles to Lake McCloud. Stay to the right on the main road, and continue for 4.1 miles around the reservoir to the dam. Cross over the dam and proceed another mile to the signed fork at the entrance to Ash Camp. GPS: 41° 7'1.50"N / 122° 3'38.63"W

The Hike

The McCloud River is one of the Mount Shasta area's great attractions. Its clear waters draw anglers, kayakers, swimmers, and general river-lovers. The McCloud is also popular with hikers, but most naturally gravitate to the McCloud River Trail, especially the section that passes the river's excellent trio of waterfalls. This part of the river, which lies upstream from Lake McCloud, is surrounded by classic volcanic terrain. Numerous basalt formations along the river indicate its volcanic past.

Below the reservoir, the river enters a different geologic zone, exhibiting rock types typical of the vast, nonvolcanic Klamath Mountains that lie to the west. Other than the tough-to-reach McCloud River Preserve Trail (Hike 50), this permutation of the McCloud is usually left unappreciated by the general hiking population. This is a shame because, with the exception of the McCloud Falls area, this is probably the prettiest section of the McCloud River.

Below Lake McCloud, the river is large, wide, and filled with huge boulders. Though there are no large waterfalls, the lower river is loaded with large cataracts created by concentrations of big rocks bottling up the water. Some of these cataracts are as high as 10 feet, giving them a waterfall-like appearance. Unfortunately, no routes directly access this awesome section of the McCloud River. However, for those

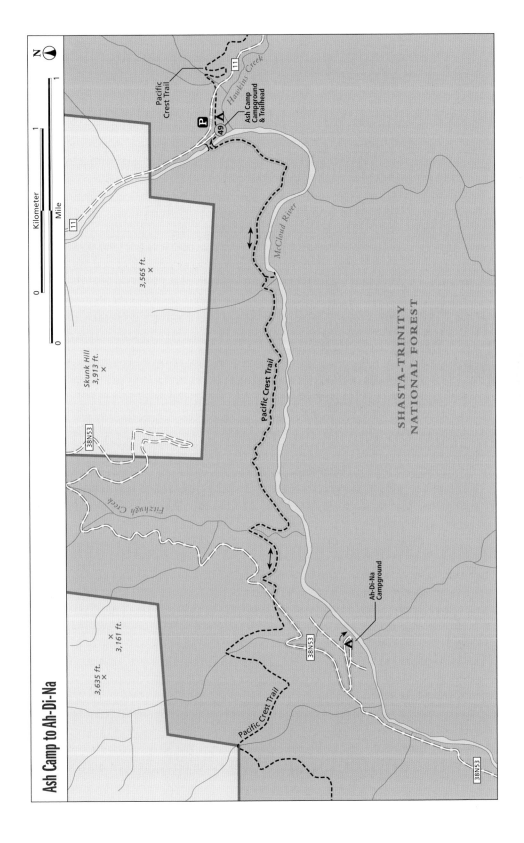

Ash Camp to Ah-Di-Na

motivated to explore this wild stretch of awesome river, the Pacific Crest Trail (PCT) offers some limited opportunities.

Beginning at the small Ash Camp campground, the PCT crosses the McCloud, and then maintains a parallel course along the river for 3 miles. Although well above the river, the hike is still quite scenic and very remote. After the trail intersects a dirt road, a short road hike leads to the isolated Ah-Di-Na campground, which has multiple places to access the river. Ah-Di-Na also has several historic ruins dating back to the early twentieth century, when it functioned as one of the McCloud River's elite fishing clubs. A short loop leads to numerous displays detailing the old fishing camp's history, which adds another layer of interest to an already worthy destination.

A couple of caveats: First, it should be reiterated that this section of the PCT does not pass directly alongside the McCloud River. The trail is nearly 300 feet above the water. Though tree-filtered views of the water occur often, it is not like other trails along the McCloud where the water is frequently just a few feet from the path. Numerous spurs lead down to the river, but these require steep ascents on the return to the PCT. Second, though the hike is level and easy, it is not a great hike for kids. This is mainly due to the presence of poison oak along some sections. It is not so pervasive that it makes passage impossible without contact, but kids may not be discerning enough to avoid it.

Ash Camp is on a spit of land nestled between the McCloud River and large and boisterous Hawkins Creek. If time permits, it is worthwhile to scramble down to the river's edge at the confluence and enjoy the watery playground. It is vaguely reminiscent of Yosemite's Happy Isles. The Pacific Crest Trail departs Ash Camp to the north, cutting downward across the slope of the canyon. Cross a large wooden bridge over the McCloud, with views of the rushing water that are among the best of the entire hike. On the far side, the trail turns to the south and begins to parallel the river, about 100 feet above the water. The sound of the river and creek's confluence is nearly deafening.

About 0.1 mile after the bridge, the PCT turns to the west and follows a westward trajectory for the duration of the hike. The river continues to the south, making a longer horseshoe bend to the west. While the trail and the river are separated, the river is still audible. Large old-growth trees abound along the route, and the forest's understory nearly surrounds the path in some places.

Be sure to look for well-established tracks branching off to the left from the PCT. These lead down to the river as it makes its wide turn. The river is at one of its most scenic manifestations along this stretch, and it is worth the time to head down to the water's edge. When the river and trail finally regain their parallel orientation, stop to enjoy some fine views down to the water roaring a couple hundred feet below the path. Another track along this section leads down to a nice campsite adjacent to some excellent whitewater.

Continuing on the PCT, the path is slung across the steep slopes that plunge down to the bottom of the canyon. There is little room for exploration off-trail and

The McCloud River viewed from the PCT bridge.

what opportunities are available are discouraged by the presence of poison oak. Thick stands of ponderosa pine, oak, and Douglas fir are ubiquitous, and are generally to blame for the lack of views down to the water. When a chance to see it does pop up, it is quite a sight since this is a particularly wild and violent section of the river.

About 1 mile from Ash Camp, an obvious track descends very steeply to the water. Hikers looking for an impressive example of the kind of rapids found on this section of the McCloud should make the effort to observe one of the river's larger cataracts. A band of massive boulders runs across the entire width of the river, forcing the water to pour over a 10-foot drop by means of a series of cascades and small plunges. The fury of the water forcing its way through the rocks is exhilarating.

Back on the PCT, continue hiking to the west. The latter half of the trail permits fewer views of the river after this point, and the tracks down to the water all but disappear. However, what the trail lacks in river views it gains in vistas of an increasingly rugged and narrow canyon. The walls on the south side of the McCloud have gotten sheer, and large crags protrude from the dense forest that blankets the canyon.

The trail travels similarly rugged terrain too. The path is often hacked into veins of rock, exposing the route to more sunshine and great views of the canyon downstream. With the river ever-audible and the intermittent views of the canyon, this is a very scenic part of the hike.

However, 2.2 miles from Ash Camp, the trail makes a sharp turn to the north, entering a side canyon drained by Fitzhugh Creek. In short order, the path converges with an old, abandoned, and overgrown road. The trail and road make common cause for about 100 yards, before the PCT breaks away and crosses the small creek. A small PCT thru-hiker campsite sits at the creek. Once across the small stream, traverse the far side of Fitzhugh Creek's canyon before turning west again. Another short dip through the small gully of a smaller stream and the PCT arrives at the edge of a road.

Across the road, a sign marks the PCT's continuation of its journey to Squaw Valley Creek and beyond. For day hikers, continue on the road to Ah-Di-Na Camp. It is slightly more than 0.5 mile down the road to the campground. The road descends gradually through another gully and then rounds the far side, marking the final drop down to the river's level. Watch for abundant locust trees along the road. These trees were favorites of pioneers and frontiersmen because the tree grows quickly, adapts to various kinds of soil, is extremely strong and rot-resistant and, when burned, give off similar Btus as coal. The presence of the trees, which are native to the southeastern United States, are indicative of early American settlement.

After passing some roadside locusts, you arrive at the entrance to Ah-Di-Na camp, 3.4 miles from Ash Camp. Situated on a wide flat adjacent to the river, it is the perfect place for a campground. Pass through a large meadow to get to the campground, which is located around a large loop. There is running water and bathrooms. Access to the river is available at various points, making this a great spot to stop, relax, and enjoy the McCloud River and its rugged canyon.

One interesting feature of Ah-Di-Na is the presence of numerous large ruins dating back to its days as an elite fishing camp. Downstream, other private fishing clubs still maintain ownership of the land around the McCloud. In the 1970s, the McCloud Fishing Club donated the area immediately downstream from Ah-Di-Na to the Nature Conservancy. The McCloud River Preserve trail travels alongside the river through the Conservancy's McCloud River Preserve.

Ah-Di-Na was once owned by the storied Hearst family, which still owns the incredible Wyntoon property just downstream from the McCloud Falls area. The family donated Ah-Di-Na to the Shasta–Trinity National Forest in 1965, likely a result of being cut off from the land by Lake McCloud. Whatever the reason, it was a gracious gift that is still enjoyed today.

The ruins include the chimney of the main lodge, several root cellars and a large, enclosed basement, cabins, some unlikely—and empty—swimming pools, and a still-productive fruit orchard. A short and increasingly overgrown trail leads to interpretive displays at each of the ruins. It is a fascinating glimpse into a bygone age.

Miles and Directions

0.0 Start from Ash Camp. Descend on the PCT to the McCloud River and cross the footbridge.

0.9 On the left, a steep path heads down to the river. It leads to one of the largest cataracts on this section of the McCloud.

2.4 The PCT crosses small Fitzhugh Creek.

2.7 The trail arrives at the edge of a dirt road. Turn left and hike down the road.

3.4 Turn left onto the dirt access road for Ah-Di-Na campground.

3.9 Arrive at Ah-Di-Na, where there is water, restrooms, a 0.3-mile loop trail through historic ruins, and access to the McCloud River. Retrace your steps.

7.8 Arrive back at the trailhead.

50 McCloud River Preserve

This beautiful hike leads through the isolated McCloud River Preserve. The trail hugs the river as it tumbles around large boulders and small cataracts in a deep canyon. The catch is that it requires a lengthy drive on a dirt road to reach the secluded preserve.

Total distance: 5.0 miles
Trail type: Out and back
Elevation gain: 100 feet
Difficulty: Easy
Trail surface: Packed dirt, rocky, rock scrambling
Hiking time: 3 hours
Season: Spring, summer, fall
Fees and permits: None

Canine compatibility: Dogs are not allowed.
Land status: Nature Conservancy
Trail Contact: Nature Conservancy McCloud River Preserve; (415) 777-0487; www.nature .org/ourinitiatives/regions/northamerica/ unitedstates/california/placesweprotect/ mccloud-river-preserve.xml
Other: Water is available in the McCloud River.

Finding the trailhead: From the main intersection in McCloud, drive south for 9.2 miles to Lake McCloud. Stay to the right on the main road and continue for 2.2 miles around the reservoir. Take a signed, dirt road to the right and proceed 4.6 miles to the trailhead. This road is long and bumpy. It climbs up and over a ridge, and then makes a long drop down to the McCloud River. The route is signed in a few places, directing you to Ah-Di-Na Campground. Be sure to follow those directions. The main road is obvious throughout, and never in doubt. Once past Ah-Di-Na, the road continues along the river and then makes a short climb through the roughest section of the entire drive. Shortly after the climb you arrive at the trailhead. GPS: N41° 6' 22.48" / W122° 6' 17.05"W

The Hike

The McCloud River Preserve is a rare opportunity to enjoy the lower McCloud River. Between the Lake McCloud dam and the stilled waters of Shasta Lake, the McCloud River flows wild and free through deep canyons, cloaked in primeval forest. Most of this stretch of the river is owned by private fishing clubs established early in the twentieth century. These privately owned sections of the river are not open to the public above the high-water mark. Rafters and kayakers can pass through, but there is no land access.

The McCloud River Preserve is one of the few parts of the lower river open to the public for hiking and fishing. The land for the preserve was donated to The Nature Conservancy by one of the fishing clubs in 1973. It was opened to the public in 1976, and permits a limited number of anglers on the land each day, but an unlimited number of hikers. Due to the length of the drive to the preserve, it is not heavily used, and hikers who make the trek will likely have the river all to themselves, perhaps bumping into an occasional angler.

McCloud River Preserve

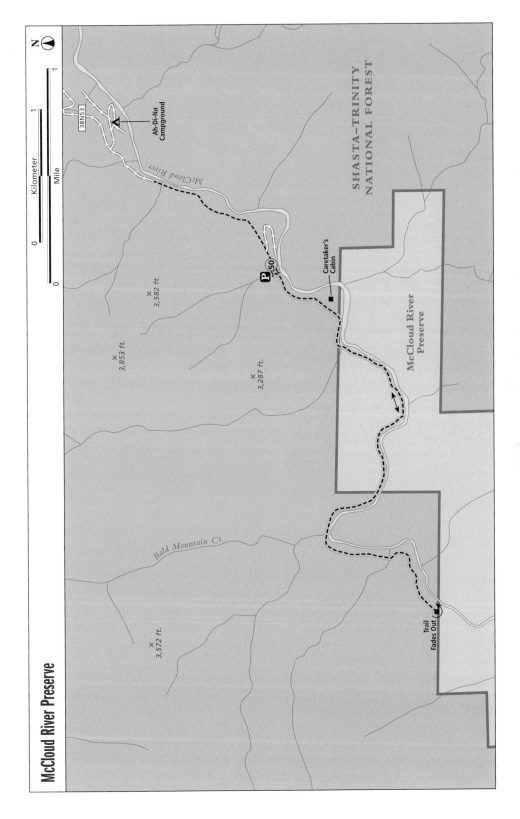

N

SHASTA-TRINITY
NATIONAL FOREST

Ah-Di-Na
Campground

38N53

McCloud River

3,582 ft.

3,853 ft.

3,287 ft.

P 50

Caretaker's
Cabin

McCloud River
Preserve

Bald Mountain Cr.

3,572 ft.

Trail
Fades Out

Kilometer

Mile

The McCloud River flows through the remote McCloud River Preserve.

This is a great opportunity to get close to the river as it crashes through rapids. The steep-sided, wooded canyon feels as far away from the civilized world . . . well, as it is. The beauty of the river coupled with its great isolation make this one of the great river hikes in Northern California.

Getting to the trailhead for the McCloud River Preserve Trail is the hardest part of the trip. The road leading to the trailhead is by no means the roughest road that leads to an established hiking trail in the Mount Shasta area, but it is certainly not a high-speed dirt road. It is windy and rough in places. Perhaps the worst part is the pittance of a parking area at the trailhead. The road simply comes to an abrupt end where a footbridge crosses a small creek. The road is, at best, slightly wider than usual here, with space for maybe three cars. This poses some difficulty for larger vehicles to turn around. About 150 yards back up the road there are a few shallow pullouts. Larger vehicles are advised to park there.

Beginning at the footbridge, the trail crosses a small seasonal creek. It immediately plunges into thick foliage. The path makes a short drop down to river level. The McCloud races by just feet from the trail. The way is narrow and flanked by rocky outcroppings on one side and the river on the other. There is only a narrow bench along which the trail passes. Poison oak becomes a threat as soon as the trail reaches the river. Be careful to pick your way around it.

Soon the rocky bench disappears and is replaced by ragged bedrock thrust up into the route. Though the trail fades out, the route across the rock is obvious. This is one of the most interesting parts of the trip. It ends all too soon and the trail resumes, continuing along the river.

A little farther downstream, the river makes a sharp bend to the west. This produces a flat in the river's elbow with an unusual sight: a house, barn, and various outbuildings. This is the residence of The Nature Conservancy's caretaker. Here you'll find a few displays explaining the geology of the river, the fish that populate it, and some Native American history. Be sure to sign in to the guest register. If fishing, grab one of the provided tags. This is also the last place for any type of restroom: A sign indicates the spur leading to a public outhouse. It also appears that the caretakers appreciate it if hikers are willing to haul a piece of firewood or two back to the residence.

Once having left the caretaker's area, the trail begins in earnest. As before, it parallels the river, at times dropping very close. A short distance from the house is a fairly rugged spot in the path, where it runs into a large boulder. Though there is no constructed trail, the route, which drops down to the left of the boulder, is obvious.

From this point on, the trail follow the curves and contours of the river. At times, well-established side trails lead down to the water. Some even continue for a fair distance alongside the river, but below the main trail. The McCloud River has few quiet spots as it races through the canyon. The placid areas are short and are quickly overtaken by more rapids. The sound of roaring water is ever-present.

About 1 mile from the caretaker's house, the trail makes its only significant climb. The path emerges from the tree cover and climbs about 100 feet above the river to bypass large rocks. Be especially careful of the poison oak along this section of the path. This stretch of the McCloud has some of the most interesting rapids in the entire preserve. Unfortunately the trail maintains a fair distance from the water at this point.

About 1.2 miles from the caretaker's house, the trail makes an unheralded departure from The Nature Conservancy's land and enters the national forest. Although more of the McCloud River Preserve is located farther down the canyon, it is not open to hikers. The rest of the trail travels across national forest land.

Once the trail drops back down to the river's level, it begins to curve around a pronounced horseshoe bend that arches around a rib in the east side of the canyon wall. This results in a sudden turn to the north, followed by an equally sudden turn to the south before the McCloud resumes its southwesterly course. Though some rapids are here, the river does not go over any as large or as interesting as when the trail rose above the river's level.

At the apex of the horseshoe, the trail crosses Bald Mountain Creek. Once across, the path begins a southward course along the big bend. About 0.8 mile beyond the creek crossing, the trail finally peters out. Though it is unmarked, the trail ends at the boundary between the national forest and more Nature Conservancy land. From here, retrace your steps back to the trailhead and make the long drive back to McCloud.

Miles and Directions

0.0 Start by crossing over a footbridge and descending to the McCloud River. Be sure to carry in a piece of firewood for the caretakers if you can find any!

0.4 The Nature Conservancy's caretaker's cabin has a sign-in sheet and restrooms.

1.4 The trail climbs about 100 feet above the trail, and then leaves the McCloud River Preserve and enters the national forest.

1.9 Cross over Bald Mountain Creek.

2.5 The trail fades away as the river reenters the McCloud River Preserve, where hiking is no longer allowed. Retrace the route back to the trailhead.

5.0 Arrive back at the trailhead.

About the Author

A native of Sonoma County in California's wine country, Christopher "Bubba" Suess grew up hiking the trails on his home turf as well as those in the famed Sierra Nevada. His first backpacking trip at age five sparked a love affair with granite and rushing water. Deeply influenced by his parents to appreciate the outdoors and by his older brother to always strive and persevere, Bubba was further moved to value the conservation of wilderness during his time in the Boy Scouts. A four-year sojourn in Texas for graduate school forced Bubba to find beauty in more subtle places and areas that are generally overlooked. Now a resident of Mount Shasta in far northern California, he loves living a rural life, centered around time spent with his wife, Harmony, and their three children.

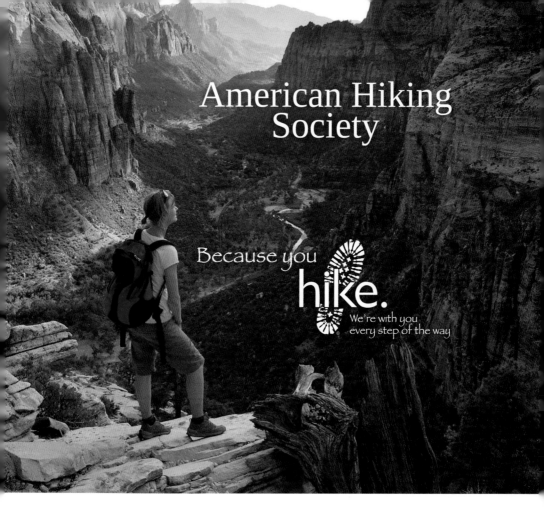

American Hiking Society

Because you hike.
We're with you every step of the way

As a national voice for hikers, **American Hiking Society** works every day:

- Building and maintaining hiking trails
- Educating and supporting hikers by providing information and resources
- Supporting hiking and trail organizations nationwide
- Speaking for hikers in the halls of Congress and with federal land managers

Whether you're a casual hiker or a seasoned backpacker, become a member of American Hiking Society and join the national hiking community! You'll enjoy great member benefits and help preserve the nation's hiking trails, so tomorrow's hike is even better than today's. We invite you to join us now!

American Hiking Society